EMPIRE AND DISSENT

AMERICAN ENCOUNTERS/GLOBAL INTERACTIONS
A series edited by Gilbert M. Joseph and Emily S. Rosenberg

This series aims to stimulate critical perspectives and fresh interpretive frameworks for scholarship on the history of the imposing global presence of the United States. Its primary concerns include the deployment and contestation of power, the construction and deconstruction of cultural and political borders, the fluid meanings of intercultural encounters, and the complex interplay between the global and the local. American Encounters seeks to strengthen dialogue and collaboration between historians of U.S. international relations and area studies specialists.

The series encourages scholarship based on multiarchival historical research. At the same time, it supports a recognition of the representational character of all stories about the past and promotes critical inquiry into issues of subjectivity and narrative. In the process, American Encounters strives to understand the context in which meanings related to nations, cultures, and political economy are continually produced, challenged, and reshaped.

A project organized by the Social Science Research Council

EMPIRE AND DISSENT

THE UNITED STATES AND LATIN AMERICA

Edited by Fred Rosen

Duke University Press   Durham and London   2008

© 2008 Duke University Press

All rights reserved

Printed in the United States of America on acid-free paper ∞

Designed by Heather Hensley

Typeset in Linotype Sabon by Achorn International

Library of Congress Cataloging-in-Publication data appear
on the last printed page of this book.

CONTENTS

ACKNOWLEDGMENTS

This volume originated in a project called "Responding to Hegemony: The Dynamics of Social Movements," sponsored by the Program on Global Security and Cooperation (GSC) of the Social Science Research Council, with funding from the John D. and Catherine T. MacArthur Foundation.

The project consisted of two international workshops and the publications they generated. I am grateful to John Tirman and Itty Abraham, the coordinators of those workshops, for conceptualizing and giving momentum to the project, which has culminated in this collection of essays. I would also like to thank Professors Eric Hershberg and Gilbert Joseph for their helpful suggestions regarding the organization of the workshops and of this volume; Valerie Millholland, the Duke University Press editor who very helpfully guided the manuscript through the acquisition and editorial stages of publication; and the two anonymous readers whose helpful, critical suggestions have been incorporated into the final versions of these essays and (to the best of my ability) into the structure of the volume.

Because the discussions herein cover so much historical ground and assume some previous knowledge of the topics at hand, Alan Knight graciously agreed to draw up a timeline of key events, a list of key individuals, and a list of key institutions, events, and places, all of which are included in "A Reader's Guide," which appears after these acknowledgments. While I contributed some items to the timeline and the lists, the comprehensive historical memory required to compile the reader's guide belongs to Knight. I am grateful for his extra effort to make the volume more accessible to the nonspecialist reader.

These chapters have appeared in several stages: they were originally drafted as workshop presentations; some were then edited or rewritten as short articles in either the GSC *Quarterly* (winter–spring 2005) or the NACLA *Report on the Americas* (September–October 2005); and all were then expanded into the chapter-length essays included in this volume.

The first workshop, "Empire and Dissent: Reflecting on History," was held in Paris, 15–16 June 2004, and explored several case histories of empire and resistance, focusing, in the words of the initial workshop prospectus, on "the current 'unipolar' moment, set in the background of the past and propelled into informed speculation about the future." Two of this book's chapters—Gregory Evans Dowd's description of Native American resistance to the imperial expansion of the eighteenth-century North American colonies and John Oldfield's discussion of the dissent and resistance engendered by the British Empire's transatlantic slave trade—are drawn from the Paris workshop.

The analytical framework constructed in the Paris workshop informed the design of the second workshop, which was held in Cuernavaca, Mexico, 4–6 March 2005, and called "Empire and Dissent: U.S. Hegemony in Latin America." In the Cuernavaca workshop, from which this volume's remaining chapters are drawn, participants discussed the concept of "empire," its relevance to both the current and the historical relationship between the United States and the rest of the Western Hemisphere, and the relationship between the exercise of U.S. power and the various forms of dissent it has generated.

While I cannot speak for individual contributors, I think it is fair to say that this volume as a whole greatly benefited from the creative, scholarly interactions that took place at both workshops. I therefore extend thanks to all the workshop participants whose work only indirectly appears on these pages.

A READER'S GUIDE

Timeline of Key Events

1823   President James Monroe proclaims the Monroe Doctrine,
           which rejects European intervention and imperialism in the
           Americas.

1833   British occupation of the Falkland Islands (Islas Malvinas).

1846–1848 U.S.-Mexican War: the United States invades and defeats
           Mexico.

1848   The Treaty of Guadalupe Hidalgo ends the U.S.-Mexican War;
           Mexico cedes half its territory to the United States.

1850   Clayton-Bulwer Treaty: an Anglo-American agreement for a pro-
           jected isthmian canal.

1882   British occupation of Egypt.

1895   Venezuela–British Guyana border dispute: the United States sup-
           ports Venezuela, invoking the Monroe Doctrine.

1895   The second Cuban insurrection against Spain begins.

1898   Spanish-American War: the United States defeats Spain at sea,
           invades Cuba, and seizes Cuba, Puerto Rico, and the Philippines.

1899–1902 U.S. military occupation of Cuba.

1901   The new Cuban Constitution incorporates the Platt Amendment,
           granting the United States the right to intervene in the island;
           Hay-Pauncefote Treaty: an Anglo-American agreement ceding
           the United States primary control of an isthmian canal, thus
           abrogating the Clayton-Bulwer Treaty of 1850.

1903	Panama, with U.S. connivance, revolts and secedes from Colombia. The United States acquires lease for the Guantánamo Bay base in Cuba.
1904	Construction of the Panama Canal begins; the Panama Canal Zone is established, under U.S. control.
1905	President Theodore Roosevelt declares the Roosevelt Corollary to the Monroe Doctrine, asserting a U.S. policing role, especially in the circum-Caribbean, which would preempt European interventions.
1906–1909	Second U.S. military intervention in Cuba.
1910	The Mexican Revolution begins.
1912	U.S. Marines are dispatched to Nicaragua.
1914	U.S. forces occupy the Mexican port of Veracruz; the Panama Canal opens.
1914–1918	World War I: U.S. trade with and investment in Latin America grow at the expense of Britain and Germany.
1915	U.S. intervention in Haiti: military occupation lasts until 1934.
1916	U.S. intervention in Dominican Republic: military occupation lasts until 1924; U.S. financial control lasts until 1941.
1916–1917	The Pershing or Punitive Expedition: U.S. forces invade northern Mexico in (futile) pursuit of Pancho Villa.
1917	The radical new Mexican Constitution is inaugurated; the United States enters World War I; the Russian Revolution takes place.
1924–1933	U.S. military intervention in Nicaragua: costly campaign against the forces of Sandino; the Nicaraguan National Guard is created.
1933	A revolt overthrows Cuban president Machado and establishes a fragile revolutionary regime, which the United States seeks to control and restrain; Fulgencia Batista rises to power; the Roca-Ruciman Pact between Britain and Argentina, designed to regulate and maintain bilateral economic relations, is signed.
1934	President Franklin Roosevelt declares the Good Neighbor Policy, renouncing intervention in Latin America; the United States abrogates the Platt Amendment; Batista installs a conservative administration in Cuba.
1938	President Lázaro Cárdenas expropriates British and American oil companies in Mexico.
1941	The United States enters World War II.

1944	The Bretton Woods Agreement makes the U.S. dollar the hegemonic (Western) world currency and establishes the principal international financial institutions: the World Bank and the International Monetary Fund.
1945	Chapultepec Conference, Mexico, on postwar Latin American economic policy and relations.
1946	Juan Perón elected president of Argentina, despite opposition of U.S. Ambassador Spruille Braden.
1947	Rio Treaty (Inter-American Treaty of Reciprocal Assistance).
1948	Organization of American States established.
1952	Bolivian Revolution.
1954	U.S.-backed and -inspired military coup against Guatemala's reformist President Jacobo Arbenz.
1958	Vice President Nixon is mobbed by hostile crowds in Caracas.
1959	The Cuban Revolution triumphs, and Castro ousts Batista; anti-American riots take place in Bolivia, provoked by a *Time* magazine article that questions Bolivian sovereignty.
1960	U.S.-Cuban relations deteriorate.
1961	President Kennedy inaugurates the Alliance for Progress; the Bay of Pigs (Playa Girón), a failed, U.S.-backed invasion of Cuba by anti-Castro Cubans, takes place.
1962	Cuban Missile Crisis.
1963	President Kennedy is assassinated; President Johnson downplays and discards the Alliance for Progress.
1964	A military coup overthrows President Goulart in Brazil; a military regime is established with U.S. endorsement.
1965	U.S. invasion of the Dominican Republic: first overt military intervention in Latin America since the inauguration of the Good Neighbor Policy in 1934.
1970	Salvador Allende elected president of Chile; the United States attempts to destabilize Allende's (Popular Unity) government.
1973	A military coup ousts President Allende in Chile, with U.S. connivance.
1979	Sandinistas topple the Somoza regime in Nicaragua.
1981–1990	United States supports Contra rebels against Sandinista government in Nicaragua.
1982	Mexican debt moratorium triggers Latin American debt crisis.

1983	U.S. invasion of Grenada.
1989	U.S. invasion of Panama: overthrow and capture of Manuel Noriega.
1994	The North American Free Trade Agreement takes effect, involving Mexico, the United States, and Canada; the United States intervenes in Haiti; the Zapatista uprising takes place in southern Mexico.
1998	Hugo Chávez is elected president of Venezuela.
2001	Argentina defaults on most of its foreign debt.
2002	Coup attempt against Chávez in Venezuela is unsuccessful; the trade unionist Luiz Inácio "Lula" da Silva is elected president of Brazil.
2005	Argentina resolves debt default on favorable terms when its offer to convert foreign bonds at reduced value is reluctantly accepted by international investors; coca-growers leader Evo Morales is elected president of Bolivia.
2006	Felipe Calderón is elected president of Mexico; Chávez is reelected in Venezuela; Lula is reelected in Brazil; Morales nationalizes Bolivia's gas reserves.
2007	Cristina Kirchner is elected president of Argentina, succeeding her husband; Venezuelan voters reject a set of constitutional changes that would have augmented the powers of the presidency and mandated progressive social reforms.

Key Individuals

Allende, Salvador: reformist president of Chile (1970–73); killed during the military coup of 1973.

Arbenz, Jacobo: reformist president of Guatemala (1951–54); ousted by U.S.-inspired coup.

Battle y Ordóñez, José: reformist president of Uruguay (1903–7, 1911–15).

Blaine, James G.: U.S. secretary of state (1881, 1891–92); advocate of Pan-Americanism and U.S. trade with Latin America.

Brady, Nicholas: U.S. secretary of the treasury under George H. W. Bush (1988–93).

Brzezinski, Zbigniew: National Security Advisor under President Carter.

Bush, George W.: Republican president of the United States (2001–).

Calderón, Felipe: National Action Party president of Mexico (2006–).

Calles, Plutarco Elías: revolutionary president of Mexico (1924–28); *jefe máximo* (big boss) of the revolutionary state (1928–34).

Carden, Lionel: British minister to Mexico (1913–14); supporter of Victoriano Huerta; hostile to the Mexican Revolution and to the United States.

Cárdenas, Lázaro: revolutionary president of Mexico (1934–40).

Carter, James (Jimmy): Democratic president of the United States (1977–81).

Chávez, Hugo: nationalist president of Venezuela (1999–).

Clinton, William J. (Bill): Democratic president of the United States (1993–2001).

Davis, Jefferson: president of the Confederacy during the U.S. Civil War.

Díaz, Adolfo: conservative president of Nicaragua (1911–17).

Eisenhower, Dwight D.: Republican president of the United States (1953–61).

Estrada Palma, Tomás: president of Cuba (1902–6).

Fox, Vicente: National Action Party president of Mexico (2000–2006).

Gaitán, Jorge Eliécer: populist Colombian Liberal, whose assassination in 1949 triggered the *Violencia*.

Haig, Alexander: national security advisor under President Reagan.

Hearst, William R.: U.S. press baron; pioneer of sensationalist mass-circulation newspapers; subject of the film *Citizen Kane*.

Huerta, Victoriano: president and military dictator of Mexico, who vainly resisted the Revolution (1913–14).

Johnson, Lyndon B.: Democratic president of the United States (1963–69).

Kemmerer, Edwin: the "Money Doctor"; Princeton academic who advised several Latin American governments (in Mexico, Guatemala, Colombia, Chile, Ecuador, and Peru) on financial matters, notably the establishment of central banks, between 1917 and 1931.

Kirchner, Néstor: Peronist president of Argentina (2003–2007).

Kirkpatrick, Jeane: U.S. ambassador to the United Nations under Ronald Reagan, whose defense of Latin American authoritarian regimes as the lesser of two evils influenced U.S. policy in the 1980s.

Lula (Luiz Inácio Lula da Silva): Workers' Party president of Brazil (2003–).

Madero, Francisco: leader of the 1910 revolution against Porfirio Díaz; president of Mexico (1911–13); ousted and killed in military coup.

Marcos, Subcomandante: principal spokesperson for the Zapatista National Liberation Army.

McCarthy, Joseph (Joe): Republican senator and anticommunist witch-hunter, late 1940s and early 1950s.

McKinley, William: Republican president of the United States (1897–1901).

Menem, Carlos: Peronist president of Argentina (1989–99).

Mossadegh, Mohammed: nationalist Iranian prime minister; overthrown by a military coup which enjoyed Anglo-American support (1953).

Nixon, Richard M.: Republican president of the United States (1969–74).

O'Neill, Paul: U.S. secretary of the treasury at the time of the Argentine financial crisis (2001–2).

Ortega, Daniel: Sandinista leader in Nicaragua; president of Nicaragua (1985–90, reelected 2006).

Patterson, Richard: U.S. ambassador to Guatemala (1949–53).

Perón, Juan Domingo: nationalist president of Argentina (1946–55, 1973–74).

Reagan, Ronald: Republican president of the United States (1981–89).

Remington, Frederic: U.S. artist and illustrator; covered the Spanish-American War in Cuba.

Rockefeller, Nelson: coordinator of the Office of Inter-American Affairs (1941–44).

Roosevelt, Franklin D.: Democratic president of the United States (1933–45); architect of the Good Neighbor Policy.

Roosevelt, Theodore: Republican president of the United States (1901–9); author of the Roosevelt Corollary.

Rubin, Robert: U.S. secretary of the treasury (1995–99); architect of President Clinton's Mexican debt bailout (1995–96).

Salinas de Gortari, Carlos: Institutional Revolutionary Party president of Mexico (1988–94); architect of the North American Free Trade Agreement.

Sánchez de Losada, Gonzalo: president of Bolivia (1993–97, 2002–3); forced to resign (2003).

Sandino, Augusto César: Nicaraguan Liberal and commander of the armed resistance to U.S. forces (1926–33); assassinated (1934).

Somoza Debayle, Anastasio: president of Nicaragua (1967–79).

Somoza Debayle, Luis: president of Nicaragua (1956–63).

Somoza García, Anastasio: president of Nicaragua (1937–47, 1950–56).

Stroessner, Alfredo: president of Paraguay (1954–89).

Trujillo, Rafael: president of the Dominican Republic (1930–38, 1942–52).

Wilson, Woodrow: Democratic president of the United States (1913–21).

Institutions, Events, and Places

Abolition Act of 1807: law passed by the British parliament outlawing the British Atlantic slave trade.

AFL-CIO: American Federation of Labor-Congress of Industrial Organizations, mainstream U.S. labor confederation.

AID (USAID): U.S. Agency for International Development, created by President Kennedy in 1961.

Alliance for Progress: U.S. program of aid and social development, promoted by President Kennedy, particularly to combat the Cuban Revolution; run down by President Johnson.

APRA: Alianza Popular Revolucionaria Americana (American Popular Revolutionary Alliance), Peruvian political party and movement created under the leadership of Víctor Raúl Haya de la Torre in 1924, originally dedicated to nationalism, Pan-Americanism, and reform.

Batllismo: Uruguayan movement and government headed by José Battle.

Bay of Pigs (Playa Girón): site of abortive U.S.-backed invasion of Cuba by anti-Castro émigrés in April 1961.

caciques: leaders and elders of Indian communities in colonial Mexico (New Spain), with responsibilities for local government and taxation; after independence, the term was applied to political bosses in general.

Chapultepec Conference: conference on postwar Latin American economic policy and relations, convened in Mexico in February 1945, at which the U.S. desire for an open economy ran counter to Latin American preferences for protection and import-substitution industrialization.

CIA: Central Intelligence Agency, U.S. intelligence agency set up under President Truman in 1947.

Contras: Nicaraguan rebels against the Sandinista regime (1979–90), backed by the United States.

CTAL: Confederación de Trabajadores de América Latina (Latin American Workers Confederation), a leftist Pan-American confederation of national labor organizations, founded in Mexico in 1938.

Ex-Im bank: Export-Import Bank, U.S. bank set up in 1934 to promote U.S. overseas trade; its responsibilities were revised in 1945 and 1968.

EZLN: Ejército Zapatista de Liberación Nacional (Zapatista National Liberation Army), armed indigenous movement based in the Mexican state of Chiapas.

Gaitanismo: movement headed by Colombian Liberal and populist Jorge Eliécer Gaitán.

GATT: General Agreement on Trade and Tariffs (1947, replaced by WTO, 1995).

Guantánamo Bay: Cuban military base leased to the United States in 1903 and still retained.

IBRD: International Bank of Reconstruction and Development (World Bank), set up as part of the Bretton Woods system in 1944 in order to promote growth within an open global economy.

IDB: Inter-American Development Bank, set up in 1959 to provide investment and promote development in Latin America.

IMF: International Monetary Fund, set up as part of the Bretton Woods system in 1944 in order to promote monetary stability within an open global economy.

IT&T: International Telephone and Telegraph Company, U.S. multinational with major assets in Chile, hence a bone of contention under President Allende.

kurakas: leaders and elders of Indian communities in colonial Andean America (Peru and Bolivia) with responsibilities for local government and taxation.

Maderismo: movement led by Francisco Madero, which initiated the Mexican Revolution of 1910.

McCarthyism: anticommunist movement headed by Republican senator Joseph McCarthy in the 1940s and 1950s.

Monroe Doctrine: 1823 doctrine proclaimed by U.S. President Monroe in opposition to European imperialism in the Americas.

NAFTA: North American Free Trade Agreement (also Tratado de Libre Comercio, or TLC), 1994 free-trade agreement involving Mexico, Canada, and the United States.

National Guard: military force established under U.S. auspices in Nicaragua in the 1920s, during U.S. occupation.

NED: National Endowment for Democracy, nongovernmental agency set up by President Reagan in 1983, with the stated aim of promoting democracy and funded by the U.S. government.

OIAA: Office of Inter-American Affairs, U.S. government agency (1941–44), headed by Nelson Rockefeller, responsible for wartime economic and political liaison with Latin America.

ORIT: Organización Regional Interamericana de Trabajadores (Interamerican Regional Workers Organization), Pan-American labor confederation set up under U.S. auspices in 1951 in order to promote pro-American and anticommunist influence in Latin American labor movements.

PCZ: Panama Canal Zone: strip of territory flanking the Panama Canal, controlled by the United States, 1904–79.

Peronism: movement created and headed by Juan Perón in Argentina, represented by the Partido Justicialista.

PJ: Partido Justicialista, party of the Peronists, Argentina.

Platt Amendment: amendment named after Senator Orville Platt and imposed on Cuba as a prerequisite of U.S. withdrawal following the first intervention (1898–1902), granting the United States a right of intervention in the island; incorporated into the Cuban Constitution of 1901 and the U.S.-Cuban Permanent Treaty of 1903; abrogated in 1934.

PNR, PRM, PRI: Partido Nacional Revolucionario (National Revolutionary Party, 1929–38), Partido de la Revolución Mexicana (Party of the Mexican Revolution, 1938–46), Partido Revolucionario Institucional (Institutional Revolutionary Party, 1946–), successive titles of the party of government which arose following the Mexican Revolution and which ruled until 2000.

Pontiac's War: named for the Ottawa leader who led early attacks on the British post of Detroit in 1763; the extent of Indian unity and power stunned British officials, forcing a reconsideration of empire.

Raj: the British imperial regime in India, from the eighteenth century through the twentieth.

Reconquista: six-century process of reconquest of the Iberian Peninsula by Spanish and Portuguese Christian forces, which culminated in the defeat of the last Moslem state, Granada, in 1492.

Roca-Runciman Agreement: 1933 bilateral agreement between Britain and Argentina relating to trade and investment.

Roosevelt Corollary (to the Monroe Doctrine): formulated by President Theodore Roosevelt, it asserted a U.S. policing role, especially in the circum-Caribbean, which would preempt European interventions.

Rural Guard: Cuban constabulary set up during the first U.S. occupation.

Sandinismo: movement led by Augusto César Sandino in 1920s Nicaragua; the name was assumed by anti-Somoza rebels in the 1960s, who finally triumphed in 1979.

Tequila Effect: the spreading withdrawal of investor confidence in Latin America following the Mexican financial crisis of 1995.

Time incident: anti-American riots in Bolivia in March 1959, provoked by *Time* magazine's report questioning Bolivia's right to exist.

UFCO: United Fruit Company, U.S. multinational with major interests in Colombia and Central America, notably Guatemala; target of the reformist Arbenz government.

UNO: Unión Nacional Opositora (National Opposition Union), center-right coalition, formed to contest the 1990 elections in Nicaragua, which defeated the Sandinistas, securing the election of Violeta Chamorro.

USIA: United States Information Agency (also known abroad as the U.S. Information Service, or USIS), U.S. agency, 1953–99, designed to promote U.S. culture and interests overseas.

WTO: World Trade Organization, replaced GATT in 1997.

FRED ROSEN

INTRODUCTION

T alk of U.S. imperialism, long marginalized as a
rhetorical excess of the "old Left," has made a
mainstream comeback over the past few years. It has
been brought back into fashion not by critics of imperialism, but by those who strongly believe that the
United States has an imperial right and obligation to
act as global guarantor not only of its own interests
but also of the interests of the entire global community. The world's strongest "market democracy," this
sentiment holds, has the ability, the authority, and,
above all, the responsibility to forcefully promote the
spread of democratic institutions, private investment,
and a secure and stable world order.

While this imperial sentiment had been growing
since the Clinton era, it bloomed after the attacks of
9/11, especially in neoconservative circles, and many
felt called upon to celebrate its "coming out of the
closet."[1] Max Boot, a senior fellow at the Council
on Foreign Relations, commented that while many
opted for euphemisms in describing the U.S. role in
the world, he preferred "the more forthright if also
more controversial term American Empire . . . sort
of like the way some gays embrace the 'queer' label."

The "more forthright term," now out of the closet, has been filtering into many corners of the ideological spectrum. In early 2003, for example, while promoting his book on the recent U.S. interventions in Bosnia, Kosovo, and Afghanistan, the liberal human-rights scholar Michael Ignatieff told a *Boston Globe* columnist that in some places in the world, "empire"—of the "lite," benevolent variety—had become "the last hope for democracy and stability alike."[2]

This sentiment played no small part in the subsequent unfolding of events in the Middle East. The invasion of Iraq seems to have been envisaged by at least some of its proponents as an easy first step toward bringing current imperial values—(constrained) free elections, (selective) free markets, and (U.S.-dominated) international security—to the Arab world, all accompanied, of course, by U.S. control of the world's second-largest oil reserves.

This view of empire has a long history within the Americas, where imperial practice and ambition have long shaped the construction of North American power. In fact, the historical role of the United States in the Western Hemisphere may well serve as a useful model for the kind of U.S. presence desired and celebrated (no matter how badly things may have gone lately) by the current proponents of empire. Long before the present-day excesses of neoconservative rule, the United States had considered it a right and a duty to exercise dominance over its "sister republics" in the Americas and to intervene when necessary to pursue its own interests, as well as to protect the "sovereignty" of those sister republics in the face of intrusion by other imperial powers. It also felt compelled to intervene when those republics faced threats from within, like homegrown communists, land reformers, labor leaders, indigenous activists—or drug lords.

Indeed, the centennial commemoration of the Roosevelt Corollary to the Monroe Doctrine occurred in 2004. "Chronic wrongdoing," President Theodore Roosevelt told the U.S. Congress in December 1904, "or an impotence which results in a general loosening of ties of civilized society may in America, as elsewhere, ultimately require intervention by some civilized nation"—namely, "however reluctantly," the United States.[3] As argued by Alan Knight in this volume's lead chapter, Washington has sought to carry out these interventions without constructing a formal empire as such. The U.S. empire, in Knight's classification of imperial modalities, has been an "informal" one, shaping the activities of its fellow American states to its own interests by means of its superior force, together with its economic, political, and cultural dominance.

Over the past century, that is, it has been U.S. policy not simply to protect its neighbors from foreign and/or evil empires (what Knight calls the "defensive" function of empire) but to exercise sufficient control over those neighbors in order to maintain U.S.-defined ties of civilization (what he calls the "engineering" function of empire). It has accomplished this by way of strategic, selective intervention, making use of what Knight refers to as the political, economic, and cultural *mechanisms* that work to fulfill the *functions* of empire. Those mechanisms are meant to increase the probability that the "ties of civilized society" will strengthen when the United States approves of actions taken by her sister republics.

The historian Greg Grandin has suggested elsewhere that, beyond its long history, U.S. imperial practice in the Americas has served as a "trial run" of sorts for the exercise of power elsewhere in the world.[4] In his recent book, *Empire's Workshop*, Grandin emphasizes both the informal and the indirect nature of much of this imperial practice, which has involved the delegation of imperial responsibility to local elites. This has been especially true of the farming out of imperial violence, a process known to Pentagon hands as the "Salvador option," after its successful use in combating El Salvador's leftist insurgency in the 1980s. The "Salvador option," discussed by Grandin in *Empire's Workshop*, thus refers to the use of native militaries and paramilitaries to do the hands-on work of imperial maintenance.[5]

And if the "Salvador option" refers to the farming out of violence, one can talk about an even more powerful "Chile option" as the farming out of economic policy. My use of the term refers to the effectiveness of training local elites to think like imperial elites in the realm of economic theory. Trained in the most "free-market" versions of neoclassical economics, Chilean economists stood ready to privatize, deregulate, remove protections, and open the economy to the easy entrance of transnational (mostly U.S.) capital once the way had been cleared by the U.S.-supported coup led by General Pinochet. "How we have come full round to the free-market absolutism now being imposed on Iraq is the back-story of our times," writes Grandin. "In important ways the road to Iraq passes through Latin America, starting first in Chile."[6] Indeed, in the "Chile option," one sees the political (the coup), the economic (the dismantling of a social economy), and the cultural (learning how to think) mechanisms working hand-in-hand to benefit the imperial relationship.

These imperial mechanisms are reflected in U.S. Secretary of State Condoleezza Rice's repeated insistence in her talks to Latin American audiences that Washington, as a democratic power, would have no choice but to "permit" elected leftist governments to take office and allow them to remain there so long as they chose to govern within a "democratic structure," leaving it quite clear who got to define "democratic structure." (This framework, of course, is relatively new. Back in the days of the Cold War, U.S. national security always trumped any notion of democracy promotion.) Democracy is a universal value, Rice now wants to be understood as saying, and the United States, as the region's benevolent great power, will do its best to protect its neighbors' ability to attain and maintain democracy, strategically intervening when governments stray from the democratic path. Implicit in this interpretation is the idea that relations between neighboring nations will also take place within a framework of institutional, democratic relations. But, for many of those neighbors, the story has always been a bit more complicated.

On 10 March 2005, for example, in a visit little noticed outside of Mexico, Rice met with Mexico's foreign minister Luis Ernesto Derbez in order to resolve a long-simmering dispute between the two countries regarding Mexico's "water debit" under a complicated water-rights treaty. Her seven-hour visit to Mexico resulted in the host country's agreement to deliver 716,000 acre-feet of river water to the United States by September of that year, thus honoring a 1944 treaty on the sharing of the water flowing along the common border between the two countries.

On the same visit, Rice dismissed Mexico's complaint that Washington had recently violated international law by abruptly withdrawing from the Optional Protocol of the Treaty of Vienna, which gives the United Nations International Court of Justice the authority to intervene in cases in which individuals imprisoned in foreign countries have not had the ability to consult with their own consular officials. Under that authorization, the court had recently directed a "meaningful review" of fifty-one convictions and sentences of Mexican citizens condemned to death in the United States, none of whom had been given the opportunity to consult with a consular official. Following that decision, Washington announced that it would simply remove itself from the court's jurisdiction.

"We will continue to believe in the importance of consular notification," said Secretary Rice in the run-up to her Mexico City meeting, but international court jurisdiction had "proven inappropriate for the United States."[7] Rice effectively told the Mexicans: while you folks have a water treaty to live up to, we can simply withdraw from any signed agreement we find "inappropriate." Rice displayed no embarrassment about the contradiction. On the contrary, one of the objectives of her visit was precisely to confirm those different levels of obligation. It was a useful demonstration of the maintenance of U.S. dominance in the Americas.

This kind of routine imperial maintenance has long generated multifaceted resentment and opposition in the hemisphere. This "dissent" has been evident in the many attempts by one or another of the "sister republics" to pull away from U.S. dominance and in the widespread manifestations of popular discontent and unrest directed against U.S. power.

Empire and Dissent examines precisely that dynamic: the interaction of imperial power with the dissent and resistance it has engendered. The contributors to this volume examine the question of "empire," the various forms of resistance, dissent, and/or accommodation it generates, and the ways it has manifested itself in the Americas. They explore the ways in which the contours of dissent and resistance have been generated by the activities of empire, as well as the ways in which the contours of empire have been given shape by opposition, resistance, and disaffection.

Since the book approaches its primary concern—U.S.-hemispheric relations at the beginning of the twenty-first century—with a historical perspective, it is divided into two sections: in part I Alan Knight, Gregory Dowd, John Oldfield, and Carlos Marichal examine empire and dissent through a historical lens; in part II the analysis moves to present-day conflicts within the hemisphere, with essays on various kinds of dissent (and, in some cases, accommodation) in Mexico (Neil Harvey), Bolivia (Silvia Rivera Cusicanqui), Brazil (Jeffrey Rubin), Argentina (Daniel Cieza), and Venezuela (Steve Ellner). The volume thus addresses the exercise of, dissent from, and resistance to imperial rule in a variety of settings, ranging from historical assessments of imperial rule in the Americas to analyses of some very different contemporary forms of domination and dissent. The contributors do not take the question of empire as a given, but rather probe its meanings and applications as a descriptive term for U.S.-hemispheric relations and, more generally, for the interplay of certain economic and cultural relations in the Americas.

Knight's lead chapter, an inquiry into the nature of imperial domination by way of a close historical examination of U.S. and British empires, sets the tone and provides a schematic framework within which the succeeding essays, both historical and contemporary, can be best understood. Knight's essay is immediately followed by three chapters that continue the historical inquiry into the nature of empire: Dowd on the conflict-laden relationship between eighteenth-century empire-building settlers and Native Americans; Oldfield on the imperial setting of eighteenth- and nineteenth-century dissent against Britain's slave trade; and Marichal on the use of financial power to bolster U.S. imperial domination in the second half of the twentieth century.

Both Dowd and Oldfield are concerned with, among other things, the cultural dimensions of imperial domination, specifically with the racial conceptions of subjected peoples held not only by ruling elites but by other, less-privileged members (or subjects) of the imperial power. Dowd discusses Native American resistance to colonial rule as generated for the most part by the inferior, subcitizen status in which they were held. This status was imposed on Native Americans in part because it was functional to their imperial subjection. By the late eighteenth century, writes Dowd, "a long history of colonial slavery and Indian dispossession had encouraged the development of notions of savagery and race that made some Britons openly question the Indians' readiness or even capacity for civility."

Oldfield writes about the shifting sentiment within the imperial power— once again, Great Britain—about the human status of the African slaves brought to the Americas, upon whom so much of England's imperial expansion rested. Indeed, the British empire's internalization of the belief that subjected populations are not qualified to retain anything but a subcitizen status has long played a role in the formation of structures of power. When that belief erodes, so, frequently, does the domination.

The question of "status" thus becomes an important subtheme of this book. A great deal of dissent in the Americas has lately taken the form of a militant assertion of humanity and citizenship by racially and ethnically excluded populations, and the chapters in part II discuss that phenomenon in Bolivia, southern Mexico, Brazil, and (with a strong component of social class) Venezuela. The issue of status extends throughout the volume in discussions of organized dissent and is especially significant in Harvey's chapter on Mexico's Mayan Zapatistas and Rivera Cusicanqui's discussion of Bolivia's Aymara and Qhichwa *cocaleros*.

In all these cases, the cultural mechanism of imperial engineering (if I may borrow Knight's terminology) attempts to link desired behavior to a certain set of cultural norms and to judge those norms deficient if they do not produce the behavior that is functional to empire. Thus, Rivera Cusicanqui's interpretation of the confrontation between empire and indigeneity in Bolivia grimly echoes Dowd's description of a similar confrontation in North America two centuries earlier. "The idea that in Bolivia," writes Rivera Cusicanqui, "the rural and urban indigenous people who led the October revolt against the government of Gonzalo Sánchez de Lozada or voted massively for Evo Morales's Movement Toward Socialism Party (MAS) were 'archaic' or 'backward'—that they were resisting modern market discipline in a kind of cultural or racial atavism—is a part of unquestioned common sense among the elites, as much in Bolivia as in the developed world."

Sources of Domination

As the essays in this volume make clear, hemispheric domination today flows both from the U.S. state apparatus and from transnational sources of power. On the one hand is the informal U.S. empire itself: Washington's determination to maintain its dominant position within the hemisphere. On the other hand is the supremacy of "the markets," frequently presented by pro-market ideologues as a kind of domination by nature, or by "reality." Critics, of course, see market domination not as a natural, but as a historical phenomenon, not as control by the abstract forces of supply and demand, but rather by those who have inordinate power within the interplay of market forces—namely, the (loosely constructed) capitalist class.

In some recent debates over globalization, as both Harvey and Ellner remind us, the ascendancy of the markets—or of capital—has been held to be the paramount form of domination in the contemporary world. In the recent work of Michael Hardt and Antonio Negri, for example, this phenomenon has been referred to simply as "Empire," a global construction with no necessary geographic or political modifier.[8] For Hardt and Negri, "Empire" is a global network of domination by an essentially transnational capitalist class that recognizes no geographical boundaries. It is a network that constantly reorganizes the logic of work, civic participation, and daily life on a worldwide basis.

This analysis has had important implications for the political organization of dissent, leading away from a focus on achieving state power (which would presumably leave one subject to the dictates of transnational capital) and toward an attempt to confront capital from below with like-minded national and transnational allies. Further, Hardt and Negri assert, just as the decentralized structure of transnational capital stands in stark contrast to the centralized structure of the imperial state, so, too, must contemporary dissident and revolutionary movements transform their vertical, centralized structures into decentralized bodies that link to one another horizontally across national and transnational space. As detailed by Harvey in chapter 5 herein, this is the strategy of Mexico's Zapatistas.

Whatever one may think of this imperial characterization of global capital and its concomitant logic of resistance, there is no question that, in addition to the relatively straightforward U.S. domination of the Americas, the more diffuse influence of global financial power has been playing an increasingly important role in the Americas.

In chapter 4 Marichal argues that these two sources of power are not so easily separated and that the hegemony of one state over others has nearly always depended on "great financial strength" on an international scale. Focusing on the financial relations between the United States and Latin America from the end of World War II to the present day, Marichal shows that Washington's establishment of its worldwide military organization has been accompanied by a succession of financial innovations that have contributed to finance its global reach, as well as to submit other nations to financial dependency in a variety of ways. These innovations, he argues, were put in place by the combined efforts of the U.S. government, private corporations, and a group of international financial institutions (IFIs) designed to construct a new international order after World War II. The new order served the interests both of the U.S. government and of global capital. While state and market forces must thus be considered together, market and corporate forces have become considerably more active than the state over the past half century. Looking specifically at Argentina and Mexico, Marichal suggests that the Latin American lending booms of the 1970s constituted a fundamental antecedent to modern financial globalization and led to the inordinate influence of the IFIs during the 1980s and 1990s.

Indeed, as is well known, in the early 1980s most Latin American countries, faced with falling commodity prices, rising international interest rates, and a sizable debt burden, found themselves unable to meet their debt obligations and were therefore compelled to adopt a series of market-based economic reforms as a condition for being "rescued" by the International Monetary Fund (IMF). Beginning in Mexico in 1982, the IFIs imposed a series of measures that were designed to impart a degree of fiscal and social discipline to Latin American governments and populations in the belief that such discipline would build confidence among the private investors whose self-interested financial activities were meant to drive the recovery and growth of their economies. The most publicly stated idea was that major industrial, commercial, and financial investors could be attracted (or reattracted) to Latin America if and only if they were given reasonable assurance that their investments in the region would be secure and profitable. A second, no less important idea behind these reforms was that recovery and growth would take place only if the region's labor force was severely limited in its ability to press its claims before private employers and the state.[9]

These market-based reforms, which came to be called "neoliberal," opened national economies to foreign (at the time, mostly U.S.) trade and investment, and included the (attempted) privatization of public activity, the deregulation of private activity, the replacement of institutional with targeted programs of social welfare, the removal of the monetary authority from elected political control, and zero-deficit public budgets that quickly became "austerity budgets" throughout the Americas. The imposition of these reforms—with the assistance and approval of at least some local elites—was made possible by Latin American governments' inability to service their debts. To this day, the foreign debt remains a major vulnerability of most Latin American countries.

Cieza, in chapter 8, narrates the events following Argentina's massive debt default of 2001, which culminated in the country's emergence from its default in such an "independent" way that it became a "bad example" for the IMF. When President Néstor Kirchner assumed office in 2003, the default he inherited allowed him to elaborate a non-neoliberal growth model, consisting of the beginnings of a reindustrialization program and a cautious reinsertion of the state in social programs and economic regulation, without having to negotiate these programs with the IMF. Then, to remove the country from default, he offered to pay foreign creditors 30 cents on every dollar of debt, to be remitted in low-interest federal bonds. Helped by the Venezuelan government's offer to buy up to three billion dollars of these state bonds, Kirchner was in a very strong position to get most of Argentina's private and public creditors to agree to his terms. With its end run around the disciplinary consequences of indebtedness, Kirchner's deal was not to the IMF's liking, but it, like most of the creditors, had little choice but to accept.

Writing about Brazil, Rubin tells a very different story: unlike Kirchner, a conventional politician who was radicalized by the times, Brazil's president, Luiz Inácio Lula da Silva, was an unconventional politician who, once in office, adopted orthodox economic policies. "Lula," writes Rubin in chapter 7, "has surprised his own supporters as well as international bankers by rigorously complying with the economic prescriptions of the International Monetary Fund (IMF). The result has been a startling political story: a long-standing leader of the leftist Workers Party (PT) has kept the Brazilian economy stable [and] gained the support of domestic and global financial leaders." He has not, however, left his own poor and working-class followers happy.

Like Cieza, Rubin focuses on the interaction of a "dissenting" state and the popular movements that have attempted to drive it to much greater levels of resistance. Brazil, argues Rubin, is a democracy that has "endured and deepened," in large part due to the activism of social movements and their ongoing ties to the Workers Party. Lula's move away from the platform on which he was elected, however, is a worrying reminder of the power of transnational capital and the limits that financial power places on formal democratic procedures.

Disciplinary Economics

Advocates of a neoliberal "consensus" among the financial institutions have generally preferred to keep their political objectives hidden behind the mantles of "efficient market theory" and "technical assistance," thereby privileging the advice of "value free" economists and technocrats over the discourse of elected politicians and political activists.[10] But the irony—or perhaps the contradiction—of the situation is that neoliberalism, with its insistence on unregulated markets, does not permit the kinds of careful government interventions the developed countries themselves have used to strengthen their domestic industries and deliberately build their own comparative advantages. The Cambridge economist Ha-Joon Chang has commented that the motto of the wealthy countries that advocate on behalf of neoliberal economics should be "Do as we say, but not as we've done."[11]

There was a time, not so long ago in the developed countries of the West, when the necessity of state intervention in the marketplace, for any number of reasons, was commonly accepted as a given. In those days, before the neoliberal era, advocates of unregulated markets were marginalized in international-development policy debates. In the past quarter century the tables have turned. Those who have critiqued free markets have been treated as though they simply do not understand the dynamics of human nature and the "real" world. They have also been accused of politicizing what should be a set of value-free, apolitical relationships. Such reconfiguration of "common sense" is another useful mechanism of informal imperial rule.

In order to understand the political logic of neoliberalism, it is therefore necessary to go beyond its discourse and to examine the relevant relations of power. The growing inequality evident throughout the Americas may not simply be a negative unintended consequence of a U.S.-based neoliberal policy consensus, but rather an intended fulfillment of the real objectives of that consensus. After all, economic "discipline" and the maintenance of a large supply of workers able and willing to work hard and cheap can be seen as one of the major motors of the North's late-twentieth-century economic recovery (which has since stagnated). This great neoliberal success story is considered the legacy of such forceful political leaders as President Reagan, Lady Thatcher, and General Pinochet. As such, the "discipline" of the neoliberal era has replaced the "security" of the Keynesian, post–World War II era as an imperial policy goal.

It is in this context that the exercise of power from both state and transnational sources has had such polarizing consequences in Latin America over the past quarter century. Indeed, one of the defining experiences of the past three decades has been the growth of income inequality both *within* countries and *between* countries. This is the case at all levels. Just as the gap between wealthy and middle-income countries has grown, so has the gap between middle-income and poor countries, and between rich and poor individuals.[12]

In response to inequality *between* countries, there have been increasing efforts to promote regional solidarity in the face of U.S. domination. The revival of the South American Common Market (MERCOSUR) and Hugo Chávez's various oil-based initiatives within the Americas all spring from a practical kind of regional solidarity: a hope that more trade and investment can be generated within Latin America itself. These moves reflect a desire to negotiate with Washington from a position of greater strength, thus reducing the South's debilitating dependence on the North.

But such efforts are not necessarily resistance. While the members and associate members of Mercosur seek to build Southern power, many would also like a non-antagonistic relationship with Washington. They promote U.S.-Mercosur negotiations as an alternative to the U.S.-promoted country-by-country negotiations to form a Free Trade Area of the Americas (FTAA), but most have voiced no opposition to the eventual enactment of a continent-wide free-trade zone that would include the United States. They are simply pursuing the promotion of regional solidarity in the face of U.S. imperial ambitions. A certain degree of pragmatic accommodation, that is, can accompany a measure of dissent.

Even the outspoken anti-imperialists of the group, Venezuela's Chávez and Bolivia's Evo Morales, know that to some extent they must respond to the imperial reality: over 50 percent of Venezuela's crude oil is still sold on the U.S. market, and following the nationalization of Bolivia's gas reserves on May Day 2006, Morales has very carefully been negotiating acceptable terms of sale with the governments of Argentina and Brazil, and terms of participation with the international investors—especially the Brazilian company Petrobras—who have a stake in the industry.

Meanwhile, Chávez has conducted a foreign policy based on regional solidarity, striking oil-based agreements with a group of Caribbean nations (an agreement called PetroCaribe), with Argentina (PetroSur), and with the countries of the Community of Andean Nations (PetroAndina), advancing ambitious proposals for the energy—and eventually economic—integration of Latin America and the Caribbean. Chávez has maintained cordial relations with the leaders of the countries in all those regions, even with his longtime ideological and geopolitical antagonist, President Álvaro Uribe of Colombia, with the aim of constructing a Latin American bloc of nations, supported by the region's ample energy resources. Members of all three pacts have approved an initiative to merge these agreements into a continent-wide initiative called PetroAmérica. This represents a movement toward a greater degree of regional sovereignty and solidarity, as well as gradual independence from the dictates of Washington.

Dissent from Above and Below

In chapter 9 Ellner draws a careful distinction between dissent from above ("the assertion of sovereignty by Third World governments") and from below ("relatively autonomous social movements and the large number of people whose daily lives clash with the logic of the established system") to elaborate on the conflicting models for extensive social change in Venezuela. Powerful elements of both types of dissent can be found throughout Latin America, and Ellner argues that both play a role in the radical movement associated with President Hugo Chávez. Ellner's chapter thus provides an insightful overview of *Chavismo*, as well as a useful elaboration of—and coda to—one of the central themes of this collection: the distinctions between government- and party-organized dissent and the dissent that emanates from grassroots popular movements.

Key to a close reading of part II is an understanding that of the many contradictions in the Americas, one of the most salient is that between the included and the excluded, between those who can regularly participate in the formal institutions of society, politics, and the economy and those who are able to do so only intermittently or not at all. This divide has become a basis of contemporary politics, partially superceding the traditional, and still-powerful, divide between capital and labor.

In some cases, as with Brazil's landless rural workers or the Andean and Mesoamerican indigenous peasantry, the exclusion of vast segments of the population dates back to the colonial era. In other cases, as with the working poor in Argentina and Venezuela, exclusion—as a form of class discipline—has been deliberately built into late-twentieth-century economic structures. Whatever its origins, exclusion has been exacerbated to crisis proportions by the region's current dominant model of social and economic development, a model premised on the systematic exclusion of certain segments of the population from meaningful participation.

In the past few decades the excluded have self-organized into movements striving for inclusion. And to the degree that participants believe inclusion to require significant changes in social, political, and economic institutions, many of these movements have engaged in radical struggles for the creation of a new set of institutions more conducive to these ends. Since the early 1990s, the disruptive, pressuring, and lobbying activities of organized popular movements have directly or indirectly played a role in bringing down governments, electing new governments, and/or influencing government policies—especially privatization policies—in at least a dozen countries in the Americas. The street protests of Argentina's *piqueteros* (most of them unemployed urban workers), for example, created the conditions for the 2003 election of President Kirchner and the subsequent implementation of (modestly) alternative policies. The protests were driven by a nationalist sector of the governing Peronist party and were supported by the social movements that emerged from the fragmented and dispersed forms of resistance against the neoliberal model—again, a mix of political-party activism (the Peronists) and "relatively autonomous" social movements.

More often than not, these movements contain a powerful racial or ethnic component. In December 2005 the coca-grower (*cocalero*) leader Evo Morales was elected president of Bolivia in the wake of a long series of disruptive antiprivatization, pro-cocalero street demonstrations. In this instance the mix of "above" and "below" was given an extra twist by the existence, in the Bolivian Andes, of local, regional, and long-distance markets for consumption of coca leaf in its natural state, as well as consumption for ritual and medicinal purposes. These markets, argues Rivera Cusicanqui in chapter 6, provided a solid basis of social organization for the grassroots movement to legalize coca—and hence the livelihood of a large part of the rural, mostly indigenous population—as well as electoral support for Morales.

In addition, Rivera Cusicanqui asserts, the continued existence and growth of these markets has provided an important affirmation of anticolonial indigenous identity. A certain amount of "traditional" coca cultivation has long been permitted in Bolivia by international convention under the assumption that, along with indigenous identity itself, it would soon die out. That this has not happened is an indication that a genuine sense of "indigeneity"—as opposed to what Rivera Cusicanqui describes as the "reified, postcard image of the indigenous culture" embodied by *el indio permitido* (the tolerated Indian)—has survived in Bolivia. This survival, she argues, alongside the popular movement to which it is linked, represents a powerful kind of resistance to the dictates of empire.

Popular mobilization—dissent from below—has not by itself created alternative policies, but over the past fifteen years or so it has served as an impetus for change. And popular movements have developed complex, frequently ambiguous relationships with the governments they have helped bring to power. While some of these movements have strongly identified with newly elected "anti-neoliberal" governments (especially, for example, the neighborhood movements in Venezuela and the cocaleros in Bolivia), many have managed to protect and preserve a significant degree of autonomy for their anti-neoliberal projects. And many movements have divided over the question.

Successful popular movements have often fragmented over whether to join progressive governments. The Uruguayan journalist Raúl Zibechi has written about this phenomenon: "When social justice movements develop the ability to mobilize large numbers of people," he writes, "and gain influence in the political arena, they create a new scenario that frequently turns against them. Too often, their success weakens and even divides them, thereby leading to a period of withdrawal and demobilization."[13] It is an understanding of the value of autonomy and independence that has made many activists uneasy about joining progressive governments that they might be willing to support from the outside, unsullied by the political compromises—some necessary, some opportunistic—that can undermine the motivating belief that "another world is possible."

Mexico's Zapatista movement represents perhaps the most deliberate attempt to organize the excluded outside the boundaries of state power. The Zapatista's "Other Campaign," which took place alongside the country's presidential campaign of 2006, was an attempt to reach out to like-minded groups at a time when people were presumably thinking about politics, writes Harvey in chapter 5. It represented their ongoing attempt, says Harvey, "to listen to the problems and struggles of a wide variety of people who are similarly searching for greater levels of coordination and solidarity, while asserting their own particular demands and goals." The Zapatistas, that is, are among the few revolutionary movements whose goal is not state power, but rather the creation of new forms of social organization outside the state.

Of course, not all active relationships between social movements and the state are alike. There is a crucial distinction, for example, between the Bolivian autonomous popular movement that carried a government to power and the Venezuelan government's successful mobilization of the population into a series of movements that, as Ellner reports, tend to come and go according to the needs of an essentially state-oriented political movement. With respect to relations between the grassroots and the state, one can identify three broad categories of popular movements: those, like the Zapatistas, that want nothing to do with state power; those, like Bolivia's cocaleros, that jealously guard their autonomy while supporting and participating in a government they have brought to power; and those, like Venezuela's electoral battle units (UBES), that are brought into being by popular governments and have no real autonomy of their own.

In all three of these cases, participation and militancy has been for many of the excluded a first step toward participation in the broader political activities of their respective countries. Further, many of these movements are, to one degree or another, integrated into global movements fighting against a neoliberal world order. Despite their local origins, virtually all of these movements have been drawn into international debates about democratic change, universal social justice, and meaningful political participation.

Social Solidarity vs. the Privatization of Citizenship

Margaret Thatcher, who tried to replace social solidarity with pure individualism, once remarked, "There is no such thing as society, only individual men and women."[14] This is not a description of life on Earth, but rather the basis for the powerful political program of neoliberalism. This program has succeeded in transforming life for many people around the world, especially those who work under conditions of "flexible" labor, without contracts, without protection, without job security or social security. But the program has not succeeded in doing away with society.

There are now about twelve million undocumented immigrants living in the United States. They are mostly from Latin America and are active members of the U.S. labor force. A great many regularly send money home, paying a kind of informal, voluntary income tax to their homeland. The Bank of Mexico estimates that total remittances from Mexicans working abroad—the vast majority in the United States—amounted to about $23.5 billion in 2006, the country's second-largest net source of foreign exchange, after sales of crude oil.[15] Of course, the money goes where the senders want it to go: to their families, their communities, their parishes, their regions of origin.

For many localities in Mexico, remittances amount to a source of income greater than any other, public or private. And in some cases, these private remittances are put to public use, improving local services and repairing local infrastructure. At the same time that many Mexican workers are slipping into informal employment and losing formal-sector health and pension benefits, remittances are strengthening local health clinics, both public and private. The system of flexible labor and benefits is thus mirrored by a system of flexible taxes and obligations. And as with informal wages, there is no guarantee that these informal taxes will be sufficient in years to come or be directed to areas where some form of public debate decides they are most needed. It all amounts to a kind of back-door privatization of public life—the privatization of citizenship itself. In an ongo-ing Web forum convened by the Social Science Research Council, Craig Calhoun refers to this process as the "privatization of risk," a process by which "efforts to replace public institutions with market mechanisms shift the burden of life's many risks disproportionately to those without sub-stantial private wealth."[16] Should the flow of remittances decline for any reason, there are no public institutions in place to pick up the slack. Thus, while many migrant workers remain tied to their homeland, they also seek rights and inclusion within the countries in which they work. This has become another popular struggle within the U.S. empire.

The existence of civil society itself has strengthened the hand of move-ments for the rights of migrant workers. In the United States migrant work-ers were never recruited as members of any community; they were never meant to be workers with connections to a definable set of social relations, with definable rights and responsibilities. They were recruited to work in the United States as members of an informal, atomized labor force, having no relation to society whatever. But civil society has its own dynamic and has come to serve as a kind of alternative public sector.

In the spring of 2006, migrant organizers, supported by many church parishes and ethnic media outlets, managed to bring an astounding number of immigrants—well over a million—onto the streets of major U.S. cities to demand rights, recognition, and legalization. This was certainly a form of "dissent from below" against the fragmentation, flexibilization, and disci-pline of the greater American workforce.[17]

These marches help reveal the underlying contradiction between the in-formal, flexible conditions under which most undocumented immigrants work and the more stable social, cultural, and political structures in which their lives are embedded. It was these stable structures—church parishes, radio stations, trade unions, hometown associations, community networks, and newspapers—that made the massive turnouts a possibility.

When all relationships are privatized and made flexible, when there are no enforceable social rights and obligations, there is little likelihood that what exists today will exist tomorrow. That may be the principal con-tradiction of the neoliberal social order. And it is the recognition of that fatal contradiction—as fatal to the undocumented workers as it is to the employers who hire them—that gave the social solidarity embodied by the migrant marches such sudden force and acceptance.

"Society" has also been recreated in the very different political setting in Venezuala, where Hugo Chávez has developed a remarkably strong rapport with poor and marginalized citizens. In his long, weekly, televised chats with the historically excluded he carefully explains current events in ways that include people who have previously been left out of political debates. He urges his viewers to involve themselves in their communities, to pressure his own government to fulfill its promises and achieve its "revolutionary" goals. The talks, frequently folksy and personal, often angry and inflammatory, create an apparent dialogue between the president and the people, and many previously marginalized Venezuelans feel included in citizenship for the first time in their lives.

There is a danger, of course, that this dialogue can become one between a *caudillo* (strongman) and his followers, but for now, Chávez has drawn on and made visible and functional the vast networks of social solidarity among those who had long felt outcast from the networks and privileges of citizenship. In so doing, he has redefined citizenship in Venezuela. The wealthy and middle classes have long excluded the poor majority from any genuine sense of participation in civic life. The poor, who have been the maids, gardeners, and delivery boys, but never the fellow-citizens of the privileged, now feel the country belongs to them. That's why the opposition by the privileged classes is so fierce. There is no gainsaying this accomplishment. Chávez's initiatives represent a kind of reconstitution of society and a kind of "dissent from above."

The multidimensional nature of empires—military, economic, political, cultural—has engendered multidimensional responses from their subjects. This has generally made for a process within the confines of those empires that is continuously unfolding, changing, and delivering surprises throughout the imperial lifespan. Both U.S. dominance in the Americas and the global dominion of capital have reached critical phases in their lifespans. The future of both is unwritten.

Notes

1. In March 2002 the neoconservative columnist Charles Krauthammer told Emily Eakin of the *New York Times*, in what became a widely quoted remark, "People are coming out of the closet on the word 'empire'" (Emily Eakin, "All Roads Lead to D.C.," *New York Times*, 31 March 2002.) Many proponents of U.S. empire prefer softer phrases like "benevolent hegemony," "unipolar power,"

or even "empire lite." See, for example, Kagan, "Benevolent Empire"; Ignatieff, *Empire Lite*. For the hard line, see Ferguson, *Empire*.

2. The comments of both Boot and Ignatieff were made to columnist Jeet Heer. See Jeet Heer, "Operation Anglosphere," *Boston Globe*, 23 March 2003.

3. For the historical context of this imperial attitude, see Grandin, *Empire's Workshop*, 15–27; Schoultz, "Latin America and the United States," 59–63.

4. Grandin, *Empire's Workshop*, 1–9.

5. Ibid., 87.

6. Ibid., 163.

7. Fred Rosen, "It's Not about Water," *Miami Herald* (Mexico Edition), 21 March 2005. Also see "No le preocupa a EU que la izquierda gane elecciones y gobierne en AL: Rice," *La Jornada* (Mexico), 10 March 2005.

8. Hardt and Negri, *Empire*.

9. See, for example, David Harvey, *A Brief History of Neoliberalism*, especially his discussion of the restructuring of the Mexican economy (98–104); also see Hershberg and Rosen, "Turning the Tide?" 9–10.

10. For a collection of early neoliberal arguments, including Mario Vargas Llosa's widely reprinted "América Latina y la opción liberal," see Levine, *El desafío neoliberal*. Also see Williamson, *Latin American Adjustment*. For current thinking of the formulators of the Washington Consensus, see Kuczynski and Williamson, *After the Washington Consensus*.

11. Ha-Joon Chang, comment at the "First Annual Conference for Development and Change," Antigua, Guatemala, 25–28 July 2003. Also see Chang, *Kicking Away the Ladder*, 1–9.

12. Gwynne and Kay, "Latin America Transformed," 8.

13. Zibechi, "The New Popular Movements." Perhaps the classic description of this process is Piven and Cloward, *Poor People's Movements*.

14. Cited by David Harvey, *A Brief History of Neoliberalism*, 23.

15. Banco de México, *Informe Annual*, 2006, 40.

16. See http://privatizationofrisk.ssrc.org.

17. The culture of informality has exacerbated the already wide income-distribution gap and thus has been targeted by many trade-union campaigns, including those in the United States. See Rosen, "From Mexico to New York, Labor Joins the Struggle," 8–11.

PART I

EMPIRE IN THE AMERICAS:
HISTORICAL REFLECTIONS

ALAN KNIGHT

I   U.S. IMPERIALISM/HEGEMONY
AND LATIN AMERICAN RESISTANCE

In this chapter I analyze the character and dynamics of the United States' putative imperialism or hegemony in Latin America and conclude by touching on the question of Latin American "resistance." However, since both topics are huge and protean and the capacity of one historian, writing one chapter, is necessarily limited, I will devote more space to hegemony. There is at least one obvious justification for this bias: hegemony is both chronologically and analytically antecedent to resistance; thus, as I argue in conclusion, the nature of hegemony affects the nature of resistance (although the story thereafter becomes dialectical, involving complicated feedback processes).

Broad comparisons of this kind demand some kind of conceptual framework.[1] I regret that the framework I suggest is rather complicated, but it is not an a priori scholastic formulation. It owes relatively little to grand theories of empire (Lenin, Hobson), of world-systems (Wallerstein), or of hegemony (Keohane).[2] It owes still less—apart, perhaps, from some emotive fuel—to fashionable advocates of U.S. imperialism (e.g., Ferguson).[3] Rather, the framework is a posteriori, based on some years of reflection on the history of empires, especially the British and the American.[4] It involves four perspectives, which may at first sight seem excessively complex and abstract, but which, I think, help organize the themes which follow.

1. The two *modalities* of imperialism (the main forms it takes: formal and informal).
2. The two *functions* of imperialism (the broad means employed by the imperialist power, what I call "engineering" and "defense").
3. The three *mechanisms* adopted to fulfill these functions (political, economic, and cultural).
4. The ultimate imperialist *goals* which these functions and mechanisms serve (which are too varied, elusive, and historically specific to permit a simple and useful typology, although the familiar triad of political, economic, and cultural could be wheeled out again).

Formal and Informal Empire

First, by *modalities* I mean the contrasting forms which imperialism assumes. In particular, I am thinking of the familiar distinction between "formal" and "informal" empire. The distinction is crucial, since U.S. imperialism has tended toward the informal, and if empire is equated solely with formal imperialism, one may wonder why the United States is being scrutinized in the first place. Also, since the fall of the Iberian empires in the New World in the early nineteenth century, Latin America—especially South America—has largely escaped *formal* imperialist rule, but has arguably experienced *informal* imperialist intervention or influence.

The notion of informal empire (or informal imperialism, hegemony, or paramountcy) is well established in both the historical and the social science literature.[5] However, different scholars use different terms, and the implications of their terminology may differ, too. The formal-informal distinction conceals (at least) two different criteria, which are too readily conflated, and which should instead be differentiated and plotted along two separate axes: one axis denotes *direct* as against *indirect* rule; the other differentiates *de jure* (legal, legitimate, hence usually durable) control from *de facto* (illegal, illegitimate, hence often transitory) control. Axes are required because, like many social-scientific categories, these are not black-and-white alternatives—separate boxes into which cases can be neatly sorted—but rather continua, along which cases are distributed in scattered fashion.

Sometimes, the formal-informal distinction differentiates direct control from indirect control (by the hegemonic, imperialist, or paramount power). The key question, to quote Dahl, is: who governs? In formal empire the imperialist power enjoys direct control; in informal empire "natives" (usually, "collaborating elites," in Ronald Robinson's words) govern in cahoots with the imperial power.[6] In fact, most of the great territorial empires of the world, painted the appropriate color on the map, have embodied large measures of informality. Metropolitan elites could not run the show single-handed, so they recruited collaborators: Mexican *caciques*, Andean *kurakas*, Nigerian emirs, Indian princes, Cuban *políticos*, Nicaraguan national guardsmen. The more formal an empire, in this sense, the more the imperial power assumed the direct tasks of administration: policing, defending, taxing, converting, educating, and developing.

French imperialism tended to be more formal, in this sense, than British. American imperialism has usually operated through highly informal control (hence, its imperial character has been denied, and more nuanced descriptives—such as *hegemony*—have sometimes been preferred). Direct administration incurs costs, in terms of both blood and treasure, and runs counter to American values of democracy and self-determination—values that were less influential when the great European empires of the nineteenth century (not to mention the sixteenth century) were being carved out. Indirect control covers a wide spectrum, ranging from semiautonomous fiefs within formal empires (e.g., the Indian princely states) to unequal and clientelist relations between "sovereign" powers, whereby one (in this case, the United States) exercises disproportionate power over another and can bend it to its own imperial will (for example, Guatemala in 1954).

The second axis corresponds more precisely to colors on the map and relates to the legality, the legitimacy, and (usually) the durability of imperialist control.[7] A sudden U.S. intervention may create a pocket of empire in which the United States temporarily exercises direct rule. In Veracruz, in April 1914, for example, the Americans landed, cleaned up the port, and drove away the vultures; then, after seven months, the Americans left and the vultures returned.[8] This occupation was short-lived and lacked both legality and legitimacy. In contrast, the huge area of northern Mexico that the United States sequestered in the 1840s was annexed, painted red on the map, and recognized as U.S. territory by the Treaty of Guadalupe Hidalgo. *Continental* expansion favored such acquisition and legitimization of conquest; thus, the U.S. land empire survived intact when the European maritime empires collapsed in the mid-twentieth century.[9] Aside from Mexico, the other site of durable and legitimate U.S. imperialism has been the circum-Caribbean, where the United States has acquired at least one colony (Puerto Rico), several bases (Panama, Guantánamo), and quite a few protectorates (e.g., Cuba under the Platt Amendment, Haiti between 1915 and 1935, and the Dominican Republic between 1916 and 1924).[10] In these cases, U.S. imperialism has been legitimized by formal cessions, treaties, and agreements which have validity in the eyes of the so-called civilized world or the "comity of nations."

This, of course, is an old story. In the past, during the heyday of European imperialism, such formal footholds often presaged more ambitious imperialist advance. A "treaty port" could afford a bridgehead for penetration of the interior; even more clearly, a formal agreement conferring partial (e.g., financial) control—like the Anglo-French condominium which controlled Egyptian finances after 1876—could be parlayed into a full-scale imperial takeover (hence, Egypt, 1882).[11] In the U.S. case, such imperial escalation—"mission creep," to use contemporary jargon—has also occurred, but it has been offset by both U.S. antipathy to full-scale imperial takeovers and the capacity of the United States for devising more satisfactory alternative (informal) arrangements. (Thus, in particular cases, one may debate whether the U.S. preference for informality is a matter of values or of self-interest. While politicians like to ascribe it to values, I see [perceived] self-interest as paramount.) Thus, the four quadrants in the table can be identified and filled in with representative examples.[12]

Both direct and indirect rule, as well as de jure and de facto control, serve imperial ends. What, in the cases under consideration, are those ends? One can frame the response in different ways (hence, my rather elaborate typology). First, one can tease out two basic *functions* of imperialism, applicable (as far as I can see) to all empires: Roman, Spanish, British, Soviet, American. Second, these functions in turn involve three *mechanisms*. Third, and finally, if one considers the historical peculiarities of each case, one can discern some ultimate *goals*, which differ from case to case (and which, by virtue of their great variation, defy simple answers). In looking at basic functions and mechanisms one is "lumping," that is, noting common features of imperialism, thus including the United States within a historical club (of imperialists), a membership that many Americans strenuously

Table 1. Modalities of Empire

	Direct Control	Indirect Control
Legitimate/de jure	Puerto Rico	Platt Amendment
	Guantánamo	Cuba, 1901–34
De facto	Cuba, 1898	Cuba, 1934–59
	Veracruz, 1914	Chile, 1973
	Panama, 1989	

deny. When it comes to ultimate goals, however, one is "splitting": stressing differences and peculiarities.[13]

The Functions of Empire

As regards basic functions, imperialist powers seek to do two things: (1) mold the "peripheral" society in such a way to suit imperial-metropolitan interests (however they may be defined); and (2) fend off rival imperial powers, thus preserving the benefits for the metropolis. The first might be called the engineering function, the second the defensive function. By and large, successful "engineering" requires a long-standing and often costly commitment to direct rule (or, failing that, some efficacious and congenial collaborators). The task roughly corresponds to what is today called, rather misleadingly, "nation building."[14] Of course, the scale of the task depends on the desiderata: does the imperialist power seek a profitable economic dependency? A loyal strategic subordinate? A society that thinks, prays, plays, dresses, consumes, and conducts its politics as the imperialist power would like? All of the above? The more ambitious the goals (and the more recalcitrant the peripheral society), the more effort must be deployed and the more durable and dogged the imperial project must become. Arguably, the Spaniards—and perhaps the Jesuits, in particular—attempted the most ambitious social engineering in the Americas; but to this end the Spaniards had a peninsular prototype to work with (the Reconquista), cadres of keen imperialists (friars, merchants, officials) on whom they could rely, and some three hundred years in which to realize their project (which they did, with considerable success).[15] In contrast, Britain's informal empire in Latin America was relatively brief and superficial. American informal empire, though more successful than the British, has yet to compare with its Iberian predecessor in terms of durable accomplishments. If this is true, one might ask whether the limits of American social engineering are set more by American incapacity or by Latin American resistance.

Compared to the social-engineering function, defense against foreign interlopers can be quite manageable. Defense involves both military and economic (and maybe also cultural) efforts. The bulk of the mainland Spanish Empire, for example, enjoyed some two hundred years of relative military security, and the Royal Navy sustained British trade and investment in Latin America for most of the nineteenth century. In the twentieth century the United States faced few serious threats to its hegemony in the Americas (although it managed to discern and exaggerate quite a few not-so-serious ones). The pre-1918 German threat, the Axis challenge of the 1930s and 1940s, and even the Soviet threat after 1945 were all successfully countered, although in the 1962 Cuban Missile Crisis the defensive function of the United States came close to triggering a nuclear war. Since the 1990s, the United States has been able to regard Latin America as geopolitically safe: no significant communist challenge, no rogue states, no terrorist threat to speak of. This resulted in the Bush administration's relative neglect of the region (compared to Asia), as exemplified by Treasury Secretary O'Neill's insouciant observations at the time of the Argentine economic—and political—crisis of July–August 2002.[16]

But the defensive function of an imperialist power must also be economic. Spain's efforts to maintain mercantilist control of her American colonies failed in the later eighteenth century; Britain, after a brief heyday in the mid-nineteenth century, had to give ground to both Germany and the United States. U.S. economic dominance has, thus far, proved durable. It was greatly helped by two costly world wars, which gravely weakened one competitor (Britain) and, for a time, entirely eliminated the other (Germany), while fortifying the U.S. economy. And despite passing fears of Japanese penetration or of systemic U.S. decline, the United States does not appear to face an imminent challenge to its economic dominance in the Americas.[17] Such a threat, however, were it to exist, would raise interesting questions. Formal imperial powers—those that undertake direct political control of their dependencies—can skew economic relations in their own favor (hence, Bourbon mercantilism, British imperial preference, the supposed underdevelopment or de-industrialization of India under the Raj).[18] However, the more informal the relationship, the harder it becomes to use political control to compensate for economic decline.[19] Would an economically embattled America—facing, let us say, a powerful federal Europe or a booming China—seek to use political (or even military) power to bolster its economic dominance in the Americas?[20] It is hard to see how it could do so successfully. The maritime supremacy of the Royal Navy, for example, was of little use in countering U.S. and German commercial competition in late-nineteenth-century Latin America. Likewise, smart weapons and stealth bombers will not help U.S. business compete with China or the European Union in the early-twenty-first century.[21]

Such speculation may be futile, but it reveals how different mechanisms can be used to pursue the twin functions of engineering and defense. A good deal of international-relations thinking—and some international history, too—operates with an explicit or, more usually, implicit threefold typology of power: politicomilitary, economic, and cultural.[22] One could summarize and colloquialize the typology thus: great powers can strong-arm their clients, bribe them, or contrive that they think along the same lines (thus, obviating the need for either strong-arming or bribery). This typology is, of course, excessively neat, and in any given bilateral relationship, all three forms of power may interact. Furthermore, there may be some complex causal links: strong-arming in the past may create a disposition to collaborate in the present (thus, "to think along the same lines" even if there are no gunboats heaving into sight on the horizon). As the Spanish proverb has it, "Gato escaldo del agua fría huye" (A scalded cat flees cold water).

In general, however, the typology makes some sense and has implications for this discussion. Strong-arming is more susceptible to sudden decision making: the U.S. government can dispatch the Sixth Fleet or invade Grenada fairly rapidly, even casually. (The occupation of Veracruz in 1914 was certainly casual: the casus belli was a mere pretext, and Veracruz was chosen because the U.S. Navy did not want to run its warships aground on the Tampico bar.) At the other end of the spectrum, winning hearts and minds is a slower process, whose dynamics are far from clear. (Nevertheless, I would hazard the random comparison that the Jesuits won many more hearts and minds in Spanish America than the Office of Inter-American Affairs [OIAA] or the CIA ever did.) Some analysts stress the importance of American "soft power," but the problem with soft power is that it is difficult both to acquire and to deploy in a conscious, purposive way.[23] The Alliance for Progress was, perhaps, the best example in Latin America of a U.S. bid for hearts and minds, but its success was both limited and short-lived. A more pervasive and durable—but very "soft"—soft power may involve American culture and consumerism. But it is far from clear how very soft power—what one might call "mushy power"?—can be utilized by U.S. administrations. Latin Americans—even Cubans—may admire and seek to emulate many aspects of American culture (its music, sports, and fashion), but that does not translate into support for American policy. Hence one sees recurrent images—from Palestine to Pakistan—of anti-American demonstrators burning the U.S. flag while wearing T-shirts emblazoned with iconic U.S. symbols, such as those for Harley-Davidson and the Dallas Cowboys. Such images do not denote some kind of weird cognitive dissonance, but rather the ability of individuals to pick and choose, to be (putting it crudely) both pro- and anti-American at the same time, depending on the aspects or incarnations of "America" that are at stake. In other words, people may evade the one-dimensional cultural stereotypes which academics wish to impose on them.

Competing Objectives of Empire

Even if all empires strive to perform these two (engineering and defensive) tasks, which may therefore be taken as diagnostic of imperialism, the metropolitan interests, benefits, and ultimate goals will vary and must therefore be treated historically on a case-by-case basis.[24] But, clearly, Spanish imperialism embodied a range of competing objectives ("Glory, God and Gold" is one succinct summation), which the British in the nineteenth century failed to emulate (they did not care much for conversion), while the Americans in the twentieth century have pursued their own shifting and sometimes confused objectives—commercial, financial, strategic, religious, domestic-electoral—and have done so amid the usual welter of conflicting interests, lobbies, policy currents, and bureaucratic factions.[25] In no case is there a national monolith systematically pursuing a clear-cut national interest. That said, the basic framework of analysis remains valid, since it depends not on a false notion of concerted, purposive policy, but rather on ex post facto analysis of actions and outcomes which, for all their muddled origins and execution, are susceptible to rational analysis and conceptualization (in this, imperialism resembles traffic jams): imperialism can be formal and informal; it necessarily adopts both engineering and defensive functions; and it uses political (including military), economic, and perhaps cultural mechanisms to achieve its perceived objectives.

The United States, like Britain, usually practiced informal imperialism in Latin America. However, elements of "formality" crept in at times, and the United States, in fact, was a more formal imperialist in Latin America than Britain had been (a somewhat counterintuitive conclusion, given usual characterizations of the political cultures of the two countries). Like Britain acquired a couple of modest territorial footholds in Latin America (the Falklands and, maybe, Belize), the United States took and retained Puerto Rico.[26] But Puerto Rico was exceptional, and U.S. administrations usually set their face against outright permanent annexation in other locations.[27] More commonly, the United States established formal controls which, while falling short of annexation, did carry a "legitimate" right of intervention, most clearly in the case of the Platt Amendment, which legitimized the second U.S. intervention in Cuba in 1906 and afforded a rough model for quasi-protectorates in Haiti, Nicaragua, and the Dominican Republic.[28] Such policy sat uncomfortably alongside American commitments to self-determination and democracy, and the Platt Amendment was abrogated in 1934. The U.S. relationship with Cuba thus shifted along the continuum from formality toward informality (what Jorge Domínguez refers to as a shift from imperialism to hegemony).[29]

The Good Neighbor Policy provided a respite from formal interventions—not, of course, from informal pressure and influence—which lasted about a generation. However, the Cold War prompted a return to direct interventions, spurred in part by the specter of the Cuban Revolution. U.S. forces invaded the Dominican Republic in 1965, Grenada in 1983, and Panama in 1989. U.S. support of local forces against supposedly hostile regimes was even more common and significant: Guatemala (1954), Cuba (1961), Brazil (1964), Chile (1970–73), Nicaragua (1981–90). Such interventions—initially modeled, it seems, on the overthrow of Mossadeq in Iran—exercised a distinct appeal, in that they avoided American casualties and maintained the fig leaf of self-determination.[30] (Indeed, the Nicaraguan Contras could be depicted as "freedom-fighters" analogous to the patriots of the American Revolutionary War.)[31]

Latin American political factions became acutely aware of the utility of great power involvement and intervention, which they might creatively exploit. A kind of geopolitical "tail-wagging-the-dog" developed, as embattled Latin American leaders, like Estrada Palma in Cuba and Adolfo Díaz in Nicaragua, angled for U.S. support and even intervention.[32] The

Platt Amendment, which was meant to shore up stability and make for a quiet life in Cuba, had the paradoxical effect of placing the United States at the center of the Cuban political stage, where it played hero and villain (sometimes both at the same time) in a plot that was not wholly its own creation.[33] Thus, U.S. interventions—exercises in formal imperialism—responded at least in part to Latin American interests and machinations. Collaboration—one might almost say seduction—thus occurred alongside resistance.

Like other imperialists, the Americans were engaged in two—not necessarily complementary—activities: molding host regimes to their own preferences and fending off rival imperialists. With regard to the engineering function, an important working distinction should be made between the circum-Caribbean (excluding Mexico, Colombia, and Venezuela) and the rest of Latin America. The differences are clear: the circum-Caribbean (thus defined) consisted of smaller, usually poorer, republics, economically tied to the United States, hence more vulnerable to American intervention, influence, and would-be engineering. They fell within the United States' "backyard" and acquired additional geopolitical significance by virtue of their proximity to the Panama Canal, which occupied a place in U.S. geopolitical thinking roughly similar to that of the Suez Canal in the British "official mind."[34] With the notable exception of Costa Rica, their political traditions inclined toward militarism, authoritarianism, and so-called sultanism.[35] On each count, the republics appeared "suitable" for direct, coercive intervention (even if, in practice, U.S. intervention proved an uphill struggle, as it did in Nicaragua in the 1920s).[36] It was one thing to grab, say, Haiti by the scruff of its unwashed neck; Brazil was a different proposition, which demanded different methods.

This distinction, rooted in objective differences, was further colored by subjective U.S. perceptions. While the old *leyenda negra* of Catholic-Hispanic perversity, coupled with racism, affected U.S. perceptions of Latin America in general, as they had British perceptions, the major countries of South America sometimes received a better press. Elihu Root, a more sober student of Latin America than most U.S. secretaries of state, "disaggregate[d] the nations of the region into two different classes—one the turbulent Caribbean region, the other the stable, progressive countries of southern South America and Mexico."[37] This view, colored by considerations of size, race, and economic development, proved enduring and influential. (Interestingly, it had been anticipated by the British and was shared by—some—Latin Americans. Argentine elites in 1910, for example, displayed "a contempt for the Central American countries, which they consider[ed] a disgrace to the very name of America.")[38] Such a view underwrote U.S. policy in the 1920s, when formal intervention was confined to the circum-Caribbean (it was no doubt easier to intervene against petty dictators who were seen as "unspeakable carrion"); and it influenced policy long after (note that the renewed interventionism of the later Cold War again targeted the circum-Caribbean).[39] By the 1950s, Brazil was warmly regarded as the "United States of the future" in South America while the Argentines, President Eisenhower generously conceded, were "the same kind of people as we are."[40]

Subjective and objective considerations therefore made intervention and coercion more likely and acceptable in the circum-Caribbean. Here, displaying an ambition and capacity which went beyond anything the British had shown (in Latin America), the United States took it upon itself to set up collaborating elites, even entire collaborative systems. The first Cuban intervention produced the Cuban Constitution (complete with the Platt Amendment), a rigged electorate, and the new Rural Guard. The Nicaraguan intervention, designed to promote political stability and correct electoral practice, resulted in the National Guard, an instrument "designed to blast constitutional procedure off the map."[41] Similar processes occurred in Haiti and the Dominican Republic. In the latter case, a decade of financial and political tutelage wrought a supposed revolution—"not a revolution of the old type, involving waste and ruin, but a revolution in the arts of peace, industry and civilization."[42]

The optimistic meliorism of the early Victorians resurfaced in the guise of Wilsonian diplomacy.[43] Like the early Victorians, however, U.S. policymakers found the political and moral regeneration of the Third World—in this case, the circum-Caribbean—to be a thankless task. Engagement engendered disappointment and, within a generation, led to withdrawal.[44] Progressive social engineering yielded to pragmatic collaboration with chosen elites, who would guarantee basic U.S. interests without necessarily uplifting the peoples they governed. As a result, when the Good Neighbor Policy brought formal disengagement from these protectorates, the United States could rest easy in the knowledge that reliable collaborators—Somoza in Nicaragua, Trujillo in the Dominican Republic, and Batista in Cuba—were securely in place, presiding over broadly congenial collaborative regimes.[45] Just such a process may be taking place in Iraq today, as the United States strives to install its collaborative partners in power; unless, of course, the country implodes, descends into civil war, or achieves some kind of stability under a far-from-congenial bunch of noncollaborating ayatollahs and warlords.

Containing Dissent

In Latin America as a whole, however, the direct fabrication of collaborators was less feasible, especially prior to the Cold War. During the first fifty or so years of the twentieth century—the period when the United States rapidly usurped Britain's previously preeminent economic role—the Americans had to reckon with a rich array of nascent popular and nationalist movements: movements of progressive middle-class reform (Maderismo in Mexico, Batllismo in Uruguay, Radicalism in Argentina); nationalist reformist movements (the Mexican Revolution, Sandinismo, the Cuban revolutionaries of 1933); populist movements (Mexico's National Revolutionary Party/Party of the Mexican Revolution [PNR/PRM], the American Popular Revolutionary Alliance [APRA], Gaitanismo, Peronism); incipient socialist and communist parties; and burgeoning trade unions, especially in the export sector—miners, meatpackers, railway men, port workers. Here was a set of political challenges—some radical, many quite moderate—which in their scale and complexity eclipsed anything the British had had to face during their brief nineteenth-century hegemony, a period of limited oligarchic politics.[46]

Not least, these movements posed problems of comprehension: what sort of challenge did they present and how might they be countered? The United States often relied on the kind of snap judgments which reached their reductio ad absurdum with Ambassador Patterson's famous duck test.[47] Thus, a variety of leftist, nationalist, and populist movements were lazily lumped together as being socialist or communist, hence deserving of strenuous resistance.[48] The British, too, had resorted to snap judgments, but in their day no rigid Cold War conceptual framework prevailed, and the chief threats to their preferred capitalist and collaborationist order came from dissident artisans, peasants, Indians, caudillos, and occasional clerics—not the organized political parties and trade unions of twentieth-century Latin America. The British therefore tended to view Latin American protest through colonialist and racist lenses. American observers, though hostile to formal colonialism, were no strangers to racism; what was novel, in their case, was their preoccupation—verging on obsession—with communism, which dated back to 1917 (and was apparent in early condemnations of Calles, Cárdenas, and Sandino), but which became the overriding filter of U.S. perception and policy during the late 1940s.[49]

Containing "communism" implied building ever closer alliances with friendly host regimes, preferably democratic, but if necessary dictatorial. These priorities, incipient in the interwar period, had clearly crystallized by the 1940s.[50] Containment meant dedicating greater resources to countering these supposed threats while inculcating good government and sound finance. In some cases, coercion was deployed; but, more important, beginning with the Kemmerer missions and burgeoning with Rockefeller's wartime OIAA, the United States also developed a barrage of noncoercive (political, economic, and cultural) agencies, which dwarfed anything the lackadaisical laisser-faire British had ever contemplated: government aid programs, which could be turned on or off at will; trade, military, and police missions; commercial benefits, such as market access; and educational and media initiatives.[51]

A swift listing of official dramatic personae gives some idea of the institutional scope and variety: Ex-Im Bank, CIA, OIAA, International Bank of Reconstruction and Development (IBRD), Inter-American Development Bank (IDB), U.S. Agency for International Development (AID), United States Information Agency (USIA), National Endowment for Democracy (NED). As befitted an age of mass consumerism and popular culture, Donald Duck and Mickey Mouse were recruited to spread the American word and further the American mission. Resolve, resources, and new technology thus made possible a variety of purposive strategies, which the British had never possessed—in Latin America, at least.[52]

Conforming to the rough geopolitical pattern just suggested, the United States could select from a range of policies that stretched from the formal (directly interventionist) to the informal (covert pressure and influence, as represented in the bottom-right quadrant of table 1). While the Guatemalan and Nicaraguan Revolutions were militarily subverted—and, of course, efforts were made militarily to subvert the Cuban Revolution, too—the Mexican and Bolivian revolutionary regimes were more subtly massaged and molded.[53] Congenial parties—the Chilean Christian Democrats, Nicaragua's

National Opposition Union (UNO)—were generously sponsored; the AFL-CIO and Interamerican Regional Workers Organization (ORIT) took on the task of combating the leftist Latin American Workers Confederation (CTAL). But while the British had pragmatically meddled in nineteenth-century oligarchic politics, the Americans had to mix in the rambunctious and ideological mass politics of the mid-twentieth century. This was a risky and sometimes costly game. Occasionally it backfired: when Perón swept to power on the slogan "Braden o Perón"; when Nixon was stoned and jostled in Caracas in 1958; when the *Time* incident broke in Bolivia in the following year.[54]

Over the long term, however, the United States was successful. Its principal bugbears—Arbenz and Allende—were ousted. Once threatening revolutions (Mexico, Bolivia) were domesticated. Populist movements (APRA, Peronism) were discredited or de-radicalized. The Cuban Revolution was slowly throttled. In two world wars and again during the Cold War, Latin America broadly supported the Allied/American cause. Apart from the Bay of Pigs, there was no humiliating defeat and certainly no protracted agony like Vietnam (or Iraq?). U.S. trade and investment grew. Economic institutions (IBRD, the International Monetary Fund [IMF], IDB, the World Trade Organization [WTO]) that broadly favored U.S. corporate interests were created; indeed, today an economic regime exists whereby the protection of U.S. capital, including flighty portfolio capital, is given a high priority (note President Clinton's swift bailout of the Mexican economy and of U.S. holders of *tesebonos* in January 1995). Latin American elites, long schooled in the arts of appealing to the Americans, now do so with even greater conviction, inasmuch as their resumés now boast backgrounds in business (e.g., President Fox and Coca-Cola) or prestigious doctorates from Harvard and MIT (Presidents Salinas and Zedillo).[55] Compared to the story in, say, Asia or Africa, this is a pretty positive balance sheet, not least because the donkey work of "containment" has been largely undertaken by Latin American elites, while the principal costs have been borne by Latin American societies more broadly.[56] Thus, in Latin America, as in Europe, American hegemony has been a species of "empire by invitation"—that is, an "empire" based on "structural" power.[57]

Containing Foreign Threats

I have focused primarily on U.S. relations with host regimes and societies (the engineering function). What of foreign threats? On the economic front, the emergent United States soon bent its efforts to supplant competitors in Latin America. Blaine's Pan-American project of the 1880s initiated this policy, which continued with reciprocity treaties; trade and banking missions (notably Kemmerer's in the 1920s); new financial institutions (the Ex-Im Bank of the 1930s; the IDB in the 1960s); the extensive governmental initiatives of the two world wars, especially the second, which targeted rivals (Germany and, indeed, Great Britain) while advancing U.S. interests; efforts to structure the postwar settlement at Chapultepec in 1945; and the regional integration projects of the 1980s and 1990s, notably the North American Free Trade Agreement (NAFTA).[58] Again, these policies, allied to the comparative economic advantage of the United States, were largely successful. U.S. economic hegemony in Latin America has, despite fluctuations, remained relatively secure; like British hegemony in the nineteenth century, it is largely voluntaristic and noncoercive, and this makes it more durable, though no less unequal.[59]

The relative security and durability of U.S. hegemony have not, however, reassured U.S. policymakers, who have often shown a sensitive—even slightly paranoid—concern for presumed foreign threats to Latin America. Such sensitivity is hardly new: it underpinned the Monroe Doctrine 180 years ago.[60] But for decades the Monroe Doctrine was a mere rhetorical document, neglected in some key instances (the British acquisition of the Falklands, the French intervention in Mexico) and ostensibly successful chiefly because, as President Kennedy noted, Monroe's rhetorical prohibition was independently upheld by the Royal Navy.[61] Meantime, the United States advanced its territorial borders (at the expense of Mexico) and staked out ambitious strategic claims in the circum-Caribbean. Cuba and Puerto Rico, as John Adams put it in 1823, were "natural appendages" of the United States; "Yucatán and Cuba," declared Jefferson Davis, "are the salient points commanding the Gulf of Mexico, which I take to be a basin of water belonging to the U.S."[62] From the 1820s—but especially following the 1840s gold rush—the United States claimed a special interest in any prospective trans-isthmian canal. In 1850 the Clayton-Bulwer Treaty recognized a joint Anglo-American interest in a future canal; fifty years later, Britain deferred to the United States and allowed the Panamanian secession to create a U.S. enclave (the Panama Canal Zone, or PCZ) within a U.S. client state, through which the new canal would run.[63] This shift in geopolitical balance was also evident in Venezuela, where the United States grandiloquently championed Venezuelan boundary claims vis-à-vis British

Guiana in 1895, and, most dramatically, in Cuba, which the United States invaded in 1898, setting up an effective protectorate.[64]

Now possessed of its "new navy"—for which it needed strategic coaling stations and for which it had to find something to do—the United States could unilaterally make the Monroe Doctrine effective, at least in the circum-Caribbean.[65] Britain pragmatically deferred to U.S. strategic pretensions, since the Isthmus of Panama was not a key British interest, and in a world of rising imperialist rivalry U.S. goodwill was at a premium. Thus, while Anglo-American *commercial* competition continued in South America, Anglo-American *strategic* rivalry was, by about 1900, resolved in favor of the United States. Those who tried to resist this trend—as British Minister Lionel Carden did during the Mexican Revolution—found themselves kicking against the pricks.[66] British deference did not, however, assuage U.S. hemispheric concerns. Like the United States, Germany now embarked on an ambitious naval program linked to an assertive *weltpolitik*, which aroused U.S. fears of German advance in the Caribbean; at the same time, fanciful notions of Japanese penetration on the Pacific coast of the Americas troubled the American official mind.[67] Theodore Roosevelt, who epitomized both American fears and American ambitions, capped his "taking" of Panama with his enunciation of the Roosevelt Corollary, which asserted the right of the United States to intervene in order to pre-empt foreign (i.e., European) chastisement of delinquent regimes in the Americas and which achieved practical expression in the Dominican intervention of 1965, inter alia.[68] Here, the engineering and defense functions of imperialism were neatly combined: Roosevelt recognized the right of "civilized" powers to chastise—hence to *mold*—recalcitrant host regimes in the Americas; but in denying such a right to European powers under the Monroe Doctrine, he asserted the right of the United States to intervene preemptively and unilaterally in order to *fend off* foreign threats.[69] This led to a slew of U.S. interventions in the circum-Caribbean from the 1900s through the early 1930s.

These interventions were confined to the minor republics of the circum-Caribbean; in South America (and Mexico) both the strategic imperatives and the coercive power of the United States were much weaker. As the State Department pointed out to an anxious U.S. banker in Chile in the 1920s, a battleship could not climb mountains.[70] Indeed, this pattern has survived to this day (i.e., during the interventions of the later Cold War and beyond): coercive U.S. invasions in the circum-Caribbean, involving the fall and refashioning of regimes (from Cuba in 1898 to Haiti in 1994); more covert politicoeconomic pressures in the larger and more remote republics of South America (Brazil, 1964; Chile, 1973). This explains the contrasting U.S. responses to the substantially similar Guatemalan and Bolivian Revolutions. In part this pattern reflected the relative weakness and vulnerability of the smaller republics of Central America and the Caribbean, but it also reflected the inexorable logic of isthmian geopolitics. Just as Britain went to great lengths to "protect" Suez, so the United States came to regard the Panama Canal as an extension of its own territorial borders, even as an emblem of American national identity.[71] As President Reagan put it, "We built it, we paid for it, it is ours."[72]

Fear of European—and Japanese—imperialism, coupled with an almost paranoid concern with the circum-Caribbean, thus motivated U.S. policy from the beginning of the twentieth century, if not before. But the Cold War greatly aggravated this fear. It had two principal effects. First, it imposed a crude dichotomous lattice on American policymaking; the fate of civilization, it seemed, was being played out south of the Rio Grande (and everywhere else around the world, of course). This was something the British had never experienced.[73] Second, the Cold War tended to fuse the two functions of imperialism: peripheral engineering and metropolitan defense. Assessing and molding Latin American regimes now became inextricably mixed up with fending off rival imperialist (i.e., Soviet) threats; the two dimensions of imperialism—analytically distinct in the days of the British— fused as never before. Nationalist challenges to U.S. hegemony were readily seen as stalking horses for Soviet (previously Nazi) imperialism.[74] This made for snap judgments, but it also enabled Latin American *políticos* to refine the old game of "tail-wagging-the-dog," now using the Red threat as an unprecedented means to extract U.S. support, even military backing, as Somoza did, literally to his dying day.[75]

Given this fusion, it is by no means easy to probe the deeper motives and higher goals of U.S. policy toward Latin America during the Cold War. Some would stress the lobbying power of U.S. corporations, hostile to nationalism and reform; others would see U.S. anticommunism as an end in itself, a geopolitical goal that transcended, and at times even stymied, the interests of U.S. business.[76] A classic case was Guatemala in 1954: in crude terms, was Operation Success the work of United Fruit or of Cold War anticommunism? (There was, of course, a third factor: Guatemalan conservatives who played on the fears of both United Fruit and the U.S. State Department.) It is certainly hard to believe that U.S. policy was principally determined by United Fruit: as the communist leader José Fortuny put it, "They would have overthrown us even if we had grown no bananas."[77] Similarly, it is hard to credit the notion that U.S. policy toward Allende was principally determined by International Telephone and Telegraph (IT&T). After all, in other times and places—such as Mexico in 1938—the U.S. government had been quite prepared to throw U.S. companies to the nationalist wolves, when realpolitik—perhaps leavened by a little residual idealism—dictated that they should.[78] At the very least, the Cold War created a climate in which corporate and national interests closely coincided, which is not to say that U.S. corporations dictated U.S. policy.

Morality and Public Opinion

This outcome reflected two final features of U.S. imperialism. These relate to "morality" and domestic public opinion. First, since the inception of the republic, U.S. foreign policy has aspired, at least rhetorically, to a moralistic and idealistic stance, linked to a sense of providential mission. (Providential missions are hardly uncommon—consider both the Aztecs and their Spanish conquerors—but the odd thing about American providentialism has been its commitment to universality, its belief that the distinctive virtues of America are readily exportable, and its readiness to deploy power in support of itself, most recently in Iraq.)[79] The United States—and, by extension, the Americas—would stand above and beyond the sordid realpolitik of Europe.

Even aggressive ambitions were justified in moral terms. A U.S. takeover of Central America, it was stated in 1859, would lead to immigration and development; war, ignorance, superstition, and anarchy would be replaced by "peace, knowledge, Christianity, and our heaven-born institutions."[80] After a lull in such expansionist sermonizing, brought on by the Civil War, the renewed expansionism of the 1880s and 1890s soon acquired a high moral tone. The decision to annex the Philippines in 1899 followed a nocturnal communion between McKinley and God. Woodrow Wilson was resolved to "teach the South American republics to elect good men"; thus—rather to his credit, I think—he blackballed the Mexican military dictator Huerta in 1913–14.[81] Franklin D. Roosevelt, renouncing intervention, undertook to be a "good neighbor."[82] And Kennedy instituted the Alliance for Progress, "a vast cooperative effort, unparalleled in magnitude and nobility of purpose," which would promote democracy, development, and social reform throughout Latin America.[83] Recurrent themes—self-determination, democracy, development—colored U.S. rhetoric and, to a degree, U.S. policy.

American idealism, of course, was never unalloyed; it coexisted with "realist" concerns, even in cases like that of Woodrow Wilson.[84] World War II and the Cold War tempered U.S. idealism: by renouncing intervention, Franklin D. Roosevelt had to tolerate authoritarian lapses (e.g., Somoza, Trujillo); and by the 1950s, when a new spate of covert interventions began, it had become clear that Washington usually preferred congenial dictators to dangerous democrats. Yet, however cynical such a policy might appear, it claimed a flimsy ethical basis, roughly along the lines of U.S. ambassador Jeane Kirkpatrick's famously casuistic defense of authoritarianism: bad though it was, authoritarianism was greatly preferable to "totalitarianism," since it was temporary, reversible, and therefore a lesser evil.[85] Indeed, the whole conceptual entity of totalitarianism was a godsend, since it enabled the United States—and the proliferating agencies, fronts, and spokesmen of the 1940s—to elide from anti-Axis to anticommunist positions with a degree of consistency and conviction.[86] Thus, even when the hard logic of the Cold War mandated support for Trujillo, Batista, Somoza, or Stroessner, U.S. policy did not entirely lose its idealistic timbre. And intermittently—usually under Democratic presidents such as Kennedy and, in particular, Carter—policy and idealism effected a somewhat closer fit, especially when the "good-neighborly" dictator seemed ripe for removal.[87]

Where British policy had been pragmatic, opportunist, even cynical, U.S. policy displayed a constant tension between a self-image of liberal rectitude and a practice which often belied that image. Though an imperialist power, the United States was a reluctant, hand-wringing imperialist (as Ferguson laments).[88] Contrasting national histories—perhaps contrasting national "political cultures"—determined this outcome. A practiced, formally imperialist monarchy could not go to Latin America preaching democracy, republicanism, and self-determination; conversely, a republican former colony, the fruit of a national revolution, unashamedly proud of its democratic mission, could not resist the temptation to preach.[89] However, just as national political culture (if such a thing exists) is maintained by institutions, not by some kind of mystical collective psyche, so the very organization of U.S. government lent foreign policy a distinctly demotic, rhetorical, and idealistic quality. And this was especially true with respect to Latin America, above all, the circum-Caribbean: "our back yard" (Brzezinski), "our doorstep" (Haig), washed by the waters of the American mare nostrum, our sea.[90]

Here I turn to the realm of public opinion and domestic politics. While British foreign policy was the preserve of narrow elites, to a degree insulated from parliamentary pressure and scrutiny, U.S. policy more readily became a political football, kicked about between Congress and the executive branch, between rival political candidates, organized lobbies (some with vested economic interests), and a fiercely competitive "yellow" press.[91] Hearst's famous riposte to Remington in Cuba—"You furnish the pictures and I'll furnish the war"—no doubt exaggerated his political clout; but, as Ernest May has shown, the U.S. decision to enter the Spanish-American War did depend on a mobilization of public opinion (not least by the press), which in turn stampeded political leaders.[92] Hard-and-fast material interests sometimes counted (policy toward Cuba and Puerto Rico might hinge on sugar lobbies), but politics and "morality" could, in the right circumstances, exert influence—certainly more influence than they had exercised in the Machiavellian British "official mind."[93]

The Cold War furnished "the right circumstances": repeatedly told that they were engaged in a collective battle for survival, it is not surprising that some—many?—Americans credited what they were told and, even if they did not proactively demand hawkish policies, at least gave politicians grounds for believing that dovish inaction could bring electoral retribution. The "loss" of China had spawned McCarthyism; the "loss" of Cuba may have won Kennedy the 1960 election (something "Nixon never forgot"); and, five years later, Johnson, "haunted by the fear of another Cuba," ordered the invasion of the Dominican Republic.[94] Recurrently, therefore, the combination of geopolitical proximity and inflamed public opinion spurred an active, interventionist U.S. policy, the Bay of Pigs being the classic case. And in recent years an additional factor has been added: expatriate communities resident in the United States who, taking advantage of their numbers and resources, try to bend U.S. policy to their will.[95] In one sense, this becomes yet another egregious case of the tail wagging the dog, the only difference being that the tail has now migrated to the U.S. mainland.[96]

Latin American Reactions to U.S. Imperialism

Finally, a word about resistance. The thrust of my argument is that the United States has exercised forms of imperialism or hegemony in Latin America; that these forms have varied by time and place (thus, interventions have clustered in certain periods, such as 1898–1934, and in certain regions, such as the circum-Caribbean rather than South America); that U.S. policy had been broadly successful in both engineering domestic compliance and fending off foreign threats; and that economic power has probably been the greatest source of U.S. success, while "soft" power is rather hard for us, as analysts, to discern or for policymakers to deploy, as it is too vague, diffuse, and unmanageable.

These risky generalizations also prompt some conclusions about Latin American reactions to U.S. imperialism, including supposed resistance. The success of U.S. policy—broadly defined to include corporate as well as U.S. government policy—suggests that collaboration is more common than resistance (hence my citation of Lunestadt's "empire by invitation"). Latin Americans may have feared the Americans, even when they brought gifts; but the gifts—trade, investment, jobs, kickbacks—have been coveted, and not just by self-serving elites. (Whether the Latin American taste for U.S. material benefits is thoroughly opportunist and self-interested, or based on some deeper cultural empathy, is a riddle I would not try to answer. Do Mexican neoliberals espouse NAFTA because they admire the United States and its values or because it lines their corporate or individual pockets? Do Protestant converts forsake Catholicism because Pentecostalism meets some deep inner need or because U.S. churches make it materially worth their while?)[97]

One reason why U.S. economic penetration and control are tolerated rather than resisted is because they are relatively discreet and impersonal, compared to politicomilitary interventions. True, there have been some egregious cases wherein the U.S. economic presence has excited vocal opposition: the Mexican oil expropriation of 1938 (oil being something of a special case); Arbenz's threat to United Fruit; Allende's nationalization of IT&T. Relative to the scale of U.S. interests in Latin America, however, these cases are hardly numerous or typical. And in the last twenty years or so the economic nationalist thrust has been blunted while the logic of contemporary political economy makes such old-style expropriations much less likely. Today Latin American policymakers have learned to mistrust statist solutions, the markets threaten swift sanctions against those who stray too far from the Washington consensus, and, compared to the extractive and agricultural enterprises of the past, today's foreign assets are less vulnerable to outright expropriation. In addition, the old nationalist constituencies are much weaker: the trade unions have lost strength and numbers (their chief bastion is now white-collar government employees such as teachers); and erstwhile nationalist parties, such as Mexico's Institutional Revolutionary Party and Argentina's Partido Justicialista, have paid the penalty for economic mismanagement and corruption. Even the new-leftist, "populist" leaders of Latin America—Chávez, Lula, Kirchner, Morales—are leery of alarming the markets.

In contrast, U.S. interventions—such as Veracruz in 1914, Nicaragua in the late 1920s, or the Bay of Pigs in 1961—excited fierce Latin American opposition. Even relatively minor slights—such as the *Time* article that suggested that Bolivia was not worthy of nationhood—could trigger nationalist resentment and protest. In such cases, both the trigger and the target can be readily identified: the United States lands marines in Veracruz, so Mexicans protest, demonstrate, burn U.S. flags, and throw bricks through consulate windows.[98] By and large they do not attack U.S. private companies or lynch their managers; the latter may not be loved, but they are not representatives of the U.S. government and they may have some positive and redeeming features. My guess is that, were a Cuban succession crisis to occur, leading to an American intervention in the island, Latin American protest would be strident and widespread.

Protest and resistance, then, are more readily provoked by American political and military interventions.[99] But right now American interventionism is directed elsewhere. The slow and more impersonal processes of U.S. economic and cultural penetration—the first, in my opinion, being much more important than the second—may be more tolerable, since they are more discreet and ostensibly more benign. For these reasons, they are also harder to resist. Economic penetration confers power and may contribute to a kind of loose informal imperialism (a relationship which used to be called "dependency," but that term has, rather oddly, gone out of fashion just as it acquired greater relevance). Supposed soft power, derived from cultural penetration, is too amorphous and uncontrollable to facilitate purposive action. Thus, to the central question—what is the basis of U.S. imperialism/

hegemony in Latin America?—the principal answer must be the old and familiar one: "It's the economy, stupid." And, pending a U.S. economic debacle and/or a sustained European (or Chinese) commercial challenge, it seems likely to stay that way for the foreseeable future.

Notes

1. "Perhaps the most fundamental, and certainly the most difficult, problem in the discussion of imperialism is the definition of the terms on which the whole edifice of argument and refutation stands" (Hopkins, "Informal Empire in Argentina," 475).
2. See Fieldhouse, *The Theory of Capitalist Imperialism*; Wallerstein, *The Modern World-System*; Keohane, *After Hegemony*.
3. Ferguson, *Empire* and *Colossus*. Note also Lal, *In Praise of Empires*.
4. When talking of the United States, I encounter the old adjectival problem: *U.S.* can be a clumsy adjective (e.g., in this sentence), *United-Statesian* is grotesque, and *American* is rather ethnocentric, since it appropriates the entire hemisphere for one country. There is no satisfactory solution, so I plead guilty to occasionally using *American* in the ethnocentric sense.
5. On hegemony, see Keohane, *After Hegemony*, and O'Brien and Clesse, *Two Hegemonies*. I am not assuming a precise identity between *imperialism* and *hegemony*; however, there is substantial overlap, which justifies initially lumping them together as a common conceptual species (which can be disaggregated as I proceed).
6. Ronald Robinson, "Non-European Foundations of European Imperialism," 124.
7. I am (again) conflating a few features. Legality, legitimacy, and durability may not correlate perfectly. However, potential empires have to get over an initial hump, after which they may enjoy legality, legitimacy, and durability. Hence, the correlation exists.
8. Quirk, *An Affair of Honor*.
9. The Russian/Soviet empire is an interesting case: while the more recent (post-1945, Soviet) dependencies in Eastern Europe have broken away, along with the Ukraine and parts of Central Asia, most of the Russian empire, created by Tsarist eastward expansion in the eighteenth and nineteenth centuries, remains, at least for the time being.
10. David Healy's *Drive to Hegemony* is a good summary.
11. Robinson and Gallagher, *Africa and the Victorians*, chaps. 4 and 5.
12. Two clarifications: (1) The bottom-right quadrant is probably the most capacious and contentious, since it contains all those cases in which imperialism or hegemony (or even dependency) is exercised both indirectly and without legal justification; such cases could be usefully disaggregated (military, political,

economic, etc.), and there would no doubt be disagreement about what to include or exclude (was U.S. connivance in the overthrow of Allende imperialistic or hegemonic? Should NAFTA figure here?). (2) Movement between the quadrants is common: de facto occupations (bottom left) can lead either to de jure colonies (top left) or to indirect but de jure protectorates (top right); conversely, decolonization can involve a passage from formal rule (top left) to either top right or bottom right (the latter corresponds to Kwame Nkrumah's "neo-colonialism"); bottom right to bottom left corresponds to the "local crisis" (e.g., Egypt, 1882), whereby informal empire becomes formal.

13. The terms *lumping* and *splitting* derive from Hexter, "The Historical Method of Christopher Hill," 241–42.

14. It is misleading because the nations are usually already there. What is usually being built is a regime, defined in the broadest sense to include a state, a political economy, and a set of relations with the rest of the world (particularly the self-appointed nation-builders). In fact, some nation building could involve nation destroying (which could be the case in Iraq in twenty years).

15. While the Spaniards were certainly successful in terms of imparting language, religion, and certain enduring legal and political features (such as administrative frontiers), this does not mean that Spanish America shares a common and ineluctable destiny derived from its Iberian inheritance. One obvious reason why Spanish imperialism has left a deeper mark than any other is because it involved sustained migration from metropolis to colony. The United States, as Niall Ferguson laments, does not export people; the demographic flow goes the other way.

16. O'Neill caused a brief diplomatic spat with remarks suggesting that some U.S. aid to Argentina and Brazil was being diverted to private Swiss bank accounts. See "Paul O'Neill Pulls Foot from Mouth," BBC News, 2 August 2002, http://news.bbc.co.uk/.

17. Compare Kennedy, *The Rise and Fall of the Great Powers*. For graphic and compendious illustrations of U.S. economic preponderance in the Americas, consult the online database associated with Miguel Angel Centeno's Princeton project on globalization (International Networks Archive, http://www.princeton.edu/~ina).

18. The question of whether, or how much, the Raj underdeveloped or de-industrialized India is, of course, contentious. See Robin J. Moore, "Imperial India, 1858–1914," 443–44.

19. The Roca-Runciman Treaty between Britain and Argentina affords an interesting case study. See Alhadeff, "Dependency, Historiography and Objections to the Roca Pact," 367–78.

20. A recent (2004) "diplomatic orgy between Buenos Aires and Beijing" held out the prospect of massive Chinese investment ($20 billion) in Argentina and even led "some [to] hope [that] China might assume the role Europe played in

the 19th century, providing insatiable demand for Latin American primary resources"; however, the economic reality is, thus far, a different matter. "Latin America and China," Lex, *Financial Times*, 14 February 2005, 20.

21. World War I gravely, if temporarily, weakened German competition in Latin America. Some rather dubious theories of imperialism suggest that the war was fought for that purpose—that is, to crush a global imperialist rival. However, extra-European imperialism was probably not so crucial, and in any event, Germany's military defeat could not eliminate German economic power, which soon recovered.

22. I cannot cite chapter and verse; this is an impression formed by rather random reading in diplomatic history.

23. Nye, *Bound to Lead*.

24. For want of time and space, I cannot attempt such a treatment here. I have deliberately refrained from trying to define *imperialism*. According to A. G. Hopkins, imperialism "involves the diminution of sovereignty through the exercise of power" ("Informal Empire in Argentina," 476). Of course, diminutions of sovereignty are common, they may involve trade-offs between countries, and they may cancel out (consider the European Union). I would add that imperialism therefore involves a "substantial and asymmetrical" diminution of sovereignty through the exercise of power; that power can assume varied (military, political, economic, cultural) forms; and that it is not just a question of state-to-state relations, important though those relations may be (Tony Smith, *The Pattern of Imperialism*, 14).

25. For examples of "policy differences . . . , rivalries of ambition and personal animosity," all of which led to "hopelessly contradictory" policy statements, see Leogrande, *Our Own Backyard*, ix.

26. The Falklands were taken from Argentina, after a fashion, and Puerto Rico was wrested from Spain; both therefore qualify as seizures of "Latin American" territory. Belize is more problematic, given the nature of Guatemala's claim, and Guyana is better seen as part of the Anglophone Caribbean. Only in the case of Puerto Rico was a distinctly Latin American society brought under "Anglo-Saxon" dominion.

27. Presidents Grover Cleveland and William McKinley, quoted in Schoultz, *Beneath the United States*, 83, 107, 129.

28. Schoultz, *Beneath the United States*, 226–33.

29. Domínguez, *Cuba*, 54–55.

30. Rabe, *Eisenhower and Latin America*, 54–55.

31. Carothers, *In the Name of Democracy*, 95–99.

32. Schoultz, *Beneath the United States*, 198, 218, 226. See also p. 117 on Venezuela's attempts to inveigle the United States into supporting her claims against British Guyana, under the guise of the Monroe Doctrine. Compare, too,

Leogrande, *Our Own Backyard*, 22–23, which describes Anastasio Somoza Debayle's "masterful" manipulation of the United States as he played out his politicodiplomatic endgame.

33. Charles Magoon, quoted in Schoultz, *Beneath the United States*, 202. The entangling and counterproductive effect of the Platt Amendment had been foreseen by some, such as Senator Joseph Foraker (see Healy, *Drive to Hegemony*, 55).

34. On the British "official mind," see Robinson and Gallagher, *Africa and the Victorians*. Was there an equivalent U.S. official mind, and if so, when did it make its appearance? Or did the United States acquire a split personality, with several minds (and several inner voices)?

35. Rouquié, *The Military and the State in Latin America*, 155–86.

36. Bryce Wood, *The Making of the Good Neighbor Policy*, chap. 1, on the Nicaraguan imbroglio and its consequences for U.S. policy.

37. Schoultz, *Beneath the United States*, 192. See also Henry Lane Wilson, quoted in ibid., 239.

38. Henry White, quoted in ibid., 194–95; and Woodrow Wilson on Latin American indifference to Haiti: "Being negroes, they are not regarded as of the fraternity" (quoted in ibid., 293).

39. The U.S. diplomat Huntington Wilson on Nicaraguan President Zelaya, quoted in ibid., 210.

40. Gaddis Smith, *Last Years of the Monroe Doctrine, 1945–1993*, 115, 122 (quoting Jack Valenti), 67 (Eisenhower to Frondizi). These attitudes had roots which stretched back at least to the end of the nineteenth century (see Burns, *The Unwritten Alliance*).

41. Pérez, *Cuba under the Platt Amendment, 1902–34*, 105–7; Schoultz, *Beneath the United States*, 271. On the durability of the National Guard as a perceived collaborator and guarantor of U.S. interests in Nicaragua during the twilight of *somocismo* in 1979, see Leogrande, *Our Own Backyard*, 26.

42. Jacob Hollander's report to the Wilson administration, quoted in Schoultz, *Beneath the United States*, 229. Emily S. Rosenberg's *Financial Missionaries to the World* offers an excellent analysis of U.S. politicoeconomic tutelage in the period.

43. Robinson and Gallagher, *Africa and the Victorians*, 1–5.

44. Bryce Wood, *The Making of the Good Neighbor Policy*.

45. Hence the telling title of chapter 13 in Schoultz, *Beneath the United States*: "Removing the Marines, Installing the Puppets." Eric Paul Roorda's *The Dictator Next Door* is a good recent study.

46. The British had faced quite different problems: underdeveloped economies with few exports, poor communications, and unstable, often violent, *caudillesque* politics. They helped overcome the problems (especially regarding exports and communications), but after a short-lived British "hegemony," their American rivals took advantage of the new opportunities.

47. That is, if it looks, sounds, and walks like a duck/communist, it must be one (Richard Immerman, *The CIA in Guatemala*, 102). For a British diplomatic critique of the duck test, see Gaddis Smith, *Last Years of the Monroe Doctrine*, 158.

48. It is worth noting that something resembling duck tests had previously been used to discern fascists in 1940s Argentina, also to British dismay (MacDonald, "The Politics of Intervention," 381–82).

49. Gaddis Smith, *Last Years of the Monroe Doctrine*, 66–67. The only possible parallel between U.S. and British policy in this regard would be the "Great Game," which, pitting British imperialist interests in Asia against tsarist Russia, meant that "throughout the nineteenth century, with a confidence born of right reasoning and equal ignorance of the facts, countless young Englishmen scoured the near east to find proof of Russian activities and explain how they might be stopped" (Ingram, *The Beginning of the Great Game in Asia, 1828–1834*, 339).

50. I am simplifying a complex process, of course: the Good Neighbor Policy involved toleration of authoritarian governments on the grounds of both principle (non-intervention) and, more important, U.S. self-interest (fear of Axis penetration coupled with commercial ambition). The Cold War changed the character of the external threat and upped the global stakes; meanwhile, by heightening fears of Latin American radicalism, it also progressively undermined the principle of non-intervention and, instead, actively encouraged U.S. (largely covert) interference designed to mould congenial regimes, whether authoritarian or democratic. See Bryce Wood, *The Dismantling of the Good Neighbor Policy*.

51. Huggins, *Political Policing*.

52. On U.S. programs and agencies, see Schoultz, *Beneath the United States*, 308–9, 313, 357; Bryce Wood, *The Dismantling of the Good Neighbor Policy*, 139–40; Connell-Smith, *United States and Latin America*, chaps. 5 and 6. Of course, this proliferation of activities reflected a broader expansion of the state—even the once modest U.S. state—stimulated by the Depression, the New Deal, World War II, and the Bretton Woods system. The result was a very different model of political economy from that which the British had operated in the mid-Victorian era.

53. Blasier, *The Hovering Giant*, chaps. 5 and 6. In Nicaragua, too, the United States, under President Carter, initially sought to tame the Sandinista revolution. As one senior State Department official put it, venturing a somewhat ill-conceived metaphor, "The Sandinistas are wearing a moderate mask. Our job is to nail it on" (Leogrande, *Our Own Backyard*, 30). However, incoming President Reagan and his crew had other ideas.

54. Schoultz, *Beneath the United States*, 321–25, 351–52; Lehman, *Bolivia and the United States*, 114.

55. Is Mexico a special case? Maybe the "acculturation" of Mexican political leadership by the United States has proceeded farther and faster. If so, this is a

fairly recent (post-1980) process. Prior to becoming president in 1934, Lázaro Cárdenas had crossed the border only once, during the Mexican Revolution, and had been briefly arrested. The revolutionary military—which supplied all of Mexico's presidents between 1917 and 1946—also had a long tradition of avoiding active collaboration with U.S. forces. One might contrast this with Anastasio Somoza Debayle, a graduate of the Lasalle Military Academy in New York State, who allegedly spoke English better than Spanish and, in the 1970s, "peppered his conversation with English slang that had disappeared in the 1950s" (Leogrande, *Our Own Backyard*, 14).

56. One way of pointing out the contrast is to note the relative absence of "blowback" in Latin America. See Johnson, *Blowback*.

57. See Lundestad, "Empire by Invitation?" 263–77. I would qualify the comparison, however, by suggesting that the European "invitation" enjoyed wider consensus (given the proximity of the Soviet bloc); the Latin American invitation, though quite effective from the U.S. perspective, was less consensual, more elitist, and at times downright authoritarian.

58. Topik, *Trade and Gunboats*, 20, 24–51; Drake, *The Money Doctor in the Andes*. See also Stallings, *Banker to the Third World*, 83, 86–87; and Humphreys, *Latin America and the Second World War*, 222–26.

59. Whether such a noncoercive—dependent?—relationship can constitute "imperialism" (of the informal, economic kind) is open to debate. Some scholars would regard coercion as a sine qua non of imperialism and would thus exclude noncoercive economic hegemony. For this reason Andrew Thompson concludes that "Britain's 'informal empire' in Argentina is in essence a myth" ("Informal Empire?" 436). If, however, imperialism "involves the diminution of sovereignty through the exercise of power" (Hopkins, "Informal Empire in Argentina," 476), then in cases of, as I put it, "substantial and asymmetrical" diminutions of sovereignty one may wish to use the term.

60. Gaddis Smith, *Last Years of the Monroe Doctrine*, 21–24.

61. Ibid., 112.

62. Schoultz, *Beneath the United States*, 48–49.

63. Ibid., 161, 165–68. As noted by Walter Lafeber, the PCZ roughly replicated the Chinese Treaty Ports which the United States had "vigorously opposed" only a few years before (*The Panama Canal*, 34).

64. Schoultz, *Beneath the United States*, 119, 137.

65. Ibid., 89, 149, 231.

66. Calvert, *The Mexican Revolution*, 1910–14. As Tony Smith notes, Germany and the United States were both serious economic rivals of Britain; however, whereas German rivalry spilled over into geopolitical tension (in Europe, the Mediterranean, and the Middle East), U.S. expansion "was taking place in regions of relatively minor concern to London: the Pacific and the Caribbean" (*The Pattern of Imperialism*, 43–44).

67. Schoultz, *Beneath the United States*, 184, 188–89; Connell-Smith, *United States and Latin America*, 117; Healy, *Drive to Hegemony*, 72–76.

68. Schoultz, *Beneath the United States*, 173, 177, 183–84. For a later invocation of the Roosevelt Corollary, by Brezinski, see Leogrande, *Our Own Backyard*, 25.

69. Gaddis Smith, *Last Years of the Monroe Doctrine*, 25–26.

70. Drake, *The Money Doctor in the Andes*, 45. Forty years later Secretary of State Dean Rusk pointed out to the U.S. ambassador in Brazil that, when it came to removing the leftist Goulart government, "obviously, in a country of over 75 million people, larger than the continental United States, this is not a job for a handful of U.S. Marines" (Rusk to Gordon, 30 March 1964 [U.S. Department of State, *Foreign Relations of the United States, 1964–1968*, 430]).

71. U.S. sovereignty over the PCZ was, as one congressman put it, "as legitimate as our owning New York City," and Panama was "an area which every grade school history book features with an American flag, a snapshot of Teddy Roosevelt, and an image of gallant engineers overcoming the mosquito" (Gaddis Smith, *Last Years of the Monroe Doctrine*, 148, 144).

72. Ibid., 149.

73. Waltz, *Foreign Policy and Domestic Politics*, 6.

74. Nazi hunting in the early 1940s provided a useful preparation for Red baiting in the late 1940s and 1950s. See MacDonald, "The Politics of Intervention," 381–82; Gellman, *Good Neighbor Diplomacy*, 226.

75. Gaddis Smith, *Last Years of the Monroe Doctrine*, 156 (and 94, for a similar ploy by Batista); Schoultz, *Beneath the United States*, 326. The most accomplished instance of the tail wagging the dog was probably that of the Brazilian military, especially Castello Branco. (Admittedly, Brazil was the biggest "tail" in the region.) In the 1960s the military cleverly played on U.S. fears of communism, won support for the ouster of Goulart in 1964, and then secured—occasionally grudging—U.S. endorsement of outright military dictatorship. The story can be closely followed in U.S. Department of State, *Foreign Relations of the United States, 1964–1968*, 398–544.

76. Thus, the question arises as to whether strident anticommunism—and its related rhetoric—is sincere, or rather a front for more material and corporate interests. Gaddis Smith wonders whether Reagan, Haig, Casey, and their compatriots "really believed" in the Red-scare stories they peddled (*Last Years of the Monroe Doctrine*, 187–88).

77. Gleijeses, *Shattered Hope*, 7. Twenty-five years later, President Reagan believed that Central America "was not intrinsically important," but derived its unfortunate salience from being "a theater in the Cold War struggle with the Soviet Union" (Leogrande, *Our Own Backyard*, x).

78. Knight, *U.S.-Mexican Relations, 1910–40*, 17–18.

79. Brogan, *America in the Modern World*, 30; Tony Smith, *America's Mission*, 144. Such attitudes may derive from the form of "civic" nationalism which

the United States, being an immigrant society, has tended to espouse (there are parallels with France and her *mission civilizatrice*). In contrast, forms of "ethnic" nationalism—or imperialism—are resistant to export.

80. Schoultz, *Beneath the United States*, 70–71.

81. Knight, *U.S-Mexican Relations, 1910–40*, 103–14.

82. Bryce Wood, *The Making of the Good Neighbor Policy*.

83. Quoted in Lieuwen, *U.S. Policy in Latin America*, 114.

84. Knight, *U.S.-Mexican Relations, 1910–40*, 107–8; Levin, *Woodrow Wilson and World Politics*, 20, 257.

85. Kirkpatrick, "Dictators and Double Standards," 34–45.

86. For example, Bryce Wood, *The Dismantling of the Good Neighbor Policy*, 200.

87. Pastor, "The Carter Administration and Latin America," 61–97.

88. Ferguson, *Colossus*, 29.

89. In *Revolutions* David Brion Davis traces the historic tension between, on the one hand, the United States' "messianic mission" (79) and "remarkable receptivity to the idea of revolution" (73) and, on the other hand, its recurrent lapses into "counterrevolutionary phobia" (59) and adoption of "neo-Metternichian" policies (3). Four of the seven instances of such policies relate to Latin America.

90. Gaddis Smith, *Last Years of the Monroe Doctrine*, 155, 189.

91. As a result, Kenneth Waltz notes, U.S. foreign policy tends to "dramatize differences," to "exaggerate dangers in order to justify action," and to "draw policies out of a series of collisions between ideas in opposition," while British policy tends to be more evasive, non-ideological, and "sidling" in its approach (*Foreign Policy and Domestic Politics*, 7–8). Note also Bryce Wood, *The Dismantling of the Good Neighbor Policy*, 205, on the tendency of U.S. administrations to strike out in new directions in order to distance themselves from their predecessors.

92. Swanberg, *Citizen Hearst*, 107–8; May, *Imperial Democracy*, chap. 11.

93. Leopold, *Elihu Root and the Conservative Tradition*, 26–28; Dye, *Cuban Sugar in the Age of Mass Consumption*, 53, 66, 259.

94. Gaddis Smith, *Last Years of the Monroe Doctrine*, 102, 127.

95. Most obviously, the Cuban lobby. See Domínguez, "U.S.-Cuban Relations," 60–65.

96. If the time comes when the Florida diaspora return in triumph to Cuba, they may constitute the first export of "prefabricated collaborators" from the United States to an informal dependency.

97. Stoll, *Is Latin America Turning Protestant?*

98. Knight, *The Mexican Revolution*, 2:158–59.

99. I have made the prudent but cowardly decision to avoid attempting any definition or discussion of "resistance," a concept that, due to overuse, may be yielding diminishing returns.

GREGORY EVANS DOWD

2 **"WE ARE HEIRS-APPARENT TO THE ROMANS"**
Imperial Myths and Indigenous Status

Empire is more than the conquest of lands; its subordinations come with complex, composite, reciprocal structures and understandings. These have been important in the history of the United States, an empire from even before its inception, as the British colonies preceding it expanded overland, displacing, absorbing, surrounding, and dominating many Indian peoples. The United States's territorial expansion continued the overall pattern, but with significant formal changes, leading to the imperial incorporation by treaty of hundreds of American Indian nations. Native American resistance is famous, even folkloric, but rarely was it a defense only of land, resources, or cultural norms. Status—political and social—has been central to American Indian struggles with both Western Europe's empires and with the Empire of Liberty. Status is the subject of this chapter, which treats the issue as it surfaced twice in eastern North America: first in the formative period immediately preceding the American Revolution, and then, more briefly, in the confederation and early constitutional eras. I focus mainly on the 1760s, a time when British claims to North American dominion were at their strongest and when armed Indian resistance to empire forced the first serious imperial consideration of the status of Native American nations and individuals.

Myths of Empire

In 1762 the diarist Horace Walpole exuded imperial confidence: "I shall burn all my Greek and Latin books; they are histories of little people. The Romans never conquered the world, till they had conquered three parts of it, and were three hundred years about it; we subdued the globe in three campaigns; and a globe, let me tell you, as big again as it was in their days."[1] Walpole was hardly alone in his exuberant delusion. When on 8 September 1760 the governor of New France signed the Articles of Capitulation of Montreal, formally surrendering his colony to British occupation, Major Robert Rogers of the Rangers boasted that he and his fellow Britons had been made "masters" of a vast land.[2] These are the sentiments of what the historian James Belich calls "False Empire": the "illusion but not the substance of empire."[3] False empire describes a highly unstable condition in which the expectations of the indigenous peoples and the colonizers are vastly and increasingly at odds, and, if I read Belich correctly, it also describes an imperial frame of mind. Britain's military conquest of French Canada may have been real in 1760, but on much ground formally ceded by France to Great Britain by 1763, the British empire was false.[4]

The fifteen years that followed the capitulation made that painfully clear. Attempting to organize itself, rather suddenly, as an empire, Britain had more success with former French subjects in Quebec than it did with those who already saw themselves as British subjects in most of the established colonies. The drive to constitute the empire—to clarify the rights, liberties, and responsibilities of British subjects and the British sovereign—brought civil war to the Anglo-Atlantic world in the form of the American Revolution. Native American peoples of the 1760s inhabited an ideological world radically different from that of the coastal thirteen colonies, but as they faced the same British imperial drive to constitute empire, they likewise imagined that it would result in their degradation and therefore struggled to prevent the materialization of an imperial reality.

Pontiac's War, named for the Ottawa leader who led early attacks at the British post of Detroit in May 1763, was resistance to degradation. An object of the early attacks was Detroit's commander, Major Henry Gladwin, an iron-willed veteran who embodied well those stubborn virtues of "cool courage" and determination that false empire celebrates. Yet those very "virtues" had steeled in Gladwin a resolve to resist Indian demands for customary respect and reciprocity, and he adopted a defiant, even violent, posture that Native Americans found extremely provocative. Detroit traders later claimed that he had treated local leaders, including Pontiac, with open contempt, refusing them hospitality and calling them "dogs" and "hogs." The charges were only hearsay, but they were numerous. It is a fact, moreover, that Gladwin would in November congratulate a fellow British officer for "the drubbing you gave the dogs" at the successful relief of besieged Fort Pitt.[5]

More alarming to the Native Americans in the neighborhood of Detroit, Gladwin hanged a woman, a Native American slave, allegedly an accomplice in the murder of an English trader, her new master. Following written orders from Jeffery Amherst, the commander-in-chief in New York, Gladwin performed the hanging in "the most Exemplary and publick manner, that thereby Others may be Deterred from Committing such Cruelties for the Future."[6] For the unnamed woman, the empire was all too real, but the local Indians' reaction to her death made Gladwin begin to worry that his empire might be false. He wrote to Amherst that the execution had affected "the Temper of the Indians."[7] Back east, Amherst was not worried; he replied that it was not in the Indians' "Power," "to Effect any thing of Consequence against Us." He only wished the man who had actually wielded the knife had met the same punishment, "for then the Example would have been Complete."[8]

But the example must have been complete enough for Great Lakes peoples to fear a future of summary and severe justice should false empire ever become real. By the time Gladwin received Amherst's assurances, he and his men were fighting for their lives. Within two months, inspired both by Pontiac's example and by the teachings of a Lenape religious prophet in the Upper Ohio Valley, Indians had eliminated most of the British posts south of the Great Lakes, west of the Niagara region, and north of Kentucky, leaving only Forts Pitt and Detroit in British hands. The extent of Indian unity and power stunned British officials, and it forced a reconsideration of empire.

Historians have long recognized that Pontiac and his allies rejected British imperial claims based on the surrender of Canada (1760) and the Treaty of Paris (1763). The Ojibwe leader Minavavana put it succinctly in

1761, making clear that status was at stake as well as land: "Although you have conquered the French, you have not conquered us. We are not your slaves."[9] Minavavana did not use the word *sovereignty*, but he could have, for he understood his people to be free of European empire and to possess their own laws and governance. British officers could no more admit that the Crown lacked sovereignty over the peoples of those regions than they could that the Crown lacked sovereignty over Shropshire, but they were inspired by the war to inquire, more systematically than ever before, into the empire's relationship with Indian nations.

Perhaps the best result of the inquiry was the promulgation of the Royal Proclamation of 1763, seen among some British imperial experts as a kind of American analog to New Zealand's Treaty of Waitangi. Each has been referred to as a "Magna Carta" of indigenous relations with the British colonial authority, as a kind of solemn promise to protect natives against rude settlers and to guarantee rights.[10] But, as Lord Chief Justice Keeling is alleged to have said to an unhappy jury in 1667, "Magna Carta, Magna Farta."[11] It does not take a very close reading of the Royal Proclamation to see that protecting Indians was not the document's only or most important purpose.[12]

The proclamation did promise to protect Indians from settlements unauthorized by the Crown, but it also established new boundaries and promoted the new settlement of colonies along the Gulf of Mexico. Explicitly temporary, it can hardly be said to have been anti-expansionist in nature. The famed boundary line established by the proclamation at the headwaters of the Atlantic drainage, a line beyond which there was to be no settlement or purchase of lands from the Indians by any other than Crown authorities, was intended not so much to separate an Indian protectorate from colonial land hunger as to leave the Crown alone as the mediator and beneficiary of future land sales. The proclamation addressed not only land but status, for it clearly distinguished Indians from subjects, a fact that some now presumptuously read as a bow to the Indians' sovereignty but a fact that also rendered the Indians' status (in the imperial view) highly ambiguous and devoid of legal remedy in the event of disputes with the colonies. The proclamation made it clear that the Crown saw itself as sovereign over Indian land, a ludicrous claim given that Indians were capturing or forcing the abandonment of ten of the king's twelve posts west of the Niagara River. The proclamation claimed that Indian country was the king's dominion, and, in full false imperial dress, it anticipated a time when the king would make that claim good.[13]

The status of Indian peoples, examined and skirted in the proclamation, was a question rarely broached previously in Whitehall, though it was not new. As European nation-states claimed possession of vast regions by right of papal grant, discovery, conquest, occupancy, or improvement, they rarely conceded that Indians possessed *dominium*, or to use the modern term, sovereignty. The sixteenth-century Spanish jurist Francisco de Vitoria came closest to such a concession. He recognized prior Indian dominion but simultaneously declared such dominion to be subject to easy forfeiture when Indian violations of Spanish rights, according to sixteenth-century Christendom's norms, gave Spain a just cause for conquest. He also left open the door for assertions that Indians might require civilized guardians.[14]

Seventeenth-century and eighteenth-century English and French colonizers did not much bother with the possibility of Indian dominion.[15] Anthony Pagden has suggested that, unlike the Spanish, the English and French avoided justifying their sovereignty with arguments from just conquest and instead denied Indian sovereignty in the first place on the putative grounds that the natives had failed to improve the land, that mere occupancy was no argument for ownership, much less sovereignty.[16] At root, European powers agreed more than they disagreed on the issue of Indian sovereignty; by the seventeenth century, it was not taken seriously anywhere east of the Atlantic. Monarchs easily gave charters to Indian lands they had never seen; rare indeed were those Europeans who, like Roger Williams, directly questioned the validity of such grants. Williams himself, moreover, saw the royal grants as deficient, not so much because they violated native rights as because the monarchs who did the granting were deficiently Christian and without access to divine favor.[17] Even William Penn, famous for his fair-minded dealings with Indians, saw his title to the land as deriving fundamentally from the Crown. So firmly did Europeans share such convictions by the eighteenth century that colonial powers formally exchanged Indian land in treaty, much to the implicated and ignored Indians' horror and disgust. In the year of the proclamation, 1763, the great Treaty of Paris, which ended the Seven Years' War and conveyed on European paper vast Native American lands to a European nation, did not even mention American Indians (though it did mention the Indian allies in India), much less involve them directly in negotiations.

Even in direct dealings with Indians, Europeans did not concede sovereignty. The "treaties" they made with Indians did nothing to admit the fundamental integrity of Indian independence, however the word *treaty* might, to modern ears, ring of a true deal between independent powers. The Dutch and the English employed the treaty mechanism much less frequently than historians assume; the word *treaty* itself was used loosely in the seventeenth century, and not very commonly.[18] To be sure, negotiations for land often enough represented a genuine European accommodation to native demands, protocols, and goals. Occasionally, Europeans recognized—however mistakenly—the autonomous leadership of Indian "kings," but this usually suited the deeper purpose of buttressing one European crown's claim to fundamental sovereignty against that of a rival crown. Sometimes, too, the public recognition of Indian kings suited metropolitan political and rhetorical purposes that actually advanced empire.[19] That the idea of Indian sovereignty went for the most part unthought speaks volumes about imperial attitudes toward Indians. Robert Williams aptly summarizes the only limitation consistently applied by European powers to their exploitation of the New World: that "imposed by a rival's superior forces. As for the indigenous inhabitants, . . . as heathens and infidels they were regarded . . . as fit subjects for conquest."[20]

Sovereignty, as a word invoking either power derived by a dread ruler from God or power derived from a people's fundamental authority through historical, legendary, or theoretical constitutional acts, was an early modern European concept alien to eighteenth-century Native Americans of the Great Lakes. But in understanding their ultimate power to govern themselves free of imperial authority, in believing that sacred powers had placed them purposefully on their lands, many Indians did take seriously what can properly be called sovereignty; Minavavana, for example, opposed Indian subordination and insisted that Ojibwes possessed the fundamental right to lands he described as "our inheritance." Europeans easily understood such frequent Indian declarations.[21] Formal independence, full dominion: it was the starting point for Indian resistance to the British Empire.

An alternative was long available to the colonizers, and, with a different inflection, some Native Americans even embraced it. Today it might easily be mistaken for a liberal position, but it is better understood, especially by 1763, as an archaic one. In this view, the Indians inhabiting Crown (claimed) lands were Crown subjects. Karen Ordahl Kupperman's examination of early English colonial writings suggests that hopes of incorporating Native Americans into the English empire were predicated upon assumptions about Indian similarities, however tortured and difficult those assumptions may have been for the colonizers.[22] Nicholas Canny finds sixteenth- and seventeenth-century English colonizers hoping to ceremonially accomplish in America what they were already accomplishing in Ireland: recognizing local leaders as Crown "subjects" and as nobles with a "legal claim over their lordships."[23]

Seventeenth-century New Englanders often assumed that local Indians were subjects and even had a certain access to law.[24] What good English law did for Indians in New England remains a question, but there were those among them who claimed the status of subject in order to gain access to courts, and as late as 1703 Native Americans served Massachusetts as justices of the peace on Martha's Vineyard. The idea that Indians were Crown subjects may have been more established in seventeenth-century New England than elsewhere, in part because Massachusetts Bay had established a more extensive mission system than had the other English colonies, but even in Virginia, the opinion that Indians "under the allegiance of the crown" were Crown subjects with "the same privilege of other English Subjects," including, especially, rights to trial by jury, could be heard into the eighteenth century.[25]

But it was heard with greater difficulty, amid an increasing and confusing din. By the 1760s, that Native Americans were even prospective subjects, much less automatic subjects by virtue of inhabiting the king's realm or by virtue of alliance and vassalage, was doubted and contested. As independent Indians understood Britons better, as they grasped meaning in terms like *subject*, and as they saw clearly varieties of British subjection, they also resisted this term.[26] By the 1760s, too, British (and British colonial) contests over politics had elevated the status of the British subject. A long history of colonial slavery and Indian dispossession had encouraged the development of notions of savagery and race that made some Britons openly question the Indians' readiness or even capacity for civility. One index to this development is that conquered Europeans became Crown subjects with little discussion. In the conquest of Canada (1760) and in the subsequent efforts to take over the Illinois territory the British made it clear that the French inhabitants would "become subjects of His Majesty" and "enjoy the same rights and privileges, the same security for their persons and effects, and the liberty of trade, as the old subjects of their [new] King."[27] Not so for Indians. At best, they would be Crown allies on Crown lands enjoying the king's protection. At worst, they would be enemies.

When colonists or officers suggested, as had been common a century earlier, that Indians were also British subjects, such imperial authorities as Sir William Johnson, one of the most influential voices in Indian affairs before the revolution, pounced: "The very word would have startled" the Indians;[28] its very meaning, he also declared, is "repugnant to their Principles; . . . no Nation of Indians have any word which can express, or convey, the Idea of Subjection."[29] Georgia's royal governor and later loyalist James Wright jumped on a limited proposal to admit Indian testimony in colonial courts, saying it would lead to the "very worst Consequences. . . . Surely no man who knows what Indians are, would ever think of admitting their Evidence as Legal, in Courts of Justice, in any Case either Civil or Criminal."[30] It is hard to imagine a British subject without at least theoretical access to the law.[31]

The Status of Enemy Prisoners

If British officials had regarded the Indians living beyond the colonies but within the king's realm as legal subjects in the 1760s, then the captured allies of Pontiac might have been legally tried for treason. This approach was considered, in fact, for Euro-American men who were alleged to have supported Indian militants. These men fell into two categories: British subjects who had been captured and assimilated by the tribes, and former French subjects who lived in the Great Lakes region. It is illuminating to contrast the fate of these men with that of militant Indians: the former presented British authorities with the question of formal trial; for the latter, such proceedings seemed to be out of the question.

In 1764 British troops separately seized the brothers Gershom and Levy Hicks, "on the Strongest suspicion that they came with Evil Intentions."[32] Gershom had appeared at the gates of Fort Pitt (now Pittsburgh) on 14 April 1764, claiming to have escaped from Indians. The garrison believed—on weak evidence—that he had a "known Attachment to Indian life" and was an enemy spy.[33] Captain William Grant, then commanding at Fort Pitt, ordered that Gershom be interrogated, a confession was "extorted from him by threats of Death," and he was even marched under arms to the place where he was meant to be hanged.[34] General Thomas

Gage, fully aware of the mode of interrogation, which was dutifully recorded, at first suggested that he be tried by a general "Court Martial for a Spy. And if he does turn out a spy he must be hanged."[35] But months later, after Gershom's brother, Levy, had also been taken, and after the two had languished together in irons at Fort Pitt, Gage reversed his decision. For one thing, he felt the evidence against them was too slim and that their testimony, having been taken under threats of death, was too tainted for the army to render a proper judgment. More important, "The Military may hang a spy in Time of War, but Rebels in Arms, are tried by the Civil Courts."[36]

Deemed rebels, the brothers Hicks were sent to Pennsylvania's Cumberland County jail to await trial. The hearty correspondence discussing these *white* men had no counterpart for captured enemy Indians, for the brothers Hicks were taken to be British subjects, while captive Indians were not subjects, not rebels, and not white. Britons might in the 1760s bring a *domestic* Indian to trial for an isolated crime against British settlers, and they might also demand the surrender for punishment of an Indian disturber of the peace, but to bring a Muskingum Valley Delaware or a Maumee Valley Ottawa to trial for fighting a war was unthinkable.

Another case starkly displays the assumption that to be a British subject was in the 1760s to be "white." In 1764 Indian Superintendent Sir William Johnson sent to Albany three enemy prisoners recently surrendered to him by the Genesee Senecas. One, "Roger," was a Delaware. A second, known variously as the "Negro," the "Indian Negro," "Tony," or "Sam Tony," had "fled many years ago from" a southern colony and then lived in a polyglot town on the Susquehanna River, where he spread "dangerous, and Treasonable" rumors that alienated Indian "Affections from the English." The third, John Eice (or Eyce), was a "German captured in Virginia years ago" who was "likewise reported to have done us much harm." The three were in the Albany jail in May 1764, but Johnson feared that they might be released "for want of white Evidences" against them. Gage agreed that the colonial courts would not proceed adequately against the men, and he reminded Johnson that the "Negro and the Indian . . . may easily be disposed of." Easily and profitably: for they could go to the West Indies as slaves. Eice was another matter. Gage could not summarily dispose of the European-American. Had Eice been either a deserter from the armed forces or a spy for a European power, he might have been tried by "a General

Court Martial as I think he would sooner meet with the Punishment which Such a Traitor Deserves, from a Military than a Civil Court." Instead, he was a white captive of Indians, taken as a "Young Lad," so a military court was impossible.

"Roger" simply disappeared from Johnson's and Gage's papers. Eice and Tony languished in the Albany jail throughout the next year, Johnson's worries about the lack of "white Evidences" notwithstanding. In July 1765 the two were sent from Albany to New York. Noting their arrival in the city, Gage planned to send the "Negro" to the West Indies. He wished that fate for Eice as well, but decided to seek the concurrence of the civil authority, asking New York's Lieutenant Governor Cadwallader Colden to settle the matter. Colden applauded Gage's decision to sell off Tony, and he gave Gage permission summarily to dispense with Eice by sending him in servitude to British Pensacola or to the Caribbean.[37] From Eice's point of view, this was a grim outcome. Eice, not only a renegade but a "German" to boot, did not get the trial by jury that, as a British subject, he should have received. Yet even this judicial miscarriage, by the racist standards of the day, demonstrates that Eice, as a white Indian, stood apart from his two fellow Indians, Roger and Tony. More thought and direct civil intervention went into his disposal. Had there been "white Evidences" against him, Eice would have stood trial; without that evidence, the authorities considered the law, bent it to their satisfaction, and shipped him off to misery. Gage, Johnson, and Colden needed no such creativity in the horror they devised for Tony. And one question remains: what did they devise for Roger?

During the war, British officers saw Indians as beyond the reach not only of British law but of the law of nations. North American Commander-in-Chief Jeffery Amherst included in his rules of engagement with enemy Indians that there be "No Prisoners." While the allied warriors of the Six Nations ignored the order and thus gave captured enemy Indians a chance of survival, it appears that British and colonial soldiers obeyed. Records of Indian warriors captured in action by British troops have yet to come to light—save for one, reported in the *Pennsylvania Gazette*, and it only proves the rule. In August, while Colonel Henry Bouquet's British troops succeeded in repelling the two-day Indian assault at the Battle of Bushy Run, they captured "only one Prisoner, and after a little Examination[,] he received his Quietus."[38]

Trying War Crimes

Pontiac's War ended without settling the question of Native American status. In imperial circles the viewpoint that the Crown reigned sovereign over protected, dependent nations whose members were not subjects became more firmly embedded in practice, but neither Pontiac nor many of his allies had explicitly yielded such dominion to the Crown. The question of the Indians' status faced Pontiac more squarely in 1767, during one of the few British investigations of crimes committed in the course of the war. The case, obscure in its details, involved the murder of a British child, Elizabeth (Betty) Fisher, who had been taken captive by Pontiac's Ottawas at the start of the war. Standing accused was a French-speaking "new subject," Alexis Cuillerier, son of Pontiac's friend Antoine Cuillerier, dit Beaubien, one of the leaders of the French community of Detroit.[39]

Alexis Cuillerier had spent the war years among Pontiac's Ottawas, first near Detroit and later well to the south near the rapids of the Maumee River, a place beyond British authority after the Indian capture of Forts Miamis and Sandusky. Not only had Cuillerier lived with these enemies of the king, but he had allegedly "assisted them in fighting against the English" at Detroit. After four years, with peace settling in, he risked a summertime visit to Detroit, where British troops promptly placed him in jail to await trial for the murder of Betty Fisher. The testimony secured against Cuillerier—particularly that given by his friend, Jean Maiet, on 4 August—was clear, according to the Indian commissary and British officer Jehu Hay. But it was also highly troubling, for it implicated Pontiac, who was then Great Britain's best hope for a lasting peace in a region still swept by rumors of war.[40]

Fisher's late father had been a retired sergeant, one of the very few Britons to stake out a farm near Detroit before Pontiac's War. In one of the war's opening raids Ottawas had captured Betty and one or two of her siblings, killing the rest of her household. When Pontiac's Ottawas retreated from Detroit to the Maumee River in late 1763, they carried the girl with them. Cuillerier and Maiet joined them and, according to Maiet, shared a cabin with Pontiac, Betty Fisher, and others during that winter. Maiet testified that on a particularly bitter night, the little girl, sick with "a flux," "beshit the blanket she lay on." The woman who cared for her washed the blanket, but before it could dry the shivering and sick child approached

Pontiac's fire for warmth, only to be seized roughly by the great man, carried out, and thrown into shallow, freezing Maumee waters. Turning to Cuillerier and Maiet, Pontiac ordered them to "Drown the Child." Both initially refused, but when Pontiac insisted, Cuillerier went to the river and submerged the child in its shallows until she was still.[41] A deeply troubled Maiet left Pontiac in the spring of 1765 and reported the murder to Lieutenant George McDougall and two prominent French supporters of the British. Nothing was done until the summer of 1767, when Cuillerier came to Detroit and was imprisoned. He soon escaped, but the investigation continued in his absence.[42]

Late that summer, two of Pontiac's own relatives confirmed Maiet's story, at least in rough outline. Detroit's interpreter, Elleopolle Chesne, further testified, on 4 September, that Pontiac had once, "in his liqor," told him the same story, adding two details: that at the time of her murder, the girl was already dying, and that she had infuriated Pontiac by soiling his clothes. When the officers told Pontiac himself of these allegations in mid-September, he neither affirmed nor denied them; he simply refused to hear such things.[43]

However helpful or unhelpful this evidence may be to one seeking knowledge of Betty Fisher's fate, it does point decisively toward another conclusion: the British understood Indians to occupy a status apart, a status unlike that held by old British colonists, his majesty's old subjects, and unlike that held by the newly conquered French of the region, the king's new subjects. After hearing repeated testimony from Frenchmen and Indians that Pontiac had ordered Fisher's death, British authorities showed not the least interest in prosecuting him. Pontiac, though he lived within the king's claimed realm and under the Crown's claimed sovereignty and protection, was not, in anyone's view, a Crown subject. He was not a new subject, nor was he an old subject—he was not a subject at all. He was instead the leading member of a separate nation that, however subordinate, had just made peace with Great Britain, a peace that obliterated the acts of war.

Lieutenant Hay explained this to Pontiac himself. Pontiac had come to Detroit to plead for a pardon for Cuillerier should he be recaptured: "I Should be glad this man could be pardon'd if caught again." Hay insisted that this was impossible. Detroit's French had, since 1760, taken oaths of allegiance to the king, had thus become subjects, and therefore had to "be ruled by the same Laws" as the old British subjects. As for Pontiac and "Other Indians," Hay said that the peace so recently formalized with the

British had buried all "that had happen'd dureing [*sic*] the war, . . . and that the Belt of friendship which he carried was a Witness of it."[44]

Hay could define the legal distinction between French new subjects and nonsubject Indians, but Pontiac would not allow the definition to work against his friends. Pontiac requested that Hay allow Chesne, the interpreter whose testimony had, along with that of others, vilified both Pontiac and Cuillerier, to winter with him on the Maumee River. This would prevent Chesne from participating in any trial of Cuillerier that might occur should the fugitive be recaptured. Chesne, meanwhile, now not only cooperated with Pontiac but filled Detroit with so many different versions of his own story that Hay felt compelled to defend the validity of Chesne's sworn affidavit against Chesne's later rumors. Moreover, Chesne absconded with Pontiac to the Maumee River, and the two later moved to a village south of Ouiatenon on the Wabash. Hay declared Chesne "a deserter from his Majesty's service," and Hay was even finally forced to undercut Chesne's credibility: "He is Capable of saying or doing almost anything." The case against Cuillerier, collapsing rapidly, weakened further when Maiet took a similarly unauthorized leave amid rumors of renewed Indian war, going to trade illegally that winter with the still turbulent St. Joseph Potawatomis. Detroit's commander, George Turnbull, would that spring again refer to the distinction between the ethnic French and the Native Americans when he promised to "treat both the New Subjects and Indians with the greatest Lenity," but the Cuillerier affair had cast doubt on the garrison's ability to make such distinctions good, and as for lenity, the affair had shown that Turnbull had little choice.[45]

Imperial authorities came to a rough conclusion regarding the status of most of the Indian nations now at war with Great Britain. When at peace, they were separate peoples inhabiting tracts of lands "secured to them under the Sovereignty Protection and Dominion of His Majesty, . . . living in Friendship with his Majesty's Subjects in America," but not subjects themselves. They possessed "the highest notions of Liberty of any people on Earth," and they retained an independence over their internal affairs. "Allies and Friends," outside the status of subject, yet tied to Great Britain by "Interest," Indians stood within the king's realm as protected, semiautonomous peoples, at least for the present.[46]

Yet the imperial authorities never expected their arrangements with Indians to last: eventually a fuller domination would follow. Sir William

Johnson understood that the temporary arrangements would end when the empire became "formidable throughout the country." The officials did not bestow the idea of full sovereignty on Indian nations and certainly did not treat them as they would European nation-states; the general disregard of Indian peoples at formal treaties in Europe underscores the point, and Indian treaties themselves never held much status in London, in its suburbs, or among its European counterparts. Nations these may have been, but they were, to use a phrase that would not have startled a man like Sir William, dependent nations. Britain already claimed full sovereignty; dependence was the claim's road to fulfillment.[47]

Before rushing to judge eighteenth-century Britons (including British colonists), one should recall that the status of indigenous nations remains an issue in the United States, Canada, and other nations rooted in European empire. Britain has hardly been alone in claiming the status of the world's greatest power or in earning the anger of those it humiliated. Prisoners of war and ambiguously situated captive enemy-combatants continue to suffer at imperial hands in our own times. The problems of the eighteenth century are familiar.

Sovereignty and North American Empire

The current discussion of the United States as an imperial power generally evokes its military, economic, and cultural reach overseas, which has been abetted by new technologies and global corporate organization. An older, even moribund, tradition treats American representative institutions and imperial strength as British legacies. The idea of the United States as "heir apparent" (to borrow from Walpole) to Great Britain is hardly current or catchy, but it is undeniably recognizable. For all its assumptions about the benefits of what was blithely called Anglo-American civilization, the moribund imperial school had the advantage, at least, of taking Native Americans seriously, if hardly on their own terms.

The composite, imperial nature of the imperial republic has been a reality to American Indians throughout its existence. Like peoples under the imperial embrace of ancient Rome or Victorian Britain, American Indians live with the protections of the imperial state, and they bear a heavy burden of its responsibilities.[48] Simultaneously citizens of the United States, their particular state, and their native nation, many Native Americans continue to possess an imperial relationship with the great republic.

Empire, with its promises and dangers, was very much on the minds of the Founding Fathers. Thomas Jefferson famously called America an "Empire of Liberty." But Jefferson also included in the Declaration of Independence an indictment of the king that characterized Indians as mere puppets beyond the laws of war: "[the king] has endeavored to bring on the inhabitants of our frontiers the merciless Indian savages, whose known rule of warfare is an undistinguished destruction of all ages, sexes, and conditions." A great many Indian peoples did fight the United States during the revolution, and when the United States secured its formal independence from Great Britain, acquiring vast western lands at a Paris treaty table, its leaders repeated the errors of Horace Walpole, Robert Rogers, Henry Gladwin, and Jeffery Amherst, imagining a conquest that was in fact merely false empire. In the aftermath of the British-American peace, Indians north of the Ohio expanded their intertribal organizing, rejected several dictated American treaties, met invading settlers with violence, and threw back several invading armies; one of them, under Arthur St. Clair, in 1792, suffered the worst defeat—ever—of any single U.S. force at the hands of Indians. The Indians' intertribal organization, determination, and capabilities were impressive, and they registered with federal officials from President George Washington to Secretary of War Henry Knox.

The successful integration of Indian country north of the Ohio into the imperial republic was accomplished, therefore, with paper and pen as much as with the sword, as American officials struggled to accommodate and not simply to conquer. Knox worried openly about world opinion, fearing that America's imperial policies, if too violent, would be associated with those of sixteenth-century Spain by some contemporary Las Casas: "If our modes of population and War destroy the tribes the disinterested part of mankind and posterity will be apt to class the effects of our Conduct and that of the Spaniards in Mexico and Peru together."[49] Knox was worried not that the United States might be called with Spain an empire, but that it might be called a cruel one. Knox and Washington insisted that treaties with Indians be made and ratified according to the process established in the new constitution for treaties generally. A degree of formal Indian nationhood, which to many has implied a degree of Indian sovereignty, became regularly acknowledged in executive treaty-making and Senate ratification, practices that resulted in hundreds of ratified treaties by 1871. The tacit U.S. acknowledgment of Indian sovereignty was tightly limited, for the United States consistently insisted, for example, on its preemptive and exclusive right to purchase Indian lands within its claimed territory as defined by the Treaty of Paris and by future treaties with nation-states.[50]

An imperial moment in the postrevolutionary determination of Indian status came in 1794–1795, when Anthony Wayne, in highly stylized Roman fashion, under the banner of the eagle and at the command of a "legion," defeated an intertribal force at the Battle of Fallen Timbers and made peace with many nations in the historic Treaty of Greenville.[51] Although this treaty was not the first made by the United States with Indians (a recent compendium lists twenty-two preceding it), it does illustrate the new American approach.[52] Secretary of State Timothy Pickering had instructed Wayne to disavow "explicitly" the interpretation that the Peace of Paris of 1783 implied a conquest of the interior. This "construction" or interpretation, Wayne was informed, was "as unfounded in itself as it was unintelligible and mysterious to the Indians." The "land is theirs (and this we acknowledge)."[53] Surveying the wreckage of twenty years of frontier war, the United States concluded that to admit the falseness of its empire was a way to make its empire real. Reginald Horsman noted long ago that "the change had been forced upon the United States by the extent of Indian resistance."[54]

When Indians signed the treaty at Greenville, they surrendered a great deal: not only land but also a measure of independence. In the course of negotiations native leaders had used Minavavana's language of sovereignty, saying that "the Great Spirit gave us this land in common." But in the end, they acknowledged U.S. protection, and they called American leaders "Father," a term that at least some of them understood to concede a degree of political authority.[55] In keeping with the republic's new practices, the treaty also brought Indian nations into the empire while recognizing their national standing. Though in different configurations and, in some cases, in very different places, many of the signing nations continue to exist *as nations*. The signing nations and several hundred other Indian nations have retained, and periodically even expanded, elements of sovereignty and self-determination. It has been no easy task, for many U.S. citizens and officials, denying an imperial past and the obligations to the colonized that that would entail, would prefer to see the nations disappear and the Indians simply be absorbed as ordinary citizens.[56]

The best scholarship on the early American republic to see the American Revolution as unleashing the forces of liberalism—forces which would eventually challenge the archaic institution of slavery and promote the legal equality of individuals regardless of birthright—has had remarkably little to say about Indians' status in the United States.[57] This is understandable, for it is difficult to accommodate the persistence of the special status of Native American tribes, legally constituted as having unique relations with the federal government, to the story of liberal democracy. But such an accommodation is possible, for the revolution did leave Indians a legacy, one based on a kind of equality, one that can be and has been sustained by liberalism, but one that rests on national, not individual rights. The legacy is more imperial than it is republican, but it reflects certain republican principles.

The United States, unlike the former British colonies of Canada, Australia, and New Zealand, assumes that recognized indigenous nations retain aboriginal rights so fundamental that the term *sovereign* can be and has been applied to them by the highest court. The idea of Indian sovereignty arises not only out of Indian achievements in defeating the American myth of conquest but also out of peculiarities in the United States Constitution. At the Philadelphia Convention of 1787 Alexander Hamilton suggested that state sovereignty could be "diminished" without ceasing to be sovereignty, an idea he repeated in the *Federalist*. Those supporters of the Constitution who would become his staunchest opponents, Thomas Jefferson and James Madison, in the late 1790s saw the republic as an arrangement of divided sovereignty.[58]

This kind of experimenting with sovereign power was less possible in Canada or elsewhere in the British Empire, which left sovereignty fully with (following another ingenious experiment) the king-in-parliament. Facing this Blackstonian notion of unitary sovereignty, Canadian First Nations have had little success arguing from aboriginal sovereignty; "aboriginal rights" are another matter. In Canadian history the idea that Native Americans might possess some residual sovereignty has been thought, and then declared, to be unthinkable: "The supposition that the Indians are not subject to the laws of Canada is absurd," said a judge in 1823. In 1839 and 1840 courts again determined that Indians had no separate legal status in rulings that tended both to extend greater civil rights to Indians and to deny the existence of their nations. In 1852 a British North American judge ruled that it could "never be pretended" that the Six Nations Iroquois "were recognized as a separate and independent nation . . . ; but yet as British subjects, and under the control of, and subject to the general law of England." In recent decades Canadian courts have recognized Indians as possessing such liberties as "aboriginal title," a liberty the sovereign is bound to protect. But north of the Great Lakes, the formal status of native people remains different than that possessed by Indian peoples of the modern United States.[59]

Legal history is not history as a whole. The Native Americans' preservation of a limited sovereignty in the United States does not mean they have somehow fared better than have the First Nations in Canada. The point is instead that the revolutionary, confederate, and early constitutional eras of U.S. history, generally seen as disastrous for Indians, did provide a foundation for a concept of Indian sovereignty that would become highly important in our time, once skilled lawyers and leaders, many of them Indians, discovered it. John Marshall most clearly articulated the semi-sovereign status of Indian nations in three cases from the 1820s and 1830s, rulings famously ignored by Andrew Jackson and less famously but just as devastatingly ignored by state courts for decades.[60] In other words, however tragic it may be that Canada disavows Indian sovereignty, the greater tragedy is that a creative revision of the concept of sovereignty in the United States, one that allowed Marshall to see Indian nations as retaining at least certain inherent powers, has been given such fitful and inconsistent attention by his heirs.[61]

Both imperial systems occasionally look back to the 1760s, when British imperial authorities faced significant challenges to their assumptions of conquest and strove with some seriousness (though without much conclusion) to ascertain the status of Indian nations. The questions they confronted, raised by a powerful Native American rejection of imperial myths, similarly vexed later generations in the United States and Canada, where the answers have been formally very different. These postrevolutionary empires, for all their creativity, have not fully escaped the conundrums of their colonial predecessors.

Notes

Portions of this chapter have appeared in the author's *War under Heaven: Pontiac, the Indian Nations, and the British Empire* (Baltimore: Johns Hopkins University Press: 2002). Used with permission of the publisher.

1. Toynbee, *The Letters of Horace Walpole, Fourth Earl of Orford*, 189, 192.

2. Peckham, *Journals of Robert Rogers*, 140.

3. Belich, *Making Peoples*, 249.

4. White, *The Middle Ground*, 50–93, 269–314.

5. Charles Moore, "Gladwin Manuscripts," 642, 647, 649, 680.

6. Ibid., 675.

7. Hamilton et al., *The Papers of Sir William Johnson*, 4:95.

8. Ibid., 10:689.

9. Henry, *Travels and Adventures of Alexander Henry*, 44.

10. Belich, *Making Peoples*, 193–97; Fleras and Elliot, *The Nations Within*, 132, 134, 137.

11. Linebaugh, "The Secret History of the Magna Carta."

12. Jones, *License for Empire*, 101–94; Green, "Claims to Territory in Colonial America," 96–124; Sosin, *Whitehall and the Wilderness*, 39, 52–65.

13. Hamilton et al., *The Papers of Sir William Johnson*, 4:214, 10:982; Green, "Claims to Territory in Colonial America," 103; Humphreys, "Lord Shelburne and the Proclamation of 1763," 241–64.

14. Vitoria, *Political Writings*, 278–79, 284–87, 290; Robert Williams, *The American Indian in Western Legal Thought*, 96–108.

15. Robert Williams, *The American Indian in Western Legal Thought*, 165–72.

16. Pagden, *Lords of All the World*, 76–93.

17. Rubertone, *Grave Undertakings*, 8, 16–17.

18. Dickason "Concepts of Sovereignty at the Time of First Contacts," 239; Savelle, *The Origins of American Diplomacy*, 205; Kent, *Pennsylvania and Delaware Treaties, 1629–1737*, 5, 6, 11, 16–18, 21–24, 34–47, 49, 58–62, 64–68, 71–74, 76–82, 99–100.

19. Hinderaker, "The 'Four Indian Kings' and the Imaginative Construction of the First British Empire," 487–526.

20. Robert Williams, *The American Indian in Western Legal Thought*, 134; see also W. Stitt Robinson, "The Legal Status of the Indian in Colonial Virginia," 258, 259.

21. Merrell, "Declarations of Independence," 197.

22. Kupperman, *Indians and English*.

23. Canny, "England's New World and the Old, 1480s–1630s," 157; W. Stitt Robinson, *Virginia Treaties, 1607–1722*, 11–22; Gleach, *Powhatan's World and Colonial Virginia*, 136–37; O'Mellin, "The Imperial Origins of Federal Indian Law," 1207–75.

24. Pulsipher, "'Subjects . . . unto the Same King.'"

25. Lepore, *The Name of War*, 137, 155, 163; Edmund S. Morgan, *Inventing the People*, 23; O'Brien, *Dispossession by Degrees*, 67; Kawashima, "Jurisdiction of the Colonial Courts over the Indians in Massachusetts, 1689–1763," 533, 533n52; W. Stitt Robinson, *Virginia Treaties, 1607–1722*, 11–22, 82, 117–18; W. Stitt Robinson, "The Legal Status of the Indian in Colonial Virginia."

26. Jennings et al., *The History and Culture of Iroquois Diplomacy*, 184.

27. Alvord et al., *The Critical Period, 1763–1765*, 10:5–7, 218, 395–96; Edmund S. Morgan, *Inventing the People*, 25.

28. O'Callaghan and Fernow, *Documents Relative to the Colonial History of the State of New York*, 7:561. See also Hamilton et al., *The Papers of Sir William Johnson*, 11:493.

29. Hamilton et al., *The Papers of Sir William Johnson*, 10:395. See also Alvord et al., *The Critical Period, 1763–1765*, 10:391–92.

30. Snapp, *John Stuart and the Struggle for Empire on the Southern Colonial Frontier*, 66.

31. Shannon, *Indians and Colonists at the Crossroads of Empire*, 12, 21, 22, 24, 59.

32. Stevens and Kent, *The Papers of Col. Henry Bouquet*, 338.

33. Hamilton et al., *The Papers of Sir William Johnson*, 11:169.

34. Alvord et al., *The Critical Period, 1763–1765*, 10:348.

35. Stevens et al., *Papers of Henry Bouquet*, 6:522–26, 539–40; Henry Bouquet to Thomas Gage, 26 September 1764, Papers of Thomas Gage, American Series, William Clements Library, University of Michigan, Ann Arbor.

36. Thomas Gage to Henry Bouquet, 15 October 1764, Papers of Thomas Gage, American Series, William Clements Library, University of Michigan, Ann Arbor. See also Alvord et al., *The Critical Period, 1763–1765*, 10:348–49.

37. Hamilton et al., *The Papers of Sir William Johnson*, 4:314, 329, 424, 439–40; 11:165–66, 174–75, 201; *The Pennsylvania Gazette*, folio 2, item 20747; John Christie to Thomas Gage, 10 July 1765, Papers of Thomas Gage, American Series, William Clements Library, University of Michigan, Ann Arbor; Thomas Gage to Cadwallader Colden, 18 July 1765, Papers of Thomas Gage, American Series, William Clements Library, University of Michigan, Ann Arbor; Cadwallader Colden to Thomas Gage, 22 July 1765, Papers of Thomas Gage, American Series, William Clements Library, University of Michigan, Ann Arbor.

38. Stevens et al., *Papers of Henry Bouquet*, 6:228–33; Shoemaker, "Bouquet Papers," 203, 261; Jeffery Amherst, *Jeffery Amherst Papers*, American Series, 2, no. 3, William Clements Library, University of Michigan, Ann Arbor; Egle and Linn, *Pennsylvania Archives*, 4:163; *The Pennsylvania Gazette*, folio 2, item 18966.

39. George Turnbull, "Examination of John Maiet," [4 August] 1767, Papers of Thomas Gage, American Series, William Clements Library, University of Michigan, Ann Arbor. See also Hamilton et al., *The Papers of Sir William Johnson*, 5:644, 723.

40. Turnbull, "Examination of John Maiet," [4 August] 1767.

41. Ibid.

42. Ibid.; Hamilton et al., *The Papers of Sir William Johnson*, 5:644.

43. Hamilton et al., *The Papers of Sir William Johnson*, 5:652–653, 671–72.

44. Ibid., 5:644, 673.

45. Ibid., 5:675, 688, 730; George Turnbull to Thomas Gage, 25 April 1768, Papers of Thomas Gage, American Series, William Clements Library, University of Michigan, Ann Arbor.

46. Hamilton et al., *The Papers of Sir William Johnson*, 4:256; Alvord et al., *The Critical Period, 1763–1765*, 10:33, 257–58.

47. Alvord et al., *The Critical Period, 1763–1765*, 10:33.

48. Wilkinson, *Blood Struggle*, 103; Holm, *Strong Hearts, Wounded Souls*.

49. Prucha, *The Great Father*, 1:43–45, 65–66; Horsman, "American Indian Policy in the Old Northwest, 1783–1812," 35–40, 53.

50. Prucha, *The Great Father*, 1:50–60; Horsman, "American Indian Policy in the Old Northwest, 1783–1812," 45–47.

51. Dowd, *A Spirited Resistance*, 113.

52. Deloria and De Mallie, *Documents of American Indian Diplomacy*, 1:183–84.

53. Jennings, "The Imperial Revolution," 44–45.

54. Horsman, "American Indian Policy in the Old Northwest, 1783–1812," 40.

55. White, *The Middle Ground*, 472–73; Horsman, "American Indian Policy in the Old Northwest, 1783–1812," 52–53; Cayton, "Noble Actors upon 'the Theatre of Honour,'" 263–69.

56. Deloria and Lytle, *The Past and Future of American Indian Sovereignty*; Wilkinson, *American Indians, Time, and the Law*, 54–78.

57. Appleby, *Inheriting the Revolution*, 52–55; Appleby, *Liberalism and Republicanism in the Historical Imagination*, 158–59; Gordon Wood, *The Radicalism of the American Revolution*, 7, 186.

58. Rakove, *Original Meanings*, 105.

59. Nichols, *Indians in the United States and Canada*, 192–93; Clark, *Native Liberty, Crown Sovereignty*, 19; *Delgamuukw v. British Columbia* [1997] 3 S.C.R. 1010.

60. Haring, *Crow Dog's Case*, 25–56, 124, 134–206.

61. Wilkins, *American Indian Sovereignty and the Supreme Court*.

JOHN RICHARD OLDFIELD

3   SLAVERY, ABOLITION, AND EMPIRE

Slavery was an unavoidable and, some might have deemed, necessary adjunct of European empire in the seventeenth and eighteenth centuries. The rise of plantation complexes in the New World that depended on enslaved rural labor forces imported from Africa underpinned imperialistic expansion in the Americas, at the same time creating important links between economic interests and state power.

The Slave Trade

All of the major European powers at one time or another entered the Atlantic slave trade, just as most of them possessed slave colonies. Yet it was the British who came to dominate the slave trade. At its height, British Empire ships carried more slaves than any other nation, their slave colonies produced vast quantities of tropical goods, and the country as a whole grew rich on the profits of African slavery. All the more remarkable, then, that during the late eighteenth century many Britons began to question the humanity of the slave trade and to call for its abolition, in the process sparking a heated and sometimes bitter debate that would ultimately refashion Britain's imperialistic ambitions, just as it would refashion the foundations of its hegemonic power.

The British probably tried some slave trading to the Spanish colonies in the Caribbean as early as the 1560s. But without major tropical colonies of their own, there was little incentive to enter the trade, at least not in any concerted or organized fashion. All of this was to change in the early seventeenth century, however, when the British claimed Bermuda and later, in 1625, Barbados. After initial experiments with tobacco and cotton, Barbados rapidly emerged as a major sugar colony—that is, as a plantation economy dependent on enslaved African labor. Barbados, moreover, set the pattern for further expansion in both the Caribbean and mainland America. The acquisition of Jamaica in 1655, and the spectacular expansion of tobacco production in Virginia and Maryland, secured the rise of plantation complexes that dominated the Atlantic economy in the seventeenth and eighteenth centuries.[1]

Spurred on by the success of Barbados, British merchants began to take a more active interest in the Atlantic slave trade. By the 1630s, the British had their first fort in Africa, on the Gold Coast, and two decades later had staked out the Sierra Leone or Upper Guinea Coast as a British sphere of influence. Perhaps just as important, in 1660 the state became involved in the slave trade when Charles II granted a thousand-year monopoly of British trade with Africa to the Company of Royal Adventurers Trading into Africa (later the Royal African Company). But the real expansion came after 1698–1713, when the last remnant of Crown control over Britain's trade to Africa came to an end. As a result of what one might call the "privatization" of the slave trade, slave exports rose from 203,000 in the decade 1710–19 to 391,200 in 1760–69. Even during the 1780s and 1790s, decades disrupted by wars with both France and America, the British exported a total of 656,000 slaves. Between 1662 and 1807, when the British Atlantic slave trade came to an end, British Empire ships carried approximately 3.4 million slaves from Africa to America, or about 50 percent of all slave exports during this period.[2]

The bulk of these slaves were shipped to the Caribbean, which proved something of a graveyard for Africans and their descendants; a smaller number (probably somewhere around 650,000) were imported into the North American colonies.[3] In each case, slaves were vital to the economic success of plantation complexes that produced large quantities of staples (sugar, rice, tobacco, indigo) for export. The value of this trade to the British is indisputable. To give one example, sugar imports from the British

Caribbean to Great Britain rose from approximately 41,000 tons in ca. 1748 to 165,000 tons in ca. 1815; in fact, between 1750 and 1825 sugar was *the* most valuable of all British imports.[4] One could cite similar figures for tobacco (in the case of the Chesapeake region) and rice (in the case of South Carolina). Annual exports of tobacco increased from 20,000 pounds in 1619 to 38 million pounds in 1700 and then stabilized at a fluctuating level of 25 to 60 million pounds throughout the eighteenth century. Not surprisingly, the importance of slave-grown produce to the British economy increased over time. According to one recent estimate, the British Caribbean's share of British exports and imports rose from 10 percent during the first half of the eighteenth century to 20 percent in 1815.[5]

The Atlantic slave system also provided a boost to British manufactures, although this is not quite the same thing as saying that it was responsible for Britain's industrial "take off."[6] As is widely recognized, slave colonies in North America and the Caribbean absorbed a bewildering array of British manufactured goods: furniture, silver, ceramics, musical instruments—the list is endless. In particular, the colonies wanted textiles to clothe their slaves and metal goods (hoes, knives, axes, not to mention instruments of torture) used in the operation of basic plantation life. Slave colonies not only stimulated demand, making up for slack periods at home, but also, as in the case of Britain's iron industry, encouraged innovation and modernization. There was also an African dimension to this burgeoning international economy. Throughout the period of the slave trade, European merchants poured vast quantities of goods into Africa, some of which, like East Indian textiles, became high-demand items, while others (brass bracelets, for instance) soon went out of fashion or aroused little interest among African traders and middlemen. Last but by no means least, the Atlantic slave system stimulated local shipbuilding and helped to reshape the urban landscape of slave ports like Bristol and Liverpool, as merchants sought to translate their wealth into property and social status.[7]

The importance of this trade to the British economy, therefore, was immense. It also followed that state interests were closely aligned with those involved in the Atlantic slave system, although British merchants, like colonial planters, leaving very little to chance, lobbied hard for their interests. Perhaps the best illustration of this was the powerful West India lobby, made up of islands agents in London (chief among them being Stephen Fuller of Jamaica), London merchants trading with the Caribbean (the influential Society of West India Merchants), and absentee planters in Britain. As Andrew O'Shaughnessy and others have shown, this lobby was closely linked with the City of London, as well as with interests in Parliament. Some Members of Parliament (MPs), like William Beckford, were themselves absentee planters. Others were merchants or else had Caribbean connections and interests. It has been estimated that between 1812 and 1830 the so-called West India interest had between fifty and sixty potential supporters in the House of Commons, with a hard core of between thirty-six and forty. These men were able to exert considerable pressure on government ministers, as well as on the course of debates on slavery and the slave trade, and could even count some ministers among their staunchest supporters. An important lead also came from the royal family, not least in the shape of the Duke of Clarence, later William IV, who was to prove one of the abolitionists' most obdurate opponents in the House of Lords.[8]

This web of interests ensured not only that the Atlantic slave system was subsidized, most obviously through advantageous taxes or duties, but also that it was protected. Without state power, and especially the military strength of the Royal Navy, it is unlikely that British merchants would have been able to dominate the transatlantic slave trade in quite the way they did. Slave colonies, particularly those in the Caribbean, were always vulnerable to attacks from European competitors: hence the importance of forts, garrisons, and naval dockyards. As James Walvin has argued, "The stability of the slave colonies was secured (or as secured as any slave society could be) by the ability of the Navy to keep out interlopers, to maintain local defenses and generally to guarantee the supplies, defense and exports of plantation society."[9] Here again, these costly operations were financed principally from London; significantly, the main fiscal pressure on the Caribbean was applied indirectly, by increasing the duties charged on colonial produce landed at British ports.

Dismantling the System

In sum, the Atlantic slave system was a critical factor in Britain's rise to global power in the seventeenth and eighteenth centuries. Yet, paradoxically, the British were the first to dismantle the system, acting decisively in 1807 to end British involvement in the transatlantic slave trade and again in 1833 to abolish colonial slavery. How and why this came about are questions that continue to puzzle historians. Early accounts, produced in the nineteenth century and early twentieth, tended to explain the abolition of the slave trade in terms of a moral crusade that pitted abolitionists (the "Saints") against evil planters and slave merchants. The first serious challenge to this "moral" interpretation of abolition came from Eric Williams in his book *Capitalism and Slavery* (1954). In brief, Williams believed that "abolition" was primarily the result of economic forces. (Williams had very little time for the abolitionists as a group or, indeed, for arguments that placed emphasis on moral as opposed to economic change.) It was "mercantilism" that created the slave system, Williams argued, and "mature capitalism" that destroyed it. Abolition, in other words, was motivated purely by economic self-interest: "When British capitalism depended on the West Indies, [capitalists] ignored slavery or defended it. When British capitalism found the West Indian monopoly a nuisance they destroyed West Indian slavery as the first step in the destruction of West Indian monopoly."[10]

This argument has some merit. But while most historians today would not dissent from Williams's view that abolition was in some way bound up with economic interests that had no direct stake in the Atlantic slave system, few would accept his contention that Britain's economic development in the nineteenth century actually required the destruction of slavery. More to the point, Williams's decline thesis—namely that calls to end British slavery coincided with periods of general economic decline in the British Caribbean—is open to criticism. Indeed, Seymour Drescher has argued that abolition, in this case the abolition of the transatlantic slave trade, took place at a time of favorable economic trends for the British Caribbean economy. Similar doubts surround Williams's assertion that "overproduction in 1833 demanded emancipation."[11] But if economic decline did not motivate abolition, what did? Since the 1970s historians of British antislavery have placed renewed emphasis on the "moral" elements in abolitionism, tracing its origins in the growth of compassionate humanitarianism and evangelical religion, within both the established church and the main dissenting sects. Still others have stressed the importance of industrialization and the growing gap between capitalist and pre-capitalist modes of production. This is not to suggest that the spread of abolitionist ideas had to rest on the growth of the factory system and free-labor ideology, but that there was a link of some sort, perhaps a "transformation of consciousness," evident in the desire on both sides of the Atlantic "to dignify and honor labor," now seems indisputable.[12]

More recently, Linda Colley and Christopher Leslie Brown have also stressed the importance of the American Revolution in stimulating abolitionist activity.[13] As is well known, the fate of Britain's North American colonies unleashed a heated debate about political representation that was quite often framed in terms of slavery (disfranchisement) and freedom (the vote). "To be free," wrote Capel Loftt, in 1780, "is to be in a condition of giving assent to the laws of the state, either in *person*, or by a representative. To be enslaved is to have no will of our own in the choice of lawmakers; but to be governed by rulers whom other men have set over us."[14] In this way, slavery began to take on a more immediate significance, related to the political condition of thousands of native-born Britons. The American Revolution, in other words, gave slavery ideological meaning. But it also had a more far-reaching effect. As Colley has argued, defeat in the American war brought with it a searching and sometimes painful reevaluation of Britain's standing as a once victorious Protestant nation. One result of the loss of the American colonies was a move to tighten the reins of empire elsewhere, notably in Canada, Ireland, and, more slowly, in the Caribbean. Another, however, was a rise in enthusiasm for parliamentary reform, "for religious liberalisation, for the reform of gaols and lunatic asylums; for virtually anything, in fact, that might prevent a similar humiliation in the future."[15]

Put a different way, the loss of the American colonies forced Britons to think about themselves and about their failings: "They had been corrupt and presumptuous, and they had warred against fellow Protestants. And they had been duly punished."[16] It only remained now to make an act of atonement. Naturally enough, slavery and the slave trade also came under the microscope, leading some Britons to contemplate alternative visions of empire, including, significantly, an empire without slaves or slavery. If the debate was rarely framed in these precise terms, one should not underestimate the impact of the American Revolution and imperial crisis on British political thought, or, indeed, the power and influence of providential ideas. Seen in this light, abolition of the slave trade was inextricably linked with the character, virtue, and destiny of the British nation and of its empire, at least until the rising tide of revolutionary violence in France shifted the terms of debate yet again.[17]

The American Revolution also had a vital impact on abolitionism because it effectively divided British America, at the same time halving the number of slaves in the British Empire. Abolitionists were well aware of the importance of these events. "As long as America was ours," wrote Thomas Clarkson in 1788, "there was no chance that a minister would have attended to the groans of the sons and daughters of Africa, however he might feel for their distress."[18] Now, of course, things were very different. Even within the British Caribbean there were signs of change. As Andrew O'Shaughnessy has recently argued, "The republican ideology of the American Revolution fostered the growth of anti-slavery sentiment in the Caribbean." Although it did not "initiate the concept of liberty among free colored people and slaves," he goes on, "it gave the idea greater currency and reality." So, eight years after the American Revolution, one could find the free colored population of Jamaica petitioning for the right to vote, arguing that taxation and representation were inseparable.[19]

The Rise of Reform

In the years immediately following defeat in the American war, this heady mix of ideas—free-labor ideology, compassionate humanitarianism, and debates about the morality and purpose of empire—prompted the first serious challenge to the cozy relationship between state interests and the Atlantic slave system. Most of those who joined the ranks of the abolitionists were members of an increasingly leisured and largely disenfranchised middle class: shopkeepers, small manufacturers, and professionals of one description or another. By and large, these were men and women who had no obvious connection with transatlantic slavery and who, if anything, defined themselves against it. Indeed, if the language of many abolitionist pamphlets is to be believed, the slave trade was considered not only immoral by many middle-class Britons but also "irrational" and an impediment to further social and economic progress. More to the point, these new interests were prepared to make themselves heard, by organizing committees, raising subscriptions, and signing petitions against the slave trade (there were large petition campaigns in 1788 and again in 1792). They also intervened in the economy by boycotting the consumption of slave-grown produce, principally sugar and rum.[20] Of course, the West India lobby fought back, but from this moment on, the state was made increasingly aware of the existence of competing interests surrounding the slavery question, interests that, in time, would force the state to make a choice between an empire with slaves and one without.

Early abolitionist activity was channeled through the Society for Effecting the Abolition of the Slave Trade (SEAST), organized in May 1787, which, with some justification, has been described as the prototype of the nineteenth-century reform organization. Its self-appointed task was to create a constituency for abolition through the distribution of circular letters, books, and pamphlets. Abolitionists were also quick to exploit the influence of the press and (in the case of Wedgwood's famous cameo of the kneeling slave) visual images and artifacts. Indeed, the full range of their opinion-building techniques is impressive, and it anticipated many of the techniques employed by reformers in the nineteenth century. By and large, these were practical men (bankers, merchants, and manufacturers) who turned out to be peculiarly suited to the task of mobilizing public opinion against the slave trade; and much the same was true of the local committees where again the "middling sort" predominated.[21]

Just as important, popular opposition to the slave trade was organized in transnational networks; indeed, foreign support and intervention were deemed vital to the success of the movement at home. In pursuit of these aims, British abolitionists made contact with the Société des Amis des Noirs, following its organization in 1788, and distributed books and pamphlets through the British ambassador in Madrid. More significant, certainly in the long term, were the links that British abolitionists established with American abolitionists, principally with the Pennsylvania Abolition Society (PAS) and the New York Manumission Society. If anything, the revolution strengthened these ties, at the same time putting them on a more formal basis. One of the first acts of PAS, for instance, following its reorganization in 1787, was to open a correspondence with Thomas Clarkson. Eager to repay the compliment, in July 1787 the SEAST wrote to the societies in Philadelphia and New York "to inform them of the measures they had taken for the abolition of the slave trade."[22]

Through these channels, which stretched from London to Paris, Philadelphia, and New York (and beyond), abolitionists exchanged ideas and information, in the process creating an "imagined community" of reformers who offered each other support, advice, and encouragement. As James Pemberton, president of PAS, put it to Granville Sharp in 1794, "It is proper to keep up a regular correspondence—the strength and encouragement afforded thereby are too sensibly felt not to be acknowledged."[23] America also provided British abolitionists with an example to follow, at least insofar as (local) state action was concerned, although one can detect a subtle shift in the relationship between British and American abolitionists, certainly after 1790 when Congress, reacting to political pressure from PAS and Quakers in New York, Pennsylvania, Maryland, and Virginia, refused to interfere directly with the slave trade (at least, until 1808, when the Constitution stipulated that a ban would come into effect) or to take any action affecting the emancipation of slaves. At a personal level, figures like Granville Sharp would continue to support attempts to test the regulatory powers vested in Congress, but increasingly abolitionists in America began to look to Britain for inspiration, and not vice versa.[24]

Of course, there is an obvious irony here. If many Britons had looked toward America for inspiration, they would have found obvious limits to the American conception of freedom, particularly where enslaved Africans were concerned. While revolutionary fervor had led to a direct onslaught against the transatlantic slave trade (arguably of less importance to Southern planters than it was to their counterparts in the Caribbean), slavery itself proved a much more intractable problem.[25] Revolutionary ideals came into conflict with a Southern plantocracy that jealously protected its economic and political power; indeed, many of the principal revolutionaries, including figures like Washington and Jefferson, were themselves slaveholders and showed little inclination to abolish the institution of slavery. Instead, the revolutionaries agreed to disagree over slavery, as part of a series of compromises that underpinned the adoption of the Constitution in 1787 and, with it, the preservation of the new republic.[26] Ironically, it would take another forty years before abolition again took hold in the United States and even then progress toward emancipation was slow and halting, at least until the Civil War.

With hindsight, one can see that the early abolitionist movement emerged during a period of anxiety for many Britons, wedged, as it was, between the American war and the mounting conflict with revolutionary and Napoleonic France, a conflict that eventually forced the movement out of the political spotlight. Ironically, however, the French revolutionary wars helped to prepare the way for final victory. The acquisition of new territories in the Caribbean, notably Trinidad, Berbice, and Demerara, led many of the old planter elites, who were increasingly fearful of competition, to desert the anti-abolitionist ranks. Capitalizing on this change of heart and on the entry into Parliament of a batch of new liberal Irish MPs, abolitionists renewed their campaign. At first, the SEAST leader William Wilberforce and his allies met with little success. But in 1806 Lord Grenville's government, the "Ministry of All the Talents," brought in a bill for prohibiting the slave trade to conquered Dutch Guiana. Seizing this opportunity, Wilberforce began to attach the provisions of his own Foreign Slave Bill to the proposed legislation. The tactic worked. The Foreign Slave Bill passed into law in 1806, paving the way for the Abolition Act of 1807, which outlawed the British Atlantic slave trade tout court.[27]

After 1807 the British anti-slavery movement entered a new phase. SEAST gave way to the African Institution, whose principal aim was to ensure that the new legislation was enforced and that other countries followed Britain's example. Thanks to the efforts of the Royal Navy, the first of these objectives was soon realized. Supplementary legislation also reinforced Britain's ongoing commitment to abolition of the slave trade; involvement in the trade was made a transportable offence in 1811 and then, in 1824, a capital crime. Persuading other countries to join Britain in outlawing the slave trade proved much more difficult, however. Despite the efforts of the African Institution, and those of British ministers, the Congresses of Paris (1814) and Vienna (1815) both failed to reach specific agreement on abolition, not least because of French opposition. The results of the Aix-la-Chapelle Congress of 1818 were equally unsatisfactory.[28]

Suppression of the slave trade, and, in particular, efforts to suppress the illegal traffic between the West Indian colonies, led, in turn, to a further innovation, namely slave registration. In 1812 an order in council set up a slave registry in Trinidad, and by 1817 all of the British Caribbean islands had a system of public registration, which in each case required regular reports of any changes in slave holdings, whether through births, deaths, purchases, or sales.[29] Despite these different initiatives, however, there was little evidence to suggest that suppression of the transatlantic slave trade had done much to improve the treatment and condition of colonial slaves, which had obviously been the intention. So it was that in 1823 some of the leading members of the African Institution, among them Thomas Clarkson and William Wilberforce, organized a new body, the Anti-Slavery Society, or, to give it its full title, the Society for the Mitigation and Gradual Abolition of Slavery Throughout the British Dominions. Modest in its ambitions, at least by later standards, the members of the Anti-Slavery Society called for the adoption of measures to improve slave conditions in the British

Caribbean, together with a plan for gradual emancipation that would ultimately lead to complete freedom. Only later, in 1832, did the more radical members of the Anti-Slavery Society embrace immediate emancipation.[30]

In organizational terms, there are obvious continuities between the eighteenth- and nineteenth-century British anti-slavery movements; in fact, some of the most successful opinion-building techniques of the nineteenth century (petitions, boycotts, pamphleteering) were first devised during the 1780s and 1790s. And, if anything, the links between British and American abolitionists became stronger, even allowing for the disruptive effect of factional rivalries.[31] But in another sense, the nineteenth-century debate was different. For one thing, during the 1820s and 1830s British colonial slavery came under fierce economic attack, as abolitionists picked over the implications of the works of Adam Smith (1723–1790), Jean-Baptiste Say (1767–1832), and a third generation of classical economists led by John R. McCulloch (1789–1864).[32] The key here was free trade and the vision of an economic order untrammeled by restrictions and controls. From this perspective, colonial slavery began to seem anachronistic; the fact that the British people effectively subsidized the West Indian planters by paying high sugar duties was particularly irksome. If anything, these frustrations, along with the declining importance of Britain's Caribbean trade as a share of national wealth, only added to the growing clamor to abolish colonial slavery.[33] Put a different way, by the 1830s the British Caribbean no longer seemed quite so vital to the state's hegemonic power or, indeed, to its imperialist ambitions, which, after mid-century would be increasingly directed toward Africa and India.

Attacks on Colonial Rule

British unease about slavery was further exacerbated by news of slave rebellions in the Caribbean. The period witnessed a series of large-scale slave insurrections, most notably the 1816 Barbados Revolution, the 1823 rebellion in Demerara in modern Guyana, led by Jack Gladstone, and, perhaps most significant of all, the 1831–32 Christmas Rebellion in Jamaica, led by Sam Sharpe, which involved over 20,000 slaves and is said to have caused more than one million pounds in damage. From 1816, in other words, the British state was faced by a new challenge, namely dissent *against* empire, as represented by the slave revolts, as distinct from dissent *within* empire, as represented by British abolitionists. The rebellions sharpened internal dissent; they were met by such fearsome reprisals from white planters (500 blacks were killed or executed in the wake of the Christmas Rebellion in Jamaica, for instance) that many shocked British observers were pushed into the abolitionist camp.[34] Slowly, the Atlantic slave system was starting to unravel, although assessing the relative importance of moral dissent, on the one hand, and slave revolts, on the other, is necessarily difficult. The least one can say is that the brutal cycle of slave discontent, upheavals, and white reprisals only added to a growing sense of imperial crisis in the British Caribbean, leading the state to question the economic cost of maintaining and protecting its slave colonies.[35]

Here again, the contrast with the United States is striking. Although there were slave revolts in the American South, chief among them being the Nat Turner rebellion of 1831, the numbers were relatively small, at least in comparison with the British Caribbean.[36] Perhaps more to the point, U.S. slave revolts served only to tighten the grip of the Southern white plantocracy on the four million slaves in its midst. Certainly, there is little to suggest that they destabilized the Southern economy, at least in the long term, any more than they destabilized the United States. These divergent experiences point to a further fundamental difference. For North Americans, slavery was always a domestic problem that could never be separated from the economic and political future of the Union, or, indeed, from its welfare. This, after all, was the meaning of the compromises hammered out at Philadelphia in 1787. For Britons, on the other hand, slavery was a colonial problem, which meant that the economic cost of emancipation could always be separated from its social and political cost, just as emancipation could always be separated from questions of "race" and identity.

By the 1830s, British colonial slavery was clearly under increasing attack, both from abolitionists and enslaved Africans. Finally giving up hope that planters might be prevailed on to improve or "ameliorate" colonial slavery, thereby staving off emancipation until some future date, government ministers threw their weight behind an emancipation bill, introduced in 1833, that significantly provided for gradual emancipation (under the terms of the bill, everyone under the age of six on 1 August 1834 was required to serve an apprenticeship of four years in the case of domestics and six years in the case of field hands), as well as £20 million in compensation to colonial planters.[37] Clearly, government ministers were not ready to embrace immediate emancipation, as many British abolitionists had wanted them to do. But equally it is clear that the government felt that it had to do something. Of course, one can speculate endlessly about the motives of government ministers, but one should not ignore the ability of abolitionists to make themselves heard or, indeed, the ability of governments to absorb opposition. As Seymour Drescher has recently argued, the alleged superiority of free over slave labor (at least, in the British Caribbean) was a fundamentally uneconomic proposition that "came without encouragement from either transatlantic economics or metropolitan economists."[38] Yet still the British went through with emancipation. That they did so is a testament to the persistence and the organizational skills of groups like the Anti-Slavery Society.

What happened in 1833 was in many ways a blip, however. If government ministers were momentarily won over by mass political mobilization around free labor, the British "experiment" was never repeated. As Drescher points out, "Even within the orbit of the British imperium, indentured servitude and a slow death for slavery became the dominant model of economic development and social change."[39] Needless to say, little of this was lost on Britain's competitors. Slaveholders in the American South, for instance, drew undoubted comfort from the fact that the "mighty experiment" (the term itself is significant) with free labor in the British Caribbean had proved such a fatal economic miscalculation, as did the French, who did not finally abandon slavery and the slave trade until 1848. Put simply, it proved impossible for "liberated" sugar colonies to compete with the slave-based economies of Brazil and Cuba, particularly when those economies benefited from the advantage of the international slave trade. The British government admitted as much when in the early 1840s it decided to permit the flow of indentured (that is, bonded) East Indian labor into the Caribbean.[40]

A Culture of Abolitionism

Anti-slavery was one of the first transnational protest movements. Moreover, it developed a range of techniques and strategies (including boycotts and petitions) that are recognizably modern. Perhaps just as important, British anti-slavery was remarkably successful and can justifiably claim to have changed the terms of political debate, committing Britain to a course of action that other imperial powers viewed with distaste and trepidation. While abolitionists operated within an imperial context, however, distance dictated that very few abolitionists visited the Caribbean or "connected" with slaves; instead, the alliances they built were with other elites that were usually defined by color and class. As a result, slavery remained very much a colonial problem, and abolition was too easily perceived as a "gift" from the imperial metropolis. None of this is to ignore or devalue the role blacks themselves played in their own emancipation. Yet, against great odds, abolitionists played a vital role, proving that the old order of things could be changed and that popular discontent could find an effective political voice.

The abolition of colonial slavery, however, necessitated a reordering of priorities as Britons adjusted to the reality of an empire without slaves. In practice, this meant absolving themselves of responsibility for transatlantic slavery and, instead, highlighting the role that the British had played in bringing slavery to an end. Perhaps just as important, it also meant placing those who were held responsible for slavery and the slave trade, both Africans and Europeans, beyond the pale of "civilization."[41] In other words, Britons substituted for the indignity of transatlantic slavery—and its role in transforming Britain into a major mercantile and military power—what might be described as a "culture of abolitionism." Emancipation marked the nation out. Such selfless actions, it was argued, legitimized Britain's role in the world, the country's stewardship over countless millions in Africa, India, and the Caribbean, and, no less important, its particular claim to speak for those who were too weak to speak for themselves.[42]

In time, this sentimental discourse would become one of the common denominators that held the empire together. Throughout the celebrations that marked the centenary of emancipation in 1933–34, Britain's decision to emancipate its slaves was variously described as a "sublime" or disinterested act and, as such, a sign of the nation's moral strength and superiority. As the Oxford historian Reginald Coupland told a meeting in Hull in 1934, the abolition of British colonial slavery was "a striking example—perhaps the most striking example one can think of in modern history—of a power of pure idealism in a practical world."[43] By this date, the link between the Atlantic slave system and Britain's hegemonic power had long been forgotten. If, in practice, this shift or transformation made little difference to the forms that British imperialism took in the nineteenth century and the twentieth (that is, in terms of direct and indirect control), nevertheless it subtly altered its rhetoric, as well as the nature of Britain's peculiar claim on the past and, indeed, the present and the future.

Notes

1. Walvin, *Making the Black Atlantic*, 19–31; Thomas, *The Slave Trade*, 154–56.
2. Richardson, "The British Empire and the Atlantic Slave Trade, 1660–1807," 441–42.
3. Ibid., 456. See also Kolchin, *American Slavery*, 22.
4. Ward, "The British West Indies in the Age of Revolution, 1748–1815," 429; Walvin, *Making the Black Atlantic*, 94; Kenneth Morgan, *Slavery, Atlantic Trade and the British Economy, 1660–1800*, 49–53.
5. Kolchin, *American Slavery*, 24; Ward, "The British West Indies in the Age of Revolution, 1748–1815," 415. Decline set in after 1815, however. According to Ward, the Caribbean's share of British overseas trade fell to 10 percent in the 1820s and 5 percent in the 1850s.
6. For this argument, see Eric Williams, *Capitalism and Slavery*.
7. Walvin, *Making the Black Atlantic*, 92, 96; Klein, *The Atlantic Slave Trade*, 86–89; Dresser, "Squares of Distinction, Webs of Interest," 21–47.
8. O'Shaughnessy, *An Empire Divided*, 15–17, 63–68, 206–8; Kielstra, *The Politics of Slave Trade Suppression in Britain and France, 1814–48*, 11–12. There was also a South Carolina lobby active in London. See Starr, *A School for Politics*.
9. Walvin, *Making the Black Atlantic*, 157–58.
10. Eric Williams, *Capitalism and Slavery*, 169.
11. Drescher, *Econocide*, 76–112; Kenneth Morgan, *Slavery, Atlantic Trade and the British Economy, 1660–1800*, 29–39.
12. Davis, *The Problem of Slavery in the Age of Revolution, 1770–1823*, 453–68, 489–501; Davis, "The Problem of Doing History by Ahistorical Abstraction," 294; Davis, *Inhuman Bondage*, 248.
13. Colley, *Britons*; Brown, *Moral Capital*.
14. Quoted in Oldfield, *Popular Politics and British Anti-slavery*, 33.
15. Colley, *Britons*, 143–45, 353.
16. Ibid., 353.
17. Oldfield, *Popular Politics and British Anti-slavery*, 117–18, 185–86.
18. O'Shaughnessy, *An Empire Divided*, 245.
19. Ibid., 244.
20. Oldfield, *Popular Politics and British Anti-slavery*, esp. chaps. 4 and 5; Midgley, "Slave Sugar Boycotts, Female Activism and the Domestic Base of British Antislavery Culture," 137–62.
21. On the activities of the SEAST, see Oldfield, *Popular Politics and British Anti-slavery*, 41–64, 155–79.
22. Ibid., 51–56.
23. James Pemberton to Granville Sharp, 6 May 1794, Pennsylvania Abolition Society Papers, microfilm edition, reel 11, Historical Society of Pennsylvania, Philadelphia.

24. Oldfield, *Popular Politics and British Anti-slavery*, 53–54.

25. Mortality rates in the British Caribbean were notoriously high, which, in turn, led to a heavy dependence on fresh supplies of enslaved Africans via the transatlantic slave trade. By contrast, the slave population of mainland America proved more than able to reproduce itself. See Walvin, *Making the Black Atlantic*, 43–45.

26. Ellis, *Founding Fathers*, 81–119; Fladeland, *Men and Brothers*, 55–58, 63–69, 72–74.

27. Temperley, *British Anti-slavery*, 5–6.

28. Ibid., 8–9; Kielstra, *The Politics of Slave Trade Suppression in Britain and France, 1814–48*, 31–57, 86–95.

29. See, for example, a Web page set up by the National Archives, London, that explains the Slave Registry and Slave Compensation Commission: http://www .movinghere.org.uk/ (accessed March 2006).

30. Temperley, *British Anti-slavery*, 9–18.

31. Temperley, "British and American Abolitionists Compared," 343–61; Mayer, *All on Fire*, 148–49, 152–65, 285–95, 372, 375.

32. For a brilliant discussion of these classical economists, see Drescher, *The Mighty Experiment*, 54–72.

33. Walvin, *Making the Black Atlantic*, 153–55.

34. Walvin, *Black Ivory*, 253–78.

35. Walvin, *Making the Black Atlantic*, 148–49.

36. Kolchin, *American Slavery*, 154–66; Greenberg, *Nat Turner*.

37. Temperley, *British Anti-slavery*, 9–18.

38. Drescher, *The Mighty Experiment*, 236–37.

39. Ibid., 235.

40. Ibid., *The Mighty Experiment*.

41. Castle, *Britannia's Children*, 64–68.

42. See Oldfield, *"Chords of Freedom."*

43. Coupland, *The Empire in These Days*: 264.

4   THE FINANCES OF HEGEMONY IN LATIN AMERICA

Debt Negotiations and the Role of the U.S. Government,
1945–2005

In Latin America it is commonly understood that the contemporary era of financial globalization began basically as a result of the loan boom of the 1970s and the subsequent debt crisis that exploded in the early 1980s. The bankruptcy of most of the governments of the region opened a prolonged period of negotiations between politicians, technocrats, and international bankers that was to continue for a decade. The Latin American debt crisis of the 1980s not only threatened the financial survival of governments of the continent but also menaced international banks and financial markets with a possible debacle. It was, in fact, a first and perilous chapter in the history of contemporary global finance, which has been marked by successive financial crises. But it was also a key chapter in the global, political history of our age.

The debt crash of the 1980s led to the most severe economic downturn in the region since the depression of the 1930s. It was accompanied and followed by a profound and radical process of political and economic restructuring that included not just debt renegotiation but privatization of hundreds of state enterprises, trade liberalization, and other neoliberal reforms. The reforms contributed to pressuring Latin American states and economies into a more intense process of globalization in the early 1990s. This, however, was followed by the multiplication of financial crises between 1995 and 2002. As it now stands, Latin America has a larger foreign debt than ever and has not been able to solve the debt quandary. If the situation continues, Latin America will confront continuing obstacles to economic and social development and will, in all probability, experience renewed and acute financial crises in the early decades of the twenty-first century.

Possible solutions to the debt dilemma have long been and continue to be debated in many political, financial, and academic forums. Indeed, the contemporary literature on Latin American finance is now enormous, consisting of daily news reports, research papers, political evaluations, and books on the recent trends of external debt. This outpouring is further amplified, as integration of the world economy advances rapidly, by the explosive growth of studies on financial globalization. But while the degree of financial globalization may be unprecedented, it has complex historical roots. Furthermore, the sizable debts assumed by Latin American states have a significant political ingredient, and therefore their analysis is critical to debates on the directions of global political economy.

Economists tend to limit their studies of debt to reviewing financial trends or to constructing analytical models with some kind of predictive potential. But since debt is a key instrument in the overall growth strategies of Latin American countries, political analysis is also essential to gauge the possible financial options, past, present, and future. Since the bulk of Latin American foreign debts have been contracted by Latin American states, these are eminently political debts, which have mortgaged public finance for their service. But, paradoxically, public external debts are not simply *national* debts. The character of external bonds—payable in foreign currencies, negotiated by foreign banks, and bought and sold by foreign investors— makes them a kind of financial instrument (and commodity) subject to international financial regulation and practice. However, this also implies that when renegotiations of Latin American external bonds take place, the governments of the most important investor groups, in particular the United States, attempt to exercise their power over such negotiations.

Another kind of foreign debt comes in the form of bank loans provided directly by international multilateral agencies such as the International

Monetary Fund (IMF), the World Bank, or the Inter-American Development ment Bank (IDB). While these may be considered international public loans, the question of sovereignty is again crucial. Despite the fact that multilateral agencies are owned by many states, in practice a few governments (those with greater voting power)—in particular the United States—have a disproportionate influence over these agencies. Hence their lending strategies are not designed independent of the U.S. government, but rather are strictly supervised by Washington.

The politics of external debts is complex and cannot be limited to an economic analysis. In this chapter I analyze the increasing role of the U.S. government in debt strategies in Latin America, particularly over the last quarter-century, by looking at the region as a whole, but focusing on Mexico and Argentina. While such a focus may have limitations, it is intended to help stimulate complementary studies on the recent history of the international debt negotiations of other countries of Latin America, as well. It is therefore the object of this chapter to encourage more research on what Louis Pauly calls "the actual political foundations of the capital markets now so prominent a feature of the international economy."[1] In the case of Latin America the works of researchers Cheryl Payer and Paul Drake, along with many classic articles published in NACLA *Report on the Americas*, constitute the pioneering literature. More recently, Oscar Ugarteche and Eric Toussaint have published important contributions.[2] But much more work is needed to provide a solid groundwork for future proposals with regard to the *political* analysis and understanding of global financial dynamics and the possibilities of reform of international financial relations.

A subtheme of this chapter, which is interwoven with the discussion of capital markets, is the difficulty faced by Latin American popular movements in confronting financial power structures and strategies. Identifying the nature of the financial strategies of the hegemonic power in the contemporary age has been particularly difficult for a variety of reasons. In the first place, market and corporate forces are more dispersed and less visible in the political debate than is the state. In the second place, financial strategies imply a complex mix of fiscal, monetary, banking, and debt instruments and policies that are managed by both public and (increasingly powerful) private actors. The complexities of the financial sphere lead most concerned citizens to focus their attention preferentially on other issues that may prove easier to grasp. For instance, it is easier to grasp and denounce the significance of sheer military power or the insidious threats of intelligence operations rather than the consequences of monetary or financial hegemony. As a result, popular movements have proved slow in the Third World (and elsewhere) to formulate programmatic critiques and strategies for the development of a new and more equitable international financial order.

It is my contention that although many studies of Latin American external debt devote adequate attention to the economics of the phenomenon, to the evolution of financial markets, and to the expectations of bankers and investors, not enough attention has been paid to a complementary and necessary look at the politics of the debt. There are two sides to debt politics: one is basically domestic and requires analysis of the individual financial and development strategies of each government that assumes significant foreign debt; the second is international and particularly involves the influence of the governments and other key actors of the creditor nations in many key debt negotiations.

In this chapter I focus attention on the latter question and, more particularly, on the role of the United States in successive debt negotiations and resolutions between 1946 and 2005. I will briefly compare the debt resolutions that took place at the end of World War II, the debt renegotiations of the 1980s, and the responses to the financial (or debt) crises in Mexico and Argentina in recent years. The U.S. government played a major role in these last two cases, though much more directly in Mexico than in Argentina. However, in order to delve into the international politics of Latin American debt of recent times, it is worthwhile first to comment briefly on the concept of hegemonic states in international finance over the last century.

The Role of Hegemonic States in International Finance: Historical Perspectives

According to standard economic textbooks, the governments of the most powerful nations did not generally intervene in international financial markets in the nineteenth century or early twentieth. Much of this literature presupposes that one hegemonic financial power, Great Britain, held sway until 1914, although research has increasingly demonstrated that its competition in global finance was intense with France from the mid-nineteenth century and with Germany from the 1880s. In any case, if one reviews the literature on the international projection of British finance and politics, it is possible to observe the prominence of arguments put forth by conservative historians such as Ronald Robinson and John Gallagher or D. C. M. Platt, who maintained that even when there were financial conflicts that led to political intervention, the real motives of the bankers and politicians of Great Britain were essentially "strategic." For instance, these writers maintain, after the bankruptcy of the Egyptian government in 1876, the takeover of the Suez Canal and the establishment of a neocolonial administration in Cairo in 1880 were simply instruments of Whitehall to guarantee continued access to British India, the jewel of the empire.

Christopher Platt even goes so far as to argue that during the nineteenth century the large number of interventions by the British Navy in Latin American ports to pressure for payments of debt (owed to bondholders or merchant groups) were not a sign of financial imperialism; Platt cites some forty such military incidents or interventions.[3] More recently, authors such as Charles Lipson, who have focused on this issue, have offered somewhat more nuanced analyses, but emphasize the *policy of restraint* by the British authorities in their worldwide expansion in the nineteenth century, at least in the financial sphere.[4] While such arguments are clearly full of holes, they constitute the orthodox contention that favors a benign view of the role of imperial powers during what one may term the age of early global finance.

Additionally, no international financial organizations (à la IMF) existed in the nineteenth century and early twentieth. In that age of free capital markets, there were few rules that governed international financial transactions outside of the terms of loan contracts themselves, which stated—as they still do today—that conflicts between debtors and creditors would be resolved in courts in the country of the creditor. But such strictures were not necessarily compelling. Hence, from the late nineteenth century, the main strategy promoted by bankers and their political allies was to attempt to stabilize international finance through increasingly widespread adoption of the gold standard. As Barry Eichengreen, the foremost financial historian on the subject, has argued, the imposition of the gold standard was possible at the time because politics and finance were, in many senses, decoupled (delinked) due to the powerlessness of social and political movements to impose fiscal and financial objectives on governments: "The pressure twentieth century governments experienced to subordinate currency stability to other objectives was not a feature of the nineteenth century world.

The credibility of the government's commitment to convertibility was enhanced by the fact that workers who suffered most from hard times were ill positioned to make their objections felt. In most countries, the right was still limited to men of property."[5] On the other hand, during the interwar period (1918–1939), Eichengreen maintains, practically all states tended to raise trade, monetary, and financial barriers, reducing the intensity of international transactions. The gold standard lost ground and was finally destroyed by the economic cataclysm of the Great Depression.

After World War II, a new international financial architecture attempted to conciliate national economic interests with international financial supervision: the IMF, which was instituted at that time, was the most powerful instrument of the latter. Furthermore, many other multilateral and national financial innovations emerged, including the establishment of multilateral development banks, with headquarters in the United States; the creation of state banks (export-import banks, development banks), especially in Europe and Latin America; and a much more active financial role for all governments in many kinds of national development programs. Coordination among central banks became standard practice, as did the promotion of an increasing number of official and unofficial financial-political instruments for coordination among creditor states and banks—for example, the Club of Paris, created in 1956, and the Group of Seven (G-7), established in the 1970s.

In the postwar world the United States clearly took a hegemonic position in the financial sphere, a fact reflected in the dollar's function as international currency reserve. In terms of international financial transactions the role of the U.S. government was fundamental; for example, with regard to the finances of its military forces on a worldwide scale, the United States transferred a large and sustained volume of funds to bases in Western Europe, Japan, Korea, the Philippines, and various points in the Caribbean, for decades. Complementary was the Marshall Plan, which implied the transfer of some $12 billion to Europe after 1947. In addition, loans provided by multilateral financial agencies were in dollars, although in the case of the IMF more flexible monetary instruments were increasingly used in transactions based on Special Drawing Rights (SDRs).

Later, in the 1960s and 1970s, the hegemony (at times, the almost monopoly) of the dollar began to cede as many international debts were contracted in pounds sterling, marks, francs, and yen, and as the circle of major financial powers broadened. As a result, the coordination of financial policies on a world scale became necessary, as witnessed by the creation of the G-7 and similar bodies. Moreover, powerful private banks from the G-7 countries all began operating much more actively on a global scale, and multinational companies also began increasing their financial investments and transactions abroad.

Due to the multiplication of international financial actors, political analysis of the financial architecture and dynamics in this period becomes more complicated. In this regard, it is worth keeping in mind that for several decades, there was no real questioning of the postwar Bretton Woods consensus on the need to maintain low domestic interest rates, convertibility to the dollar (at a fixed parity of $35 dollars to the ounce of gold), and bank stability, all of which were tied, in varying degrees, to protectionism for trade and industry. Yet by the 1960s, with increased trade competition among the United States, Japan, and Europe, accompanied by the expansion of multinational enterprises and, later, multinational banks, the development of the eurodollar markets, and a rising complexity of international transactions on leading capital and money markets, this consensus began to break down. The large deficits of the U.S. government during the Vietnam War constituted another factor leading to the breakdown of the Bretton Woods architecture, and attacks on pegged exchanged rates became common.

The result was that in 1973 the postwar monetary agreements came tumbling down, and a new period of increasing financial instability, rising interest rates, and rapidly expanding international capital flows presaged the age of financial globalization. Some authors have designated this period "Bretton Woods II," although others would argue that it was not until the 1980s that the brave new world of global finance really came into its own, provoking an enormous increase in financial instability, particularly in the indebted countries of the Third World.

In any case, the Latin America lending booms of the 1970s constituted a fundamental antecedent of modern financial globalization and reflected the enormously pernicious consequences of adopting debt policy as the preeminent priority of government development finance strategies.

The Latin American Debt Negotiations at the End of World War II

World War II and the postwar era led to an intense politicization of international finance, under the hegemony of the U.S. government. The Latin

American debt negotiations that took place in the 1940s reveal the historical antecedents of the political nature of many foreign debts. Most Latin American governments had suspended payments on their foreign debts in the years 1931–33 as a result of the Great Depression. A wide array of debt renegotiations took place during the 1930s, but generally speaking the restructurings did not produce a resumption of debt service. As a result, the Latin American defaults generally continued until the end of the war. At that time, authorities in Washington resolved to adopt a much more activist role in the negotiations between Latin American debtor states and mainly European private creditors. European investors, in fact, had no option but to accept the preeminent role of the U.S. government and its banker allies in the successive restructuring of Latin American debts between the end of World War II and 1950.

The first major debt negotiations were those conducted with Mexico during the years 1942–46. Bankers and private creditors were forced at this time to accept the advice of the U.S. government, which tied these renegotiations to other important accords between the U.S. and Mexico that had been necessitated by World War II. At the end of the war, the U.S. government virtually obliged creditors to accept a substantial discount on their outstanding bonds, and the Mexican foreign debt was thus reduced by 80 percent. There followed the Brazil debt negotiations in 1945, which allowed for a reduction of 50 percent on the value of that nation's external obligations, and those with Chile in 1948, also with a partial reduction in external debt stock and service.[6]

Quite different was the case of Argentina, which was at loggerheads with the U.S. government. Juan Domingo Perón had huge cash reserves, which had accumulated in the Bank of England during the war, against Argentine exports. In 1947 Perón nationalized the foreign-owned railways and the telephone companies, and paid off the entire debt in gold at 100 percent of its nominal value. This was a major populist coup, but a Pyrrhic victory, as it wiped out a good deal of the country's reserves. Argentina had been, until then, the richest government in Latin America.

After these negotiations, Latin America did not receive much foreign finance in the way of loans for almost twenty years. Beginning in 1955 the IMF offered several bridge loans to different Latin American governments when confronted with the balance of payments problems, and from the early 1960s development loans began to flow from the World Bank and the recently established IDB. But very little came to the region in the way of private bank loans (except U.S. commercial bank loans to companies in Mexico in the 1960s).[7] There were also very few issues of Latin American government bonds abroad until the late 1960s.

The weak demand in Latin America for external finance during more than a quarter of a century can be attributed to the fact that import-substitution industrialization (ISI) was for the most part domestically financed and reasonably successful despite emerging problems generated by inflation-driven growth policies, which had begun to be adopted in the 1950s.

This situation changed in the 1970s as a sizable new loan boom gained strength throughout Latin America. This boom has been attributed to various causes, the most important being the recycling of petrodollars, as bankers sought new investment outlets following the drop in international demand for credit caused by economic recession in Europe and, to a lesser extent, the United States. In most other regions of the world demand for external finance was either limited or not feasible: in Japan and Korea domestic banks financed industrialization; in the nations of the socialist bloc, the U.S.S.R., Eastern Europe, and China, domestic state-controlled finance was the agent of industrial development; in Sub-Saharan Africa the volume of external financial flows was reduced, although there was a rising current of official credits. During the 1970s, then, there was much pressure by bankers and other private financial actors to invest the rapidly accumulating petrodollars, preferably with state guarantees on repayment. As a result, the bulk of the loans went to Latin American governments, state enterprises, and banks which demanded financial support for their fast expansion plans in the 1970s, and in other cases to cover deficits and arms expenditures by local military governments.

The Latin American Loan Boom of the 1970s: Finance and Politics

No region in the world absorbed such large debts as Latin America did in the 1970s, a fact that merits more comparative reflection and discussion. Remarkably, almost all Latin American governments and public enterprises sought easy money at what were argued to be low interest rates. The supply-side explanation of the lending boom was emphasized in particular by Robert Devlin, who argued that the excess sums of petrodollars in Western banks stimulated ferocious competition to obtain clients who would take loans. On the other hand, the lemming-like behavior of all Latin American governments in seeking loans has yet to be adequately explained in theoretical terms, although both the supply and demand sides of the equation were clearly important. In any case, any such explanation requires a political component (or, more precisely, a *political economy* component) to account for why different types of regimes in Latin America all became engulfed in the financial frenzy.

In the case of Argentina the expansion of foreign debt took place basically during the bloody military dictatorship of 1976–83, although it had begun on a small scale before. In 1975 the Argentine foreign debt stood at $7.9 billion, but rose to $45 billion by 1983. A review of the bond issues of those years reveals that a large part was guaranteed by state companies such as the oil company, YPF, and the state-owned water, electrical, and telephone companies. Great sums were expended in hydroelectric projects and highways, and an unknown amount in military expenditures. Private corporations also took debt abroad, although these debts were mostly absorbed by the state by means of exchange-rate insurance schemes in the years 1982–83.

The funds that flowed into Argentina from abroad spurred a tremendous speculative boom in local financial and real-estate markets that paradoxically allowed for a substantial exit of local capital. Capital flight was predicated on the inflow of foreign currency as a result of rising government indebtedness. The finance minister of the dictatorship, José Alfredo Martínez de la Hoz, gave his blessing to this peculiar and perverse financial casino. The result was that sizable fortunes were accumulated by members of the private sector (including entrepreneurs, rentiers, technocrats, and generals) while the state became increasingly weighted down with foreign debts. The economic strategies adopted by Martínez de la Hoz—whose tenure became known as the era of *la plata dulce* (the sweet money) because of the extraordinary financial profits earned by local elites and international bankers—were well known by the IMF and the U.S. government, which provided full support to the military dictatorship and its high-level servants.

Mainstream political and economic analysts have generally argued that there was virtually no connection between international finance and the geostrategic priorities of the U.S. government. However, this argument is clearly undercut by the historical fact that international and multilateral

Table 1. Long-term foreign debt (private and public) of Latin American countries, in millions of U.S. dollars

Country	1970	1980	1985	1990
Argentina	5,171	16,774	41,902	48,731
Brazil	5,132	57,500	91,915	90,432
Chile	2,568	9,398	17,628	14,619
Mexico	5,966	41,215	88,448	81,161

Source: World Bank, *World Debt Tables, 1992–1993* (Washington: World Bank, *1993*), vol. 2: *Country Tables.*

banks funneled substantial sums of money precisely to the military dictatorships and authoritarian governments that reigned in Latin America in the 1970s, most of them with clear support of the Pentagon and of the U.S. government. This point was raised in *New Chile*, a book-length report by the North American Congress on Latin America (NACLA), which demonstrated how multilateral lending agencies had decreased loans to the Allende government, but had quickly shifted gears after the coup headed by General Augusto Pinochet, soon offering the dictatorship loans for infrastructure projects. This perverse strategy has also been remarkably well illustrated by Eric Toussaint in recent articles, published on the Web site of the Committee for the Abolition of Third World Debt (CADTM), which demonstrate how loans were awarded to authoritarian governments in Chile and Argentina after the military coups.[8]

In the case of Mexico the reasons for increasing foreign indebtedness were linked to the needs of the state political party, the Institutional Revolutionary Party (PRI), to reinforce populist strategies and guarantee the immense, undemocratic party bureaucracy and its allies their long-standing monopoly of political power. One of the key instruments was the financing of state companies that provided jobs, bureaucratic plums, and thousands of supplier contracts. In the 1970s two public enterprises—Petróleos Mexicanos (PEMEX), the profitable state petroleum monopoly, and Comisión Federal de Electricidad (CFE), the state electrical consortium—took the greatest number of loans. The foreign debt of PEMEX had stood at barely $367 million in 1970, but by 1981 had surpassed $11 billion, representing 27 percent of total long-term Mexican public debt. Promoting electrical expansion was also a major government priority under the administrations of Presidents Luis Echeverría (1970–76) and José López Portillo (1976–82), which led the external obligations of the public electricity corporation, CFE, to rise from $990 million in 1970 to over $8.2 billion by the end of 1981.

The 1970s thus marked a major change in international financial operations. This was no longer the *bond finance* age of the nineteenth century and the early twentieth.[9] Now it was *bank finance* that dominated. All the major U.S., European, and Japanese banks were recycling petrodollars to Latin America, and not surprisingly in this decade Latin America stood out as the developing world's leading region in terms of loan flows from abroad.

The Debt Crises of the 1980s: The Increasing Role of the U.S. Government in Financial Negotiations

The loan boom came to a close in 1982 with the outbreak of the debt crisis, provoking panic on world markets. This grim prospect spurred a series of international financial agencies to produce a rescue package, which could serve to deter a possible debacle. This undertaking involved the U.S. government, but not, initially, as the most prominent actor.

Mexico, which had declared itself virtually bankrupt in late August 1982, was the talk of the town among the hundreds of bankers and high-level technocrats who met in the IMF–World Bank meetings at the end of September, and there was much trepidation about the fallout this situation would create for world financial markets. By November, the key actors—Mexican technocrats, international bankers, and U.S. Treasury Department officials—had reached agreement on an $8 billion package (approximately the amount Mexico needed to service its debt in 1982 and early 1983): the IMF would provide $4.5 billion from its extended drawing facilities to help guarantee debt-service payments on the Mexican debt; the Bank of International Settlements (BIS) would extend $1.85 billion in credits; and the Commodity Credit Corporation and the Stabilization Fund of the U.S. Treasury would each provide $1 billion in additional short-term funds.[10]

Subsequently, negotiations began to restructure part of the external debt. In the spring of 1983 two groups of commercial banks provided an additional $7 billion in credits to Mexico in order to stretch out the November rescue package and to guarantee interest payments for the rest of 1983.[11] During the next several years, an intense sequence of talks allowed for a series of renegotiations, but provided no definite solution. Despite the initial intervention of the multilaterals, it was the private international banks that took the drivers' seat and first renegotiated, rescheduled, and then securitized

Table 2. Mexico's foreign public debt, 1970–1996 (selected years), in millions of U.S. dollars

Year	Federal Gov't	State Companies	State Banks	Others	Total
1970	701.10	1,886.70	1,264.90	409.30	4,262.00
1973	1,386.10	3,026.20	1,909.10	749.00	7,070.40
1975	2,169.30	6,005.00	4,336.40	1,938.30	14,449.00
1980	5,622.60	16,287.20	9,907.00	1,996.00	33,812.80
1982	12,476.10	27,239.00	15,348.50	3,810.60	58,874.20
1985	25,634.30	29,187.80	14,221.00	3,037.00	72,080.10
1990	46,560.40	8,141.20	21,523.30	1,545.40	77,770.30
1995	60,017.00	11,696.70	29,217.50	2.10	100,933.70
1996	75,636.00	12,853.00	9,795.50	0.00	98,285.00

Source: Ibañez Aguirre, *México: ciclos de deuda y crisis del sector externo* (Mexico City: Plaza y Valdes, 1997), 140–42 (tables 8a and 8b).

and/or sold their stakes in Latin American loans. Walter Rhodes of Citibank exemplified the debt renegotiator, heading a great many of the banker teams that negotiated with the Latin American governments in the 1980s. In the case of Mexico he headed the Bankers' Steering Committee, which represented the 530 international banks that had interest in Mexican debt.

Writing in 1989, Charles Lipson argued ingenuously, "In the case of debt renegotiations (of the 1980s) and security issues, the de-linkage has been almost complete. Even though dozens of countries, including virtually all of Africa and Latin America, have required substantial debt restructuring, only rarely have security issues intruded on the formulation of U.S. debt policy." According to this view, the U.S. government did not participate very openly in most of the other debt negotiations until 1987, although its presence was felt. But even Lipson recognizes that "given Mexico's strategic and diplomatic significance, the U.S. government has been willing to do far more in debt restructuring and temporary financing than with other major debtors."[12]

In 1988, with the establishment of the Brady Plan—beginning first with Mexico—it became evident that the U.S. Treasury was increasing its role in the resolution of the debt crisis in order to stabilize world financial markets and assure the banks that they would recover most of their money. Following new restructuring agreements with the international commercial banks, a series of proposals made by successive secretaries of the U.S. Treasury,

James Baker and Nicholas Brady, served as the basis for a more long-term resolution of the Mexican debt crisis in 1988. The basic accord was based on the exchange of the old bonds for new, so-called Brady bonds, which were Mexican long-term debt instruments, but with a U.S. Treasury guarantee. The net result was a limited discount of the total capital owed to banks and a drop in debt-service payments.[13]

The Mexican debt restructurings reflected the success of the alliance of the IMF, the U.S. Treasury, and the international private banks in assuring continued debt-service payments by the Mexican government and at the same time impelling a dramatic restructuring of the public sector, including privatization of state enterprises and liberalization of foreign trade. This set of neoliberal policies, which was, in part, the offspring of the debt crisis and which was applied in many developing nations, came to be known as the Washington Consensus.[14] Once neoliberalism was adopted by most Latin American political and financial elites, it became possible to carry out new programs of financial engineering like the Brady Plan, which, it was expected, could help reconcile debtor countries and their numerous international creditors.

The initial stages of the debt-relief package that would become the basis of the Brady Plan were negotiated by President Miguel de la Madrid (1982–88), but the new debt program was actually put in place by his successor, Carlos Salinas de Gortari (1988–94). The Brady plan thus became operative for Mexican debt in 1989, serving as the basic model for subsequent financial arrangements in most other Latin American nations.[15]

Furthermore, the Brady Plan was key in launching the age of "equity finance" in the Third World.[16] Much of the money that began to pour into Mexico in early 1990 was from pension and mutual funds now interested in so-called emerging markets, but a fair amount was also from Mexican plutocrats who had stashed away billions of dollars in the United States or in offshore banking accounts. A major attraction for the return of these funds to Mexico was the privatization of numerous state-owned industrial and banking firms.

Financial Crises of the 1990s: Bailouts and the Perverse Connection of Mexico-Washington Elites

According to the IMF, between 1990 and 1993 Mexico received $91 billion, or "roughly one fifth of all net inflows to developing countries."[17] Of this sum, portfolio inflows amounted to $61 billion while foreign direct investment was only $16.6 billion. The bubble in the Mexican stock exchange continued to attract money from the United States as a result of stability of the pegged exchange rate, carefully nurtured by the Mexican Central Bank and the Finance Ministry. But that apparent stability was not based on solid economic fundamentals; by the early 1990s, Mexico had a cumulative commercial deficit of over $100 billion as a result of the General Agreement on Trade and Tariffs (GATT) in 1984 and subsequent negotiation of the North American Free Trade Agreement (NAFTA), which was ratified in November 1993. Commercial deficits were mainly covered by the inflow of portfolio (hot) capital. But the money could as easily leave as it had entered. This instability soon contributed to the most severe financial crisis in recent Mexican history.

The history of events in 1994 in Mexico provides an excellent case study of how politics can accentuate the course of financial developments. But not all political events have the same impact. For instance, some observers argued that the launching of the Zapatista rebellion in Chiapas on 1 January 1994 had a major impact on Mexican financial markets but, in fact, *this was not the case*. It was, rather, the March assassination of the presidential candidate Luis Donaldo Colosio, which provoked panic among wealthy Mexican and foreign investors, who took more than $10 billion out of the country in a few weeks. This was the moment for a devaluation to have been implemented, but President Carlos Salinas and Finance Minister Pedro Aspe did not want a blemish on their administration; instead, they held out until the end, in a kind of financial Russian roulette, which finally resulted in the devaluation of December 1994 and the subsequent collapse of the Mexican economy in 1995, with one million people losing their jobs, thousands of firms being driven into bankruptcy, and eventually almost the entire banking system going into technical bankruptcy.

The Mexican government's financial bankruptcy in December 1994 not only led to a general economic crisis but also represented a more general threat to international financial markets, particularly because of the large amount of Mexican debt that had been issued on the emerging markets. Bankers and investors everywhere were terror stricken by the prospect of capital flight from Latin America back to Europe, Japan, and the United States. As a result, the head of the U.S. Treasury, Robert Rubin (by profession a banker who had been heavily engaged in global finance), convinced

President Bill Clinton that a Mexican rescue program was urgently needed. It is now a historical cliché that the February 1995 rescue plan, which initially involved a guarantee of almost $40 billion for Mexico, was the first of the great bailouts of the mid-to-late 1990s and represented one of the largest loan operations ever to be provided to an individual country. The total actually disbursed during the years 1995 and 1996 by the U.S. Treasury (using the Monetary Stabilization Fund) was $12.5 billion, with slightly over $17 billion disbursed by the IMF, some $4 billion by the World Bank and the IDB, and lesser sums by commercial banks.[18]

By organizing such a sizable financial package for Mexico, the U.S. Treasury, in the person of Robert Rubin, and the IMF, in the person of Michel Camdessus, were rather dramatically informing investors and bankers worldwide that they should not pull out of Mexico entirely since stability was preferable to a prolonged international financial crisis. Camdessus labeled the Mexican cataclysm as only the first of a series of twenty-first-century financial crises, and he was certainly not mistaken, as many others soon followed.

The objective of the rescue package, however, was not simply to help the government confront the financial crisis unleashed by the devaluation. The immediate object was quite simply to bail out the foreign and national investors who in 1994 had bought a huge volume of *tesobonos*, Mexican government short-term public debt, indexed to dollars. The affluent lenders (each tesobono cost $100,000) did not lose money after devaluation, for they almost immediately got their funds back in dollars. In fact, many wealthy Mexican investors made enormous profits, for they had bought large quantities of tesobonos with pesos in the weeks before the devaluation, but afterward got twice their money back, as the value of these peculiar securities doubled. In effect, the U.S. Treasury–IMF financial rescue package allowed for a substantial transfer of funds to Mexico, which allowed these lenders to get their money. The financial authorities of the Mexican government paid off each of the successive monthly amortizations of the dollar-indexed tesobonos on schedule during the year 1995.

If the government of Ernest Zedillo had had the courage, it could have found a much less costly solution by calling for a restructuring of this enormous very-short-term debt with an offer to repay in five or ten years instead of the incredibly brief amortization schedule of less than one year. But neither Zedillo nor Rubin was in a mood to provoke any irritation in the investment community. The bills for the bailout were passed on to Mexican taxpayers and the state oil company, PEMEX. These policies were, clearly, the most incompetent adopted in the modern financial history of Mexico. The men most directly responsible for generating the conditions that led to the colossal debacle at the close of 1994, Miguel Mancera, director of the Bank of Mexico, and Pedro Aspe, Mexico's finance minister, got off scot-free.

The cost of repayment to creditors was substantial. During 1995 and 1996, Mexico repaid over $14 billion to the U.S Treasury to liquidate the emergency loans of early 1995, winning the applause of the Clinton administration for having fulfilled its financial obligations ahead of schedule. Repayment of the huge sum of $17 billion to the IMF was also covered by the Mexican government in the 1996–98 period, the bulk of petroleum revenues being used for this purpose.

If one compares the mechanisms used to manage the debt crisis of 1982 with the financial collapse of 1995, one finds significant parallels in the responses adopted, especially with respect to the international mechanism of lender of last resort. The actors involved in organizing the financial rescue plans for Mexico in November 1982 were basically the same as those involved in February 1995, including the U.S. Treasury, the IMF, the World Bank, and representatives of private international banks, all of them participating actively because of the importance of Mexico in the international financial and political arena. However, the U.S. government, in particular, had to make much larger commitments in the crisis of 1995. The IMF also had to increase its emergency support by a large factor, which helps explain the IMF decision to double the fund of special drawing rights that could be made available for dealing with financial crises in the future.[19] And these crises were soon in coming.

In fact, the IMF virtually exhausted its resources when it organized similar bailouts to confront the subsequent financial crises of the late 1990s in Indonesia, Korea, Russia, Brazil, and Turkey. Of particular interest with regard to the Mexican crash is the extraordinary role assumed by the U.S. government, especially by the heads of the Treasury Department, in providing what they considered to be a necessary rescue mechanism for Mexican finance. Indeed, what this financial collapse (as well as other crises in emerging markets of the late 1990s) demonstrates is that as financial markets have become more complex and integrated in recent decades, the role of governments has been crucial. In this regard, it is clear that, despite the rhetoric of official IMF reports, the U.S. government, in alliance with the IMF, played an increasingly decisive role in the *regulation* of financial markets, although the traditional view was that the IMF should act essentially as lender of last resort, in times of major emergencies. In other words, the orthodoxy argued, governments should not interfere with thriving financial markets and speculation, but that they, and more particularly the U.S. Treasury, should be obliged to rescue faltering markets. In the 1990s, then, the metaphor for governmental market intervention was clearly that of the fireman, rather than of the policeman. The financial rescue operation organized in Mexico in February 1995 by Secretary of the Treasury Rubin was a prime case in point.

Turn of the Century: The Argentine Financial Crash and the Wavering Financial Game of Washington

The Argentine financial debacle of 2001–2002 demonstrated the limits of the global financial roulette that had been played to the hilt in the 1990s. It also revealed increasing contradictions in the strategies of the United States with respect to management of Latin American foreign debts. The IMF, confronted with a potential default, had initially offered sizable financial guarantees to the administration of President Fernando de la Rúa in 2001. However, the IMF subsequently reneged when the Stanford economist Anne Krueger was named subdirector of the powerful multilateral agency. She called a halt to future lending to Argentina, arguing that the moral hazard was unacceptable. As a result, the IMF soon forced the Argentine government to default, but paradoxically with its own, unspoken blessing. This unprecedented decision was taken in consultation with the Treasury Department and the White House. For the first time, the IMF had decided to stop playing the fireman, but in so doing, it obliged the Argentine authorities to adopt a new game plan. The largest default in history began, and its resolution was unexpected.

It is now recognized, even by the IMF, that lack of adequate supervision in the 1990s by the multilateral agencies was heavily responsible for the financial debacle in Argentina. By allowing enormous increases in Argentine indebtedness during times of global and domestic financial uncertainty, the international financial institutions made the tragedy inevitable. Even in the midst of the Mexican crisis of 1995, the Argentine government, under the administration of Carlos Menem, devoted itself to financing growing deficits with rising foreign debts. International investors took loan after loan, confident that they would get their money back because of the stability of the fixed-exchange regime (with a dollar currency board) that had been adopted in Buenos Aires in the early 1990s. But the foreign debt had begun increasing at the rate of almost $10 billion per year from late 1992, continuing until 2001 and the subsequent meltdown. From $59 billion in 1990, Argentina's total debt rose to almost $160 billion by 2002.

After the fall of the de la Rúa government at the end of 2001, an interim presidential administration, headed by the Peronist party leader, Eduardo Duhalde, attempted to confront the crisis by suspending convertibility and debt service on foreign bonds. Debt-service payments continued to the IMF and other multilateral agencies. Nonetheless, resolution of the default remained in suspense until after the national elections in the spring of 2003, which brought to power another, more leftist Peronist politician, Néstor Kirchner. The new president adopted an extremely hard line with the foreign bondholders, maintaining the default on half of the foreign debt until early 2005, when an offer for conversion of the bonds at reduced value was offered to and accepted by the majority of international investor groups.

The negotiations surrounding Argentina's debt have been incredibly complex and have spawned a new polemical literature in the press, in financial journals, in the publications of specialized financial agencies, and in recent books, a good number published in Buenos Aires.[20] While it would appear that in the Argentine-debt negotiations the IMF and the U.S. government are affirming that markets should resolve the financial debacle, it has instead been the strategy and actions of the Argentine government that have resolved the default and obliged the markets to accept its proposals. In this case, a Latin American state gained strength by making a firm offer and by not backing down. The results proved successful and represented a major setback to bankers, investors, and speculators.

The Argentine case is a major turning point in Latin American financial history and points to the possibility that other governments in the Third World will likewise demand more equitable treatment from bankers, investors, and financial markets. Thus, as new crises emerge, the governments of the leading industrial powers may find that they can no longer simply impose their views and financial policies, but will gradually be obliged to accept the need for substantial changes in the regulation of world finance and in the policies of the multilateral agencies. In this regard, there now exist strong doubts as to whether there is any intention of reinforcing the IMF as international lender of last resort. Hence, without a strong fireman, it is clear that policing of the foreign debt of Third World countries by the G-7 will become more difficult. The need for more equitable political and financial negotiations in global debt finance will inevitably became a major issue in the future. The prospect of genuinely equitable negotiations poses a fundamental challenge to neoliberal doctrines, but the implications have yet to be widely discussed.

The Slowly Emerging Popular Response to the International-Debt Game

Political activists have begun to play an important role in debt-finance negotiations, principally in many counterglobalization mass meetings and protests. In addition, some taxpayer groups in Third World countries have begun to protest against financial exploitation, although not yet on a large scale. There are very few analyses of popular responses to the debt crises, whether in the 1980s or in more recent times. The academic literature on the subject is scarce. Information on popular protests can be derived basically from the press and from activist organizations. Most protests against external debts, common throughout Latin America in the last two-and-a-half decades, have been of relatively short duration and have had a limited degree of political effectiveness. As has been noted by most specialists, popular opposition to the debt negotiations of the 1980s failed in most cases, although in the debt renegotiations of Nicaragua and Bolivia, popular pressure did eventually influence the outcomes, which were somewhat better than expected.[21] Economists and political scientists have written quite a large number of research papers to explain why creditors in the 1980s were in such a strong position, focusing on the success of bank cartels, supported by the international financial institutions and by the G-7, in successive negotiations.

Nonetheless, in the last few years, particularly in South America, popular repudiation of debts has had at least two significant impacts. The first was the Peruvian Congress's establishment of an investigative committee on the foreign debt in 2003, the reports of which demonstrate the corruption and lack of legitimacy of many loans taken in the 1990s. Oscar Ugarteche was coordinator of the committee, and his reports merit full attention, as never before in the history of Latin American parliaments have such investigations taken place.[22] The second concrete indicator of popular mobilizations against the old debt policies has been the widespread popular support given to the steadfast negotiating strategies of President Kirchner of Argentina, who has managed the largest sovereign default in world history with notable ability. That the negotiations with bondholders reached a successful conclusion for the Argentine government speaks tomes regarding future debt negotiations by indebted Third World nations.

But beyond the specifics of financial renegotiations, it is also worthwhile to discuss some new ways in which public opinion has been responding to financial instability and the perverse effects of financial globalization. A review of the numerous activist sites on global finance—most particularly, the Committee for the Abolition of Third World Debt, based in Brussels and directed by Eric Toussaint—demonstrates how among new generations (particularly in forums like those of Porto Alegre and Mumbai) there is a growing rejection of orthodox finance and of the strategies of the majority of international financial banks and agencies. The growing stream of articles and books by Toussaint and his colleagues, as well as by members of the international Association for the Taxation of Financial Transactions for the Aid of Citizens (ATTAC), now constitute an important critical literature on the subject. Frequently, the tone of these texts can be quite radical, but this is a response to the radical-right positions of the traditional spokespeople of the Washington Consensus.

In addition, it is impossible to neglect other, more reformist groups that have pushed for debt reduction, led initially by the Catholic promoters of the Jubilee debt-reduction campaign in the year 2000. At that time, the G-7 countries promised reductions on debt to many of the poorest countries in the world, but did not provide much relief in practice. On the other hand, from early 2005, the Jubilee Debt Campaign regained steam as certain leading politicians in Europe—in particular, the British prime minister, Tony Blair—began touting the need for reduction of African debt. In the early summer of 2005, at a G-7 meeting in Scotland, agreement was formally reached to reduce debts owed to official and multilateral agencies by a sum close to $40 billion, the largest debt relief that had ever been contemplated. Despite leftist criticism of this program, these measures represent a significant advance in the regulation of global finance and can help to reduce the suffering of highly indebted countries.

More orthodox, and also at loggerheads with the leftist proposals to abolish foreign debts, a considerable number of academics in Washington think-tanks also recognize the political problems faced by global finance. They propose limited reforms, but in recent years have become increasingly aware of the need to introduce real political and social concerns and to reduce technocratic behavior in the realm of multilateral finance. A key spokesperson of the trend is Nancy Birdsall, president of the Center for Global Development in Washington, who has repeatedly emphasized the need for political reform of multilateral institutions. She takes note of Third World popular critiques of the skewed political architecture of international financial organizations, which are, in principle, public entities and thus accountable to taxpayers. She says,

> Those activists see the Financial Stability Forum, the Bank for International Settlements, the International Monetary Fund and the World Trade Organization as undemocratic. They see the overall system as controlled by corporate and financial insiders, not by the world's median income voter; by the United States Treasury and Wall Street, not middle-income consumers; by Ministers of Finance and Governors of Central Banks, not Ministers of Health, Labor, and Social Affairs.[23] They are suspicious of the Bretton Woods institutions, where country votes reflect economic power, compared to the more democratic United Nations, where in the General Assembly at least, every country has a single vote.[24] Independent of the merits or demerits of these various views, they all contain a core truth, namely that the global economic and financial system overall is not particularly representative of the poor of the world.

In the final analysis Birdsall does not call for radical reform, but simply points to the fact that the IDB is considered more responsive to its participating government members than is the more bureaucratic and rigid World Bank. She thus points to a key governance issue, but sets an agenda for limited political reform of the international financial architecture.

The vaguely reformist discourse of the mainstream and center-Left think-tanks is clearly at odds with many activists and popular movements around the world. The drama of world poverty, of increasingly uneven income distribution within most societies, of the growing power of global companies, and of the decreasing capacity of states to maintain equitable social, educational, and health policies all point to the need for a much more profound transformation of the dynamics of international finance, in particular as it relates to new options for a more just social order. The relevance of the radical critiques of the debt burden in the case of Latin America is obvious. Extremely slow growth has accompanied the last quarter-century of constant increase of total debt stock and enormous debt-service payments.

The international financial and investor communities are clearly not well-disposed to any further debt reductions like those obtained in the Argentine case. They will fight tooth-and-nail to assure, for example, that Brazil and Mexico continue with their substantial debt payments. Nonetheless, a simple survey of the overall debt burden in Latin America suggests that restructuring is indispensable to allow for greater economic growth. However, given the tremendous instability being generated by the current trends of global finance and, in particular, by the U.S. government (with its own huge debts), the prospects for further reform appear remote. It is, in fact, possible that only a world financial crisis (a gruesome possibility, which does not now seem so unlikely) can force radical change, as did the Great Depression of the 1930s.

Notes

1. Pauly, *Who Elected the Bankers?* Pauly also calls attention to the burgeoning literature on politics and international finance that is of great use for our purposes.
2. Toussaint, *Deuda externa en el Tercer Mundo*; Ugarteche, *El falso dilema*; Ugarteche, *Adios Estado, Bievenido Mercado*.
3. Platt, *Finance, Trade and Politics in British Foreign Policy, 1815–1914*.
4. Lipson, "International Debt and National Security."
5. Eichengreen, *Globalizing Capital*, 31.
6. For summary details on all the debt negotiations of Latin American countries in the 1930s and 1940s, see Marichal, *A Century of Debt Crises in Latin America*, chap. 8.
7. For details on U.S. commercial bank loans to Mexico in the 1960s, see the important but little-cited study by E. Sánchez Aguilar, The International Activities of U.S. Commercial Banks.
8. NACLA, *New Chile*; Committee for Abolition of Third World Debt, http://www.cadtm.org/.
9. The concepts are from Eichengreen and Fishlow, "Contending with Capital Flows," 23–68.
10. Data from Gurría, *La política de la deuda externa*, and Secretaría de Hacienda, *Deuda externa pública mexicana*, final appendix.

11. Gurría, *La política de la deuda externa*, and Secretaría de Hacienda, *Deuda externa pública mexicana:* final appendix. In March commercial banks provided $5 billion to Mexico and in June the Club of Paris advanced another $2 billion in the way of commercial credits.

12. Lipson, "International Debt and National Security," 212.

13. The most detailed analysis of the origins and implementation of the Brady bonds can be found in Cline, *International Debt Reexamined*. A journalistic account of the 1987–88 negotiations between the Mexican negotiating team led by Angel Gurría and the U.S. commercial bankers and government officials can be found in Fernández Sotelo, "El último rescate."

14. An interesting critique of the Washington Consensus is found in Krugman, "Dutch Tulips and Emerging Markets," 28–44.

15. Cline's *International Debt Reexamined* is the basic source here.

16. The concept is taken from Eichengreen and Fishlow, "Contending with Capital Flows," 47–60.

17. International Monetary Fund, *International Capital Markets*: 53.

18. A detailed analysis of the rescue package is in Marichal, "La devaluación y la nueva crisis de la deuda externa mexicana."

19. Among the more detailed recent analyses is Eugenio Andrea Bruno's *El default y la restructuración de la deuda*. But also see the extensive recent literature published in Buenos Aires, including Bonelli, *Un país en deuda*; Juliá et al, *La memoria de la deuda*; Elespe et al., *Default y reestructuración de la deuda externa*; Lozada, *La deuda externa y el desguace del Estado nacional*; Vicario, "Argentina y el FMI"; Galazo, *De la Banca Baring al FMI*; Arriazu, *Lecciones de la crisis Argentina*.

20. Michael Mussa, *La Argentina y el FMI*.

21. See Abendroth et al., *La deuda externa de Bolivia*. Oscar Ugarteche has announced that he will publish, in 2008, a new book on the debt of Andean nations. On the CADTM Web site, Eric Toussaint has various articles on the Nicaraguan debts (Committee for Abolition of Third World Debt, http://www.cadtm.org/).

22. Ugarteche, *Adios Estado, Bievenido Mercado*.

23. Nancy Birdsall, "Why It Matters Who Runs the IMF and the World Bank," Center for Global Development (Washington), Working Paper 22, 2004. She notes that Joseph Stiglitz makes this point.

24. Ibid. Birdsall notes that on some questions before the United Nations, the powerful countries of the North have been divided on security issues, and thus unable to push through decisions they favored on development issues.

PART II

EMPIRE AND RESISTANCE
IN THE TWENTY-FIRST CENTURY

5   BEYOND HEGEMONY
Zapatismo, Empire, and Dissent

In June 2005 the Zapatista Army of National Liberation (EZLN) issued its Sixth Declaration of the Lacandon Forest. As with their previous declarations, the Zapatistas called on Mexican society to participate in a national movement to build popular alternatives to the existing political system and the continued implementation of neoliberal economic policies. The Zapatista leadership hoped to capitalize on the growing discontent with the weaknesses, corruption, and opportunism of the major political parties during the run-up to presidential elections in the summer of 2006. The Sixth Declaration was preceded by a series of communiqués by the leading Zapatista spokesperson, Subcomandante Marcos, in which he criticized the political establishment for failing to respond to the needs of the majority of the population. Marcos included the center-left Party of the Democratic Revolution (PRD) in his critique and pointed out that the party's presidential candidate, Mexico City mayor Andrés Manuel López Obrador, did not represent a radical change from the ongoing implementation of neoliberalism in Mexico.

The Zapatistas have therefore sought to occupy the political space of the Left, calculating that the political parties would continue to lose legitimacy and popular support, while more and more people would look for alternatives outside the party system. The Sixth Declaration reaffirmed the Zapatistas' commitment to peaceful and political struggle through dialogue with other individuals and groups at both national and international levels. The main goals are to develop a national program for the political and economic transformation of Mexico, the formulation of a new constitution, and the promotion of new forms of political engagement.

In August and September 2005 a wide variety of groups and individuals traveled to Zapatista communities in Chiapas in order to participate in five meetings in which they began to outline the national campaign. Following these meetings, the Zapatistas announced that they would send delegations to different communities throughout Mexico, beginning with a national tour by Delegado Cero (Delegate Zero, Subcomandante Marcos himself) in 2006. The Zapatistas called this latest initiative the "Other Campaign," in order to highlight its alternative nature in comparison to the official electoral campaigns of the political parties. In addition, the Zapatistas called for an international meeting against neoliberalism. Planning for this meeting has taken place in discussions held in Chiapas during the first half of 2007.

The Other Campaign is another example of the ways in which the Zapatistas are attempting to link local, national, and international experiences of neoliberalism in novel forms of political organization. It involves meeting with other groups in every state of Mexico in order to listen to the problems and struggles of a wide variety of people who are similarly searching for greater levels of coordination and solidarity, while asserting their own particular demands and goals. The Zapatistas are using the Other Campaign not to provide solutions, but, rather, as a collective effort to build a strong grassroots movement that is opposed to capitalism and prepared to work for a new political constitution for Mexico.

The Zapatista movement is probably one of the best-known examples of dissent against the neoliberal model of economic globalization. On 1 January 1994 more than three thousand indigenous people staged an armed uprising against the government of then president Carlos Salinas de Gortari and issued a list of demands for basic social and political rights. The rebellion was timed to coincide with the start of the North American Free Trade Agreement (NAFTA), an accord that reduced most tariffs on trade between the United States, Canada, and Mexico. Subcomandante Marcos argued that NAFTA represented a death sentence for Mexico's indigenous people and called on all Mexicans to participate in their own ways for a more democratic, just, and sovereign nation.[1]

Over twelve years have passed since the Zapatistas caught international attention. In that time, other social movements have expressed similar demands for social justice and greater participation in decision-making bodies. Meetings of the Group of Eight (G-8), the World Economic Forum, and the World Trade Organization have been met with large-scale protests that have highlighted the common perception that economic globalization is occurring without the kinds of constraints that are necessary for ensuring popular participation and democratic debate over the economic, political, and cultural models that the world's societies need and desire. Although the precise demands and forms of organization are different, protesters have often referred to the Zapatistas as a source of inspiration. The Sixth Declaration reasserts such linkages by analyzing the national and international effects of neoliberalism, with the political goal of promoting an alternative program from the Left. As such, the Zapatistas present an important opportunity to critically assess the challenges facing dissent in the age of globalization.

Zapatismo, Empire, and Multitude

One of the most striking aspects of the Zapatista movement is the fact that its demands immediately resonated with many people around the world. In part this was due to the rapid transmission of its communiqués and analyses via the Internet, but it was also related—perhaps more so—to the growing realization of the linkages between decisions taken in one part of the world and events in another.[2] The Zapatistas proved adept in connecting their own experiences with those of other communities, within and beyond Mexico, that were also faced with the prospect of economic exclusion and political marginalization.

Although the Zapatistas emerged from complex and conflictive local histories of dissent, their rebellion is also a sign of the crisis and transformation of capitalist states around the world, including in Latin America.[3] At the global level has been the decline of state-led development models in which various degrees of national economic regulation have allowed for redistributive programs of a broadly supported welfare state. The dismantling of this model in favor of greater deregulation, trade liberalization, and private enterprise has been a common experience for many countries, including Mexico.

Focusing on the global level of international relations, Michael Hardt and Antonio Negri have argued that this transition is best conceptualized as a passage from imperialism to Empire (which they always write with an upper-case E).[4] In their analysis, imperialism refers to a system in which dominant nation-states compete for control of territory and resources in order to enhance their own national power. Empire, on the other hand, has no national home, although some nations are clearly more influential than others in directing its operations. Instead, Empire is a global network of power relations that perpetuate capitalism through the constant reorganization of social life and natural resources. With Empire, dissent is not "outside," combating the imposition of a foreign power, but rather it is already "inside," where it is placed under permanent surveillance. Empire does not have an outside, so any alliances of political dissent must be made with the same goal in mind: to expose and transcend Empire, rather than reform national governments by winning state power.

Hardt and Negri add that the way we think about dissent has also shifted away from the idea of a unified people to the recognition of diversity. From their perspective, this change opens up greater possibilities for more novel and creative forms of political dissent. In doing so, we value the uniqueness of each person and group as they confront Empire in their own ways. The unified "people" turns out to be a diverse "multitude" with little desire or need for centralized organization and leadership.[5]

Are the Zapatistas an expression of the multitude? Some authors have adopted this line of argument. For example, John Holloway stresses the Zapatistas' search for a different approach to politics itself. Rather than seeking power for themselves, the Zapatistas call on all people to construct new spaces for dialogue in which the dignity of each is upheld.[6] Their strategy is not to seize power and wield it over others, but to democratize power relations in every sphere of society. This, continues Holloway, will remain an "uncertain revolution" in which definitions, programs, and theories will always be displaced by the ambiguities and contradictions of any social movement. The novelty is that the Zapatistas have recognized this lack of definition and, with a strong dose of irony, have turned it into one of their main sources of strength. In Holloway's words, "The [Zapatista] revolution is a moving outwards rather than a moving towards."[7]

How convincing are these arguments? Some would say not very. Why would any group, particularly one that aspires to change the basic structures of a highly unequal society, try to avoid the exercise of power? Atilio Borón claims that the postmodern celebration of diversity and local autonomy is symptomatic of the Left's retreat from class struggle.[8] For him, the popular movements cannot afford the luxury of ignoring the struggle for state power. This is particularly relevant in Latin America, where national sovereignty has so often been undermined by U.S. imperialism in direct or indirect forms. It can also be argued that nationalism and imperialism have not given way to Empire. Instead, U.S. imperialism is still the dominant force in international politics, particularly so after the attacks of 9/11. U.S. policies have been deliberately unilateralist rather than directed toward a global concert of interests. In the current context Tariq Ali has argued that the Zapatistas are failing to make any serious gains, and the proposal to "change the world without taking power" is only a moral slogan that does not pose any threat to the dominant groups in Mexico nor to their foreign allies.[9]

In Chiapas power and dissent do not conform entirely to the global analyses discussed above. What they reveal is the extent to which modern imperialism and postmodern Empire overlap with each other. The distinction made by Hardt and Negri is useful in that it highlights the qualitative differences between globalization and domination by a single country. However, the particular influence of the United States in Mexico cannot be underestimated, and any discussion of Empire should make explicit the extent to which the United States still exercises imperialist power. What is required is a differentiated analysis of the degrees to which Empire is inflected by U.S. imperialism in particular countries or regions. Although Empire may be globally present, it does not necessarily assume the same form or force in every location. In Latin America the relative importance of the United States in the transition to neoliberalism may help explain the presence or absence of "dissent from above."

In this regard the Mexican and Venezuelan governments occupy opposite ends of the spectrum, the former hoping to participate in Empire rather than resist it, while the latter strives to exploit the weaknesses of Empire through popular mobilization and an independent foreign policy. Timing also turns out to be crucial here. In Mexico the fraudulent elections of 1988 denied the Cardenista coalition the chance of exercising "dissent from above." Instead, the Salinas government moved rapidly to dismantle the vestiges of "revolutionary nationalism" and redirect economic and foreign policy in ways that facilitated Empire's reach into Mexico. NAFTA effectively locked in the basic features of a markedly U.S.-led integration. In contrast, Venezuela's economic and political crises of the late 1980s solidified a strong political force opposed to neoliberal reforms, leading eventually to the election of the Chávez government and the intense mobilization of a popular base of support to prevent the return to power of members of the pro-U.S. oligarchy. The presence of NAFTA and the absence of the Free Trade Area of the Americas (FTAA) mark two different realities and reflect two different time periods, the former characterized by the height of neoliberal hegemony, the latter by the growing opposition to U.S.-led Empire and the search for alternatives (local, regional, national, and global).

Indigenous Rights and Mexico's Rural Crisis

The earlier and more extensive integration of Mexico into U.S.-led globalization helps explain why dissent has taken on different forms. In Mexico, unlike in Cuba or Venezuela, dissent is a decidedly nongovernmental affair. However, the debate over whether dissent should primarily target the nation-state or global capital can obscure the constant effort to build grassroots support at the local level. In the case of the Zapatistas, to paraphrase Holloway, the revolution is not solely about "moving outwards" but also about "moving inwards." The Sixth Declaration is clearly an effort to articulate local, national, and international struggles, but it rests on the Zapatistas' success in consolidating their own experiments in self-government in Chiapas.

It can be argued that the Zapatistas have always been concerned with strengthening their local bases of support. This was evident during the peace talks of 1994 and 1995, and became particularly important in showing support for the Zapatista delegation as it negotiated with the government a set of minimal accords on indigenous rights and culture. The San Andrés Accords, named for the town where they were signed in February 1996, represented a historic moment for Mexico and the hope of achieving political and peaceful solutions to the Chiapas rebellion. However, the government of Ernesto Zedillo failed to implement the accords, arguing that the provisions for indigenous autonomy potentially threatened national unity. Further talks were suspended and, as the conflict worsened in 1996, a multiparty legislative body (the Commission for Peace and Reconciliation in Chiapas, or COCOPA) produced a revised document that met with the approval of the Zapatistas, but still failed to get Zedillo's support.

The historic defeat of the Institutional Revolutionary Party (PRI) in the 2000 presidential elections raised the hope that the new president, Vicente Fox of the National Action Party (PAN), would get congressional backing for the COCOPA law. However, in April 2001 the Congress passed a watered-down version that restricted indigenous autonomy to communities within single municipalities, denied constitutional recognition of indigenous peoples as collective subjects with the right to decide on their own forms of governance and development, and maintained a paternalistic relation in which the federal government would provide social services to indigenous communities.[10]

The Zapatistas rejected these revisions and suspended all contacts with the federal government (a situation which continues to the present). Nevertheless, the constitutionally requisite number of state legislatures subsequently ratified the reforms, although, significantly, they were rejected in those states with the largest indigenous populations (including Chiapas, Oaxaca, and Guerrero). In addition, anomalies in the ratification process led to a series of legal appeals concerning the validity of the entire procedure. Despite the fact that these appeals were still awaiting a ruling from Mexico's Supreme Court, President Fox decided to promulgate the new law, which entered into effect on 14 August 2001. A year later, the Supreme Court declared that it could not rule on the legal appeals that had been submitted, and the new law continued to stand.

After April 2001, the Zapatistas focused their efforts more on the internal aspects of their movement. The consolidation of autonomy became the main goal and relationships with other groups were reorganized with this task in mind. In July 2003 the Zapatistas announced the creation of five regional autonomous governments that encompassed over thirty autonomous municipalities. In part, this reorganization was seen as important for ensuring greater inclusion and fairer distribution of the resources provided by solidarity groups among all Zapatista communities. The new "councils of good government" (*juntas de buen gobierno*) are seen as an experiment in local democracy, attending to the day-to-day conflicts that emerge in areas where Zapatistas coexist with supporters of other political organization and parties. In making their services open to all, the Zapatistas aim to defuse local opposition and gradually establish autonomy as a viable alternative to the official political system. Programs in healthcare, education, and organic agriculture are supported through networks of community-level *promotores*.[11] Autonomy may not have gained the kind of constitutional recognition that would demonstrate the impact of the Zapatistas at the level of the state, but this does not mean that it is a politically weak form of dissent. In Chiapas the demand for self-government has only increased since 1994, as demonstrated by the large number of efforts to establish new municipalities, multiethnic autonomous regions, or autonomous rebel municipalities.[12]

The struggle for local and regional spaces of self-government is one of the most important ways in which rural communities are resisting neoliberalism. In contrast to the European Union, where governments now recognize the noncommercial values of small-scale food production (such as its role in protecting biodiversity and cultural diversity), Mexican policymakers have tended to follow the dominant U.S. position that privileges competitiveness over other considerations. Despite the evident hypocrisy of U.S. trade policy, which simultaneously demands access to Mexican markets while protecting the wealthiest U.S. agribusinesses, the PAN government has failed to demand more equal relations and has simply continued the PRI's neoliberal policies of abandoning rural producers to the effects of vastly uneven competition.

The underlying assumption of agricultural policy is that "inefficient" producers must suddenly become globally competitive or else find other sources of income. This basic position has remained unchanged from the Salinas government to the present. The overall impact on small producers has been devastating. The value of Mexico's corn imports from the United States increased by 200 percent between 1994 and 2004, depressing prices paid to local producers by 46 percent in the same period.[13] As Armando Bartra has pointed out, the increasing flow of migrants to the United States reflects the short-sightedness of macroeconomic decision-makers who have solely been concerned with controlling inflation through large-scale imports of basic grains.[14] New productive investments have been insufficient to create the number of jobs needed to absorb this new rural exodus. In this context, indigenous people are not only displaced from their land, but are also forced into the lowest-paying jobs at the service of agribusiness in northern exporting zones or in the United States and Canada.

One alternative is to continue growing corn for subsistence needs. Hallie Eakin and Kirsten Appendini have documented the preference of many small producers to plant at least half of their available land with corn as a means to ensure food security during the year.[15] Confounding neoliberal theorists, millions of rural Mexicans produce corn instead of converting en masse to lucrative cash crops. Significantly, their decisions are based not only on economic calculations to offset market vagaries but include cultural and ecological considerations that proponents of NAFTA have so far failed to understand. These include the preference for nutritionally superior and locally produced white corn over the yellow corn imported from the United States, the sharing of knowledge between family members that enables communities to grow different types of corn in a wide array of ecological niches, and the cultural importance attached to corn in local rituals and fiestas.

Bartra laments the fact that while the European Union has begun to recognize such noncommercial values, the NAFTA countries continue blindly down the path of mass production at all costs.[16] Social movements, including the Zapatistas and a large number of producer organizations, have been pressing the Mexican government for reforms to NAFTA ever since the agreement came into effect. In late 2002 and early 2003 a coalition of rural organizations called The Countryside Can Endure No More (El Campo No Aguanta Más) led large-scale marches, demonstrations, and road blockades to demand the renegotiation of the agricultural chapter of NAFTA. The demand failed to win support in the Mexican senate, although other measures were agreed on in order to attend to short-term needs of small producers.

The result was another illustration of how Mexico's relationship to Empire is shaped primarily by its overdependence on trade with the United States. Currently, over 80 percent of Mexico's imports come from the United States. A similar percentage of its exports go to the U.S. market. This is very different from the more diversified trade relations found in Venezuela, for example, where the Chávez government has been able to resist such dependency on a single market, leaving greater opportunities for alternative agricultural policies. The relationship with the United States, therefore, gives Empire a more constraining form in Mexico than in Venezuela. Whereas Mexico appears locked into a permanently unequal relationship with little room for negotiation, Venezuela can exploit some of the contradictions of Empire by playing competing nations against one another, testing the limits of a system that is less monolithic than it seems from either a theoretical or Mexican perspective. While this analysis may be comforting for those who still hope for a national road to liberation from imperialism, it also suggests the need for alternative paths in Mexico.

Inclusion through Autonomy

In the spring of 2002 I had the opportunity to meet with a group of indigenous farmers in the municipality of Tumbalá in northern Chiapas. The group included Zapatista supporters as well as members of other social organizations. We shared our views about the local effects of the Zapatista rebellion of 1994, the problems facing small producers today, and the potential impact of a recently announced large-scale development project known as the Plan Puebla-Panamá (PPP). One of the older men expressed his concern for the future: "The PPP is not like the war in 1994, but it is a cold war. It is carried out no longer with bombs and aircraft, but it is a cold war, where we do not understand how it works. It is a war of low prices, so that we die off, but we are going to continue fighting. We have to create our own new plans in order to defend ourselves."

This man's use of the term "cold war" is obviously not in reference to the conflict between the capitalist West and communist East prior to 1989, but a way of describing the local experience of economic globalization, a phenomenon that conceals its inner workings while pushing down commodity prices and threatening the viability of indigenous communities. As such, this testimony is not unique to Chiapas, but could be recounted by millions of people around the world, many of whom have organized to demand inclusion and participation in the decisions that affect their lives, cultures, and environments.

Although the demand for inclusion is a common one, its meaning is not reducible to any single form. The appeal of earlier forms of inclusion, such as those provided by official labor unions and mass parties, has increasingly been eroded—in part as a result of the shift toward pro-market economic policies. These older forms of inclusion were also limited in most Latin American countries due to the relatively small size of the formal workforce, and they tended to reproduce authoritarian control to the benefit of co-opted leaders, rather than of workers, peasants, and voters. Independent unions and grassroots movements have long struggled for inclusion through the expansion of the number of channels for public participation. In Chiapas such struggles were traditionally met with arrests, harassment, and violent repression of dissent, leading many to support the Zapatistas as they prepared their rebellion.

The comments by the farmer in Tumbalá also reveal a desire to build and defend viable alternatives to globalization. Rather than see their communities dismantled by the impact of low prices, indigenous people are also experimenting with their own forms of economic and political organization. Access to common property and social solidarity are central to such dissent. Globalization advances through the enclosure of more and more areas of social activity, through the division of tasks and resources among specialized groups of community members. The flexibilization of rural labor is a necessary part of contemporary capitalism, as production is geared to particular segments of global markets. In this model, labor is still seen as another factor of production, but it is valued for particular skills in unregulated markets, rather than as a permanent feature of a stable economy. This precariousness is expressed in the way that people become interchangeable and frequently disposable. Autonomy can therefore be seen as an attempt to defend access to common property in the face of corporate strategies that rely on flexible labor, competitive specialization, and cultural fragmentation.

At first sight, these twin demands for inclusion and autonomy seem to contradict each other. However, the contradiction arises only if one assumes that the two are mutually exclusive, a form of reasoning that continues to block full recognition of indigenous rights in Chiapas and around the world. Until the 1980s, the political importance of cultural diversity tended to be subordinated to other concerns related to matters of state formation and economic development. In Mexico and other Latin American countries inclusion assumed adherence to a single national identity, which was decidedly non-indigenous. Attempts to depoliticize ethnic identities were not entirely successful, however, and the government's own social programs led to the emergence in the 1970s and 1980s of new indigenous leaders who began to demand a much greater role in the design and implementation of policies. By the end of the 1980s, this demand was voiced in local, national, and international arenas and led to the first step of constitutional reform that recognized the multicultural nature of Mexico in 1992. For indigenous organizations that had emerged in the day-to-day battles over land, crop prices, bilingual education, and health services, inclusion first required reform of the legal and institutional forms of the state. This effort was given a great boost by the Zapatista uprising, although the results remain uncertain and highly contested. At stake is the scope of indigenous autonomy and its relationship to the existing form of constitutional government in Mexico.

This issue is not unique to Chiapas and Mexico. Throughout Latin America, national governments have responded in different ways to the demand for indigenous autonomy. In some cases, constitutional reforms were more far-reaching, at least on paper, because of favorable conjunctures that allowed indigenous organizations and leaders a greater presence in national debates. For example, the depth of political crises in Colombia and Ecuador led to the holding of constitutional assemblies in both countries in the 1990s. At the time of the constitutional debates, indigenous movements could count on an important bloc of allies in political parties that were sympathetic to their goals. This moment of political opening allowed for the inclusion of some provisions for indigenous autonomy.[17]

In contrast, Mexico has not held a constituent assembly, and there have been much more limited opportunities to present proposals for constitutional reform. The majority of deputies and senators belong to parties that, for the most part, opposed the San Andrés Accords after they were signed in 1996. Crucially, senators of the only party that had agreed to continue backing the COCOPA proposal, the PRD, failed to keep their commitment at the moment the bill was discussed in the committee stage. By backing the watered-down version, the PRD senators displayed a lack of political will that the Zapatistas interpreted as a simple act of betrayal. Although the PRD members in the Chamber of Deputies voted against the new law, their opposition was too late since the main principles of the law had been established in the senate bill. Despite this unsatisfactory outcome, the long-term viability of indigenous autonomy may depend more on its appropriation at the local level rather than on the revision of legal statutes. In this regard, autonomy is best thought of as a set of practices that uphold an independent political identity, rather than being a purely constitutional norm.

The Zapatistas have raised important questions regarding the future of indigenous peoples in Mexico. At the same time, many of their demands have resonated with individuals and groups from other parts of the world. The lack of secure access to work, education, and adequate healthcare are common problems facing many people today. If the nation-state was traditionally seen as the main institutional guarantee of human security, it is becoming apparent that this is no longer the case. The privatization of social services will benefit only those who can afford to pay, while the rest will find their situation increasingly precarious. Although it is important to keep reminding the state of its social obligations, it is also necessary to recognize the role played by social movements, new labor unions, indigenous organizations, independent media, and transnational migrant networks in the continual experimentation with novel forms of social inclusion and political autonomy.

Whether such a strategy will succeed in Mexico depends on how people respond to the Sixth Declaration of the Lacandon Forest as well as the lessons learned from similar efforts in previous years. Among these, it is important to take into account the ways in which relationships between the Left and indigenous peoples have evolved from being characterized by mistrust and separation to being characterized by a search for novel elements of mutual support, such as the defense of autonomy, collective property, and social solidarity in the face of economic globalization and the privatization of natural resources. Another historical task is that of finding ways to unite the great diversity of popular movements around a national program that remains open to debate and grassroots participation. After all, the gulf between party leaders and the majority of the population is seen as one of the root causes of dissent. In this context the Zapatistas and their supporters have an important opportunity to create different relationships that provide people with attractive alternatives to the currently widespread disengagement, depoliticization, and uncritical pragmatism.

The Other Campaign and the Social Life of the Multitude

The Sixth Declaration was preceded by Marcos's damning critique of all the political parties in Mexico. While his criticisms of the PRI and PAN were well known, his attacks on the PRD—which continued throughout subsequent months—caught many by surprise, particularly those who considered themselves part of the Left. For the latter, the popularity of former Mexico City mayor and PRD presidential candidate Andrés Manuel López Obrador represented a strong possibility that he would win the presidency in July 2006. They felt that although the PRD might have a weak national presence, a victory for its presidential candidate would indicate popular rejection of the economic policies in place since 1982 and lead to a shift in public policy toward the social needs of the majority.

However, Marcos criticized López Obrador and PRD for three reasons. First, as Marcos pointed out, López Obrador had declared in newspaper interviews that he was "of the center" and had committed to the same macroeconomic variables favored by the International Monetary Fund. Second, López Obrador's campaign managers were former PRI politicians, many of them close to former president Ernesto Zedillo (including Socorro Díaz and Adolfo Orive, who both actively opposed the EZLN and the San Andrés Accords during 1994–2000). For Marcos, the PRD could not be forgiven for betraying their commitment to defend the COCOPA bill in 2001, and the composition of López Obrador's campaign team only served to confirm the impression that the party leaders had little interest in reversing their position if they were ever to win national office. Third, the PRD failed to take action against its own members who had violently attacked unarmed Zapatistas in the municipalities of Zinacantán and Las Margaritas in Chiapas. Marcos pointed out that these local PRD members were the ones in charge of organizing support for López Obrador's presidential campaign in 2006.

Supporters of López Obrador decried Marcos for his tone, his accusations, and, most of all, his timing. They felt that his polemic would only have the effect of spoiling the Left's best chance of winning the presidency. Some even suggested that members of the PRI and the PAN were supporting Marcos. Rank-and-file PRD supporters also criticized Marcos for not accepting that they could support the Zapatistas as well as the PRD. However, some did accept the criticisms directed against the party leadership, noting that Marcos was right about the way the PRD had been taken over and had lost its popular agenda. It was unclear whether the party could be won back by its grassroots supporters, as was the case with many social democratic or labor parties in other countries. Difficult questions began to be raised among grassroots PRD supporters. For example, would a victory for López Obrador help swing the party back toward the left, or would it simply consolidate a new group in power, with a better chance of implementing neoliberalism than the discredited PAN or PRI? For Marcos, the answer was clearly the latter, a conclusion that he had reached after the vote on the indigenous law in 2001.

The Marcos-PRD debate reveals some deep divisions between popular movements and political parties in Mexico. For the Zapatistas, the PRD does not represent a viable form of "dissent from above," even if (or especially if) López Obrador were to become president. From their perspective, the only possible form of dissent in Mexico for the foreseeable future is "dissent from below," and they no longer expect to gain anything from negotiations with parties or the institutions of the nation-state. Once again, their hopes are invested in the diversity of civil society, nationally and internationally. In this regard, the Zapatistas are helping to construct new connections between a wide variety of groups that similarly feel disenfranchised by unrepresentative parties and media conglomerates.

The Other Campaign seeks to link autonomy and inclusion in ways that modern theories and practices have failed to recognize. This is probably the Zapatistas' greatest challenge. How can the governance practices of indigenous communities be of relevance to city dwellers far from Chiapas? In other words, how can a popular and democratic left build points of unity and solidarity while recognizing the uniqueness of each context and situation? The Zapatistas have constantly declared that they are uninterested in occupying a leading role in such an endeavor. They want to participate on an equal footing with other groups, but are opposed to the idea that they can or should direct this process.

Their interactions with other groups is therefore part of what Hardt and Negri have called the "social life of the multitude."[18] The concept of multitude reflects the convergence of different experiences. Rather than positing some inherently unifying element of the "people," the multitude relies on the unique capabilities and desires of each individual. Some authors argue, however, that the dissent of the multitude can only come into being through the kinds of articulation that are decided among different groups. For example, Ernesto Laclau argues that collective action requires the construction of political identities that define supporters and opponents in the struggle over hegemony.[19] Laclau believes that Hardt and Negri fail to theorize this moment of articulation and therefore lack an explanation of when disparate groups and individuals become unified multitudes.

In contrast, Hardt and Negri, like the Zapatistas, appear suspicious of the way that politics has traditionally been reduced to a question of who exercises hegemony. By combining elements of their indigenous forms of government with the global tendency toward network movements, the Zapatistas are contributing to non-instrumental ways of relating to others, not unlike the "democracy to come" that Jacques Derrida described in his critique of pragmatism and the friend-enemy distinction that informs so much of Western political thought.[20] Is there another politics before or beyond hegemony? This is the question posed by the Zapatistas and the Other Campaign.

Events in 2006 sharpened this question with unpredictable force. The year began with a clear demarcation between the Other Campaign and the presidential campaigns of the political parties. The PRD not only hoped but also expected to win power in the 2 July elections. Its leaders cited several polls that placed López Obrador a full ten points ahead of his nearest rival, Felipe Calderón, of PAN. Confident of victory, the PRD and most of Mexico's intellectual Left tended to ignore or minimize the Other Campaign. When Marcos began his tour of the southern states in January, several commentators stressed the limitations of his "new way of doing politics": relatively low turnout, the lack of policy proposals, and seemingly endless presentations of local economic or political problems. As the months went by, and the television media remained focused on the presidential candidates, only the supporters of the Other Campaign bothered to document the testimonies of the people who turned up for meetings with Marcos. Listening to these testimonies was an inversion of the traditional political rally where the candidate speaks and everyone else listens. While local workers, students, women, farmers, and teachers took turns to share their grievances, Marcos and the accompanying independent media took notes, filmed, recorded, and instantly disseminated these words and struggles.[21]

Telling an important political figure your day-to-day problems is not particularly new in Mexican politics. For example, hundreds of campesinos sent letters and requests to Cuauhtémoc Cárdenas during his campaign for the presidency in 1988. However, those petitions were directed to someone in the hope that, as president, he could solve their problems, a tradition continued by López Obrador. Marcos, on the other hand, insisted that solutions would not come from a leader, but instead from grassroots organization and mutual support. During a meeting of the Other Campaign in Puebla, one woman said that she was confused because she thought that López Obrador and Marcos basically wanted the same things. Marcos responded by saying that the difference between him and the PRD candidate was that "López Obrador wants to be your president, while I want to be your *compañero*."

The idea of becoming a compañero is central to a politics that does not seek to take power. In Hardt's and Negri's analysis the shift from highly centralized revolutionary movements to "network movements" is partly about the form that dissent takes today, but it is also a matter of content, or what they term "biopolitical production." By this, they mean the kind of activity that produces the social life of the multitude, the bringing together of a wide range of individuals and groups who resist global capitalism and, through collective resistance, build new forms of social cooperation and communication. Indeed, for Hardt and Negri, the Zapatistas are one of the clearest examples of this tendency toward network movements.[22] The Other Campaign has sought to move outward from Chiapas, but also inward, in the sense of building new subjectivities and capabilities.

For the Zapatistas, the kind of subjectivity needed to resist capitalism and construct democracy in Mexico is that of a compañero. This explains the decision of Marcos to temporarily suspend the Other Campaign following the brutal police repression against the Popular Front in Defense of the Land (FPDT), in San Salvador Atenco, state of Mexico, on 3–4 May 2006. In the police attacks several people were killed, more than a hundred were arrested and beaten, and many women were sexually abused. Marcos, rather than continue his trip through northern Mexico, stayed in Mexico City until late September and made the release of those detained at Atenco a central demand of the Other Campaign.

The use of force in Atenco was justified by the presidential candidate of the PAN, Felipe Calderón, as necessary for upholding the rule of law, an argument that was fully supported by the two main television networks, Televisa and TV Azteca. López Obrador, for his part, was not very vocal in his criticism of the police and the government. The television media were ready to use any potential connection between the protest movement in Atenco and López Obrador in order to further taint him as a danger to Mexico's future stability.

As it happened, the real threat to stability came from the electoral process itself. Rather than ensuring the legitimate transfer of power, the elections were marked by uncertainty over the official results, which gave Calderón victory by less than 1 percent of the vote. López Obrador claimed fraud and led a widespread national movement to demand a total recount. The occupation of downtown Mexico City by tens of thousands of protesters provided support for the PRD's legal petitions, although the electoral court decided in favor of only a partial recount of 9 percent of polling stations. This resulted in the confirmation of Calderón as president-elect, and, searching for a longer-term strategy to confront the new government, López Obrador called for the formation of a National Democratic Convention (CND), which duly recognized him, rather than Calderón, as the "legitimate president."

The Other Campaign tended to stay out of this dispute. Although Marcos noted that López Obrador had been cheated out of the presidency, he also argued that the project of the Other Campaign was different from that of the PRD for all the reasons noted above. This distance from a popular mobilization that was one of the biggest in living memory was criticized by many commentators. Marcos, it was argued, was out of touch with the new political reality. For Marcos, however, the popularity of López Obrador was not due to any solid grassroots organization, but simply to a populist style of leadership that would be unable to satisfy social demands. Noticing that some previously supportive groups had begun to shift their allegiances more clearly in favor of López Obrador and the CND, Marcos called on adherents to the Other Campaign to reflect on their political commitments and, through a national-level consultation in early December, define more clearly the identity, structure, and alliances of the Other Campaign.

This process is also shaped by the increasingly authoritarian style of politics used to suppress local and regional dissent. In June the state governor of Oaxaca, Ulises Ruiz, ordered state police to violently break up a peaceful encampment of striking teachers in the central plaza of the state capital. The repressive tactics of the PRI governor led to the growth of discontent as many groups throughout Oaxaca (including members of the Other Campaign) mobilized in support of the teachers and together formed the Popular Assembly of the Peoples of Oaxaca (APPO). This movement demanded the resignation of Ruiz, but the federal government refused to act against the PRI, since the PAN needed the PRI's support in ensuring that Calderón would take office as president of the republic on 1 December.

Instead of negotiating a peaceful solution, the government again used federal police in an attempt to suppress the APPO. In November (President Fox's last month in office), over one hundred APPO supporters were arrested and taken to jails in other states, many were beaten and tortured, homes were illegally and indiscriminately searched and ransacked by police, and twelve people were killed by local paramilitaries. Any hope of negotiations was undermined by one of Calderón's first actions as president:

the arrest of the main leaders of APPO one day before they were due to meet with representatives from the Interior Ministry.

As 2006 closed, it appeared that the regime was prepared to sacrifice democratic rights in favor of the violent defense of a privileged minority. If this is the case, democracy becomes thinkable only from the perspective of those who, like the Zapatistas, struggle to realize its promise of freedom and social solidarity.[23]

Notes

1. Collier, *Basta!*; Neil Harvey, *The Chiapas Rebellion*; Leyva and Ascencio, *Lacandonia al filo del agua*; Womack, *Rebellion in Chiapas*.
2. Olesen, *International Zapatismo*.
3. Rus, Hernández Castillo and Mattiace, eds. *Mayan Lives, Mayan Utopias*.
4. Hardt and Negri, *Empire*.
5. Hardt and Negri, *Multitude*.
6. Holloway, "Dignity's Revolt."
7. Ibid., 165.
8. Borón, "Poder, contrapoder y antipoder."
9. Rodríguez Lascano, "¿Slogan Moral?"
10. Higgins, "Mexico's Stalled Peace Process."
11. Múñoz Ramírez, "Los Caracoles."
12. Burguete, "Chiapas."
13. Eakin and Appendini, "Subsistence Maize Production and Maize Liberalization in Mexico."
14. Bartra, "Rebellious Corn Fields."
15. Eakin and Appendini, "Subsistence Maize Production and Maize Liberalization in Mexico."
16. Bartra, "Rebellious Corn Fields."
17. Van Cott, "Explaining Ethnic Autonomy Regimes in Latin America."
18. Hardt and Negri, *Multitude*.
19. Laclau, "Can Immanence Explain Social Struggles?"
20. Derrida, *Politics of Friendship*; Derrida, "Remarks on Deconstruction and Pragmatism."
21. They are all available at the Other Campaign's Web site, http://enlacezapatista .ezln.org.mx/.
22. Hardt and Negri, *Multitude*, 85.
23. Organization of the Other Campaign is coordinated through a special commission (see http://enlacezapatista.ezln.org.mx/). The international component is organized through a separate commission (see Zezta International, http://zeztainternazional.ezln.org.mx/). See also Revista Rebeldía, http://www

.revistarebeldia.org/, for full summaries of meetings between the Zapatistas and supporters of the Sixth Declaration, as well as for updates on related events and new communiqués. For updates and English translations of Zapatista documents, including the Sixth Declaration, see the *Narco News Bulletin*, http://www.narconews.com/.

6   **COLONIALISM AND ETHNIC RESISTANCE IN BOLIVIA**
A View from the Coca Markets

In October 2003 an unprecedented indigenous and popular uprising brought down the Bolivian government after an indiscriminate massacre that took the lives of sixty-seven people in the city of El Alto and the outskirts of La Paz.[1] Two years later, in December 2005, an Aymara coca growers' leader from the Chapare region, Evo Morales, won the presidential election with almost 54 percent of the vote. Both events attracted unusual attention from the international media, and several reports and editorials, especially in the United States, referred to them as unwelcome triumphs of forces opposed to the free market.

The idea that in Bolivia the rural and urban indigenous people who led the October revolt against the government of Gonzalo Sánchez de Lozada or voted massively for Evo Morales's Movement Toward Socialism party (MAS) were "archaic" or "backward"— that they were resisting modern market discipline in a kind of cultural or racial atavism—is a part of unquestioned common sense among the elites, as much in Bolivia as in the developed world. This common sense is beginning to break down, as a new sense of self-identification emerges. Following the election of Evo, as he is popularly known, indigenous-peasant identity has become a political force to be reckoned with. This political agency is also an expression of long-term indigenous participation in regional and long-distance markets.[2]

Indigenous Identification in the National Censuses

Who are these indigenous people? An oblique way of answering is by way of the representation made of them by the dominant mestizo-criollo elites. Iconographies like monuments and exhibits represent indigenous people in a certain manner, as do other state products, like maps, museums, and censuses.[3] One can consult many censuses and general enumerations of the country's population during the last century in order to see how the notion of the Indian has been constructed by the hereditary elites who have presided over the Bolivian state.

Thus, in the census of 1900 the criteria for ethnic classification were race and location, implicitly signals of class: "Blancos" (urban proprietors, businessmen, or absentee landowners); "Mestizos" (urban workers or low-rank employees); and "Indígena" (rural or mining workers, female servants). In addition, the census registered "Negros" and "No Consta" (no answer). According to these definitions, the indigenous population of Bolivia represented 48.5 percent of the total.[4] Although these figures can be attributed to a gross underestimation of the indigenous population all over the country, the authors of the census nevertheless engaged in an elegy to the disappearance of the Indian race in line with the social Darwinist interpretations of the science of those days. War and successive epidemics and famines had decimated the Indian populations since 1879, and those populations were considered to be condemned to extinction.

Nonetheless, as Ervin Grieshaber has indicated, these predictions were not to be fulfilled.[5] Half a century later, in the 1950 census, ethnicity continued to be defined by race, but this time occupational categories played a role, including not only rural indigenous people but also indigenous workers in towns, cities, and mining centers. Thus, the percentage of those classified as indigenous in the 1950 census rose to 63 percent of the population.[6] The census takers no doubt made use of a kind of racialized common sense, applied to those who seemed to be indigenous, contributing to this apparent rise in the proportion of Indians in the overall population.

Beginning in the 1950s, major changes took place in the country. An armed popular and miners' insurrection defeated the army of the oligarchy in three days of fighting, and on 11 April 1952, established the mestizo-criollo leaders of the Nationalist Revolutionary Movement (MNR) as the rulers of the country. The new government nationalized the mining industry and undertook a radical agrarian reform, expropriating land from the great *latifundios* and allotting it to hundreds of thousands of peasant and indigenous families. In the cultural sphere the government decreed an educational reform that universalized primary education in Spanish and granted formal citizenship rights to women and indigenous people via universal suffrage. In addition, centralized cultural institutions were created, such as the Instituto Cinematográfico Boliviano and the Instituto Boliviano de Cultura. Their main task was to establish the Indian's past as the genealogy of the modern nation-state. Cultural artifacts that documented this past were to be preserved in museums and archives, and the contemporary indigenous cultures were to be considered only as passive culturalist ornaments lying in the backdrop of the active, modern, and Eurocentric dominant culture of the urban elites. Thus, the agency and vitality of indigenous social movements were erased and neutralized, as their autonomous presence in the political arena became entangled in the networks of patron-client relations which tied the peasant and miners' unions to the state via the nationalist political party.

The populist state of 1952 was succeeded by a series of military coups, which culminated in the dictatorship of Col. Hugo Banzer Suárez in 1971. Five years later, in 1976, another national census was undertaken. Since the late 1960s, anthropologists and nongovernmental organizations (NGOs) had undertaken demographic and qualitative investigations on the indigenous population, both urban and rural. The well-known four-volume study by Xavier Albó, Thomas Greaves, and Godofredo Sandóval, *Chukiyagu: La cara Aymara de La Paz* (Chukiyagu: The Aymara face of La Paz), indicated the existence of an Aymara urban subculture that reproduced a series of networks, family relations, and mutual aid and economic organizations within the city's world of work. The study confirmed the habitual use of the Aymara language and its diffusion through radio stations whose broadcasts reached the cities as well as rural areas.[7] A new sense of indigenous pride emerged, based in the practice of broadcast Aymara through radio programs dealing with daily news, dramatizations, native music festivals, and the like. Together with the organization of migrant cultural centers and Aymara student unions, a multifaceted process of recovering a public voice and self-representation was in full force when the new census was launched.[8]

The 1976 census adopted a linguistic criterion as the basis for the definition of ethnicity. The anthropologist and linguist Xavier Albó, then the director of the Center for Research and Promotion of the Peasantry (CIPCA), was hired as an advisor to the National Institute of Statistics (INE) to conceptualize the variables and formulate the questions on ethnicity. Questions were introduced about the language spoken and learned during childhood, language presently spoken, and so on. The results showed that 68.5 percent of the Bolivian population spoke an indigenous language.[9] This figure possibly underestimates the actual indigenous population since it doesn't recognize the specificity of the indigenous lowland populations, many of whom, like the Moxeños, identify themselves as indigenous although they no longer speak their own language. In the census of 1992, language continued to be the main criterion for ethnic identification, and the population that spoke an indigenous language declined to 58.8 percent, although there was an increase in the total number of people bilingual in Spanish and a native language.[10]

This light but significant decline was situated in the context of the consolidation of neoliberal reforms. At that time it was assumed that the liberalization of the market, relocation, and migration would precipitate a massive conversion of indigenous people into mestizo "citizens," though situated at the lowest levels of citizenship.[11] International cooperation, with its many millions of dollars, also fed a process of partial citizenship and *capacitación* (training)—that is, acculturation and modernization—aimed at indigenous populations that would have an effect on their identification as indigenous peoples. It was in this context that the United Nations Development Program (UNDP) launched a national survey that introduced another criterion of ethnic classification: self-identification. Based on the work of the anthropologist Frederik Barth, self-identification is based on a critique of the application of discrete and fixed "diacritical" indicators as markers of ethnicity (language, dress, etc.).[12] Insofar as these are changing and historical, they don't explain the persistence of "ethnic boundaries" among groups.[13]

In 1996 a national UNDP survey, applying this criterion, found that only 16 percent of the Bolivian population self-identified as indigenous. The Bolivian state had finally found a mechanism to prove that the indigenous populations were a demographic minority. Two years earlier, the UNDP had co-financed the Censo Indigena de Tierras Bajas (Indigenous Census of the Lowlands), in which it had applied, curiously, the same criterion of locality as used in the census of 1900, in addition to self-identification. Taking into account only those villages and towns that had less than 2,000 inhabitants, the census succeeded in reducing the lowland and, in fact, the overall indigenous population of the country to only 100,000 out of more than 6 million. Combined, the two criteria reflected a colonial vision of the Indian. The 1996 survey took the same approach, and both censuses seem to corroborate the long process of acculturation and degradation of ethnic identity that has resulted from the advance of world capitalism and rural-to-urban migratory processes.[14]

Nevertheless, a few years later, these expectations were found to be in sharp contrast with the data of a new census. Using the criteria of self-identification, the 2001 census found that a surprising 62 percent of the population identified itself as indigenous, which radically contradicted the results of the 1994 Indigenous Census of the Lowlands and the expectations projected by the UNDP in the 1996 survey. In fact, these statistical representations used the tool of self-identification as a mechanism for the consolidation of hegemonic forms of citizenship, based in the dominant male-centered Eurocentric urban culture and the uprooting of migrant populations from their ethnic origins through a process of "acculturation from above."[15] The surprising result of the 2001 census can nevertheless be explained not only by changes in criteria for classification; a deeper analysis reveals how Indian self-perception was also tied to the wider changes in the political and historical conjuncture at the end of the twentieth century.

In 1996 the unquestioned hegemony of neoliberal thinking was expressed in the pragmatics of structural adjustment policies. In spite of the cracks and crevices brought by the privatization of Bolivian natural resources and state enterprises, the elites were still naïvely confident in IMF and World Bank recipes for overcoming the critical situation of the Bolivian economy. Such illusions had evaporated by 2000. In that year two massive rural-urban mobilizations—one that ran from February to April, the other from September to October—for the first time shattered the consensus of the ruling classes and shook the apparent conformity of the popular and indigenous organizations, especially in the western part of the country. In the first mobilization the so-called water war—an unprecedented alliance among factory workers, farmers on irrigated lands, coca growers, and the marginalized urban population—took place in the streets of Cochabamba to depose Aguas del Tunari, a subsidiary of the transnational Bechtel Corporation. In the highlands the movement opposed to the law privatizing water led by the Confederation of Bolivian Rural Workers (CSUTCB) decreed a massive road blockade, which reached its climax on 9 April with a bloody confrontation in the highland town of Achacachi. Two leaders of the blockade had gone to meet with the army and were assassinated in cold blood by the troops. In response, the indigenous multitude brutally lynched an army captain, provoking a wave of racist outrage and fierce commentaries in the media.

Following a few months' truce—achieved with the expulsion of Aguas del Tunari and the postponement of the debate over the water law—a new blockade took place in September, both in the highlands of La Paz and in the tropics of Cochabamba. In this second mobilization, which lasted almost a month, the routes that connected Andean cities, both with one another and with the rest of the country, were completely cut off. The interruption of supplies reached critical limits, and indigenous self-consciousness in El Alto and La Paz became evident in the demands of the demonstrators: they rejected military service, formed an indigenous government in the rebellious region, and decreed a "state of siege" in a vast territory, prohibiting entrance for state officials and assuming day-to-day control within the region. This event, which Pablo Mamani Ramírez has called the "territorialization of the indigenous-state conflict," revealed the ideological context of those moments, with an increasing amount of space controlled by a tight network of local indigenous leaderships and with the participation of entire families in a process of expelling colonial invaders.[16] During this process, the Andean region of the country had in fact evolved from sustaining a situation of residual indigenous identity to self-affirming ethnicity as a political strategy with which to face the imposed burdens of corporate capital along with the cultural impositions of the Eurocentric elites and their neocolonial styles of managing the country.

The census of 2001 reveals, then, a kind of "ethnic availability" of the population, as much among the rural indigenous as in the urban migrant population, and also among the broad mestizo layers of the popular and middle classes, who were disillusioned by the false promises of neoliberal well-being. Indigenous self-identification had become a matter of pride and dignity; it is therefore no surprise that it rose from a mere 16 percent in 1996 to 62 percent in the 2001 census.[17] A significant change in the political momentum and in the collective mentality—the rebirth of political and cultural resistance—mediated between the survey and the census. The idea of using an alternative strategy to face the neocolonial impositions of the developed world and thus to prevent the dismantling of the Bolivian economy by the structural-adjustment reforms had in fact replaced feelings of resignation and subdued ethnicity that were typical of the 1990s.

During the government of Sánchez de Lozada (1993–97), the vice president, an Aymara pedagogue named Víctor Hugo Cárdenas, was instrumental to the multiculturalist strategy of turning indigenous majorities into ornamental minorities. This strategy can be termed the *indio permitido* (the tolerated Indian), endorsed by World Bank projects of the ethno-ecotourist type, reflected in poverty-alleviation policies that deny the subject position to a vast majority of the rural population, both in the highlands and in the lowlands.[18] The strategy of the indio permitido enshrines a reified, postcard image of the indigenous culture while preserving the unquestioned cultural hegemony of the mestizo-criollo elites in the daily fabric of social life. The roadblocks of 2000 shattered this comfortable and sanitized image of the good Indian and reminded the world of the unfulfilled promises of liberal, populist, and neoliberal reforms. The massive mobilizations of 2000–2003 also prepared the terrain for a radical turnabout in the self-perception of the mestizo population. The allure of a "politics of ethnicity" that could also express the mestizo's frustrations with the dark side of neoliberal reforms became a powerful tool for antihegemonic practices that were soon to bear fruit. During this process, a shift from the indio permitido or World Bank multiculturalism to a hegemonic indigeneity capable of problematizing mestizo identity would end up making its mark in the political arena.[19]

In December 2005 the ethnic availability of the population turned into a massive vote for Evo Morales for president, inaugurating a new political situation that many have termed a *pachakuti*, a reversal of time-space and the beginning of a new cycle in history.

The Uses of Tradition

To ask about ethnicity today in Bolivia is to allude to concrete localities and territories of the indigenous-state conflict. One of these localities, the region of the Yungas of La Paz, serves as a setting for the nexus between the collective action of the peasant population and the classification of the insurgents as "indigenous." The coca growers (*cocaleros*) of the Yungas, who are originally from the diverse provinces of the highlands and the valleys of La Paz, as well as descendants of the migrant slaves brought from Africa in the colonial period, have for centuries supplied coca leaf to a huge, legitimate, and legal interior market that crosses Bolivia's borders into the north of Argentina and other regions. It is a market that has existed since colonial times.

I will attempt to connect the question of the construction of the image of the Indian and the existing politics of ethnicity, with the resistance of the Bolivian cocaleros to the repressive measures of the war on drugs pressed on Bolivia by the United States, and with the electoral turn that the politics of ethnicity took at the end of 2005.

In 1988, in the *United Nations Convention against Illicit Traffic in Narcotic Drugs and Psychotropic Substances*, the notion of "licit traditional uses" of coca leaf was introduced. Article 14, paragraph 2 reads, "Each party will take appropriate measures to prevent the illicit cultivation of, and to eradicate plants containing narcotic or psychotropic substances, such as opium poppy, coca bush and cannabis plants cultivated illicitly in its territory. The measures adopted shall respect fundamental human rights *and shall take due account of traditional licit uses, where there is historic evidence of such use*, as well as environmental protection."[20] Thus, the Vienna Convention of 1988 protects a certain type of residual coca consumption by indigenous populations, which would presumably disappear, along with the indigenous populations themselves, under the influence of modernization and westernization of the coca-leaf producers and consumers. The 1988 formulation appears to be a concession to reality, since in 1961 the *United Nations Single Convention on Narcotic Drugs* had established that "coca leaf chewing must be abolished within twenty five years from the coming into force of this Convention."[21]

Ironically, a few years after this deadline passed, not only did the coca leaf continue to be massively consumed by millions of Indians and non-Indians in Bolivia, Peru, and southern Colombia, but even in Argentina a federal act issued in 1989 decriminalized the consumption and possession of coca leaf in its natural state if used as *coqueo* or *akhulliku* (which is similar to, but not precisely "chewing"), herbal teas, rituals, and so on.

This legislation forms the basis for the widening of the legal and quasi-legal market of the coca leaf, which turns out to be ideal for the Yungas coca growers, until then only intermittently involved in supplying the illegal market. Since 1989, prices have steadily risen, testifying to the vitality of an internal and transnational market that has surpassed the notion of "traditional consumption" and incorporates modern urban consumers in Bolivia and the north of Argentina, as well as new groups of consumers—sugarcane workers, chestnut pickers, logging-company workers, and so on—within the scope of akhulliku or coqueo.

How do cocalero families react to this expansive market demand, which is increasingly quality oriented and urban? Can one call the method of production and market participation of these families "traditional"? What strategies do they employ to increase their supply of the product? Who are the "traditional" coca growers, and what do they do? The same questions can be asked about the so-called surplus producers, located in the zones of colonization of Asunta and Caranavi, in the department of La Paz, and in the Chapare region of Cochabamba.

In answering these questions, one must also ask if the notions of tradition and *modernity* are colonial misrepresentations of the Indian that deny their condition as political and historical subjects, coeval with the modern elites and perhaps more prepared than they are for the challenges of a postcolonial modernity. There is an ideological overtone to the discussion about tradition, which covers up contradictory policies and practices in the face of the reality of a global market and its multifaceted impacts in indigenous societies. The reality of the market inevitably involves *all* indigenous and peasant production within the Andean area, not just the cocaleros of the Yungas, and has done so since colonial times.[22] In the present-day context of a new and intense cycle of dynamic market rhythms, one can see exactly what the term *traditional* tries to conceal. To elaborate this point, I first describe the new legal markets of coca consumption in the modern cities of Santa Cruz, Cochabamba, and La Paz. One can appreciate that these cities are spaces for the active questioning of the essentialist notion of tradition; they become sites for a genuine modernity anchored in long-term legal markets, as well as for expressions of new, intercultural market trends. I then trace the challenges facing the cocalero enterprise Departmental Association of Coca Growers (ADEPCOCA) and the broad lines of the new government's policy on the coca issue. I conclude by re-elaborating the theoretical notion of the "prose of counterinsurgency," focusing on the perverse use of the idea of tradition as a part of state and supranational policies oriented toward a museumlike and ecotourist version of the indio permitido of the 1990s.[23]

My reading of indigenous modernity, as expressed in the cocalero experience of Bolivia, points to another form of the indigenous presence in the regional and global markets. Beginning with a commodity that was once global, but that throughout its "life history" was also incessantly connected with intense cultural dynamics through ritual, alternative medicine, and strategies of political identity in the Andean-Amazonian indigenous world, one can associate it with the idea of a "modernity of our own" based in interregional market circuits more organic and healthy than those brought by the imposed and colonized version of liberal and neoliberal modernity.[24]

There is no question that in the Yungas the coca producers and their peasant enterprise, ADEPCOCA, along with their union matrix, the Council of Federations of Peasant Coca Growers of the Yungas (COFECAY), have opted for a Bolivian-style modernity, a "development with coca," which will allow the cocaleros to reenter internal, regional, and global markets with a product whose actual intrinsic value cannot be overlooked.[25]

The production of coca leaf for this market, shadowed by illegality and prohibition, involves a notion of entrepreneurship and management that are entirely the cocaleros' own, anchored in long centuries of weaving the social networks that allowed them to compete in internal, interregional, and bi-national markets. Today this process rearticulates new identities and new political realities in Latin American regions and countries. At the same time, it involves the possibility of establishing cross-border networks that facilitate the long-distance circulation of coca leaf, avoiding the inconsistencies of Argentine legislation, which legalizes consumption and possession, but not the "trafficking" of coca. All these economic processes were behind the massive vote for Evo Morales. The Aymara cocalero leader represents that "other" modernity pursued by the urban and rural indigenous populations of the country, as well as by vast sectors of the mestizo middle-classes. In fact, one could say that Evo's symbolic power lies in his being an Indian, as much as in his emblematic representation of coca-leaf modernity. Beyond the indio permitido of neoliberalism, and in opposition to the satanic view of the war on drugs, cocaleros and their legal commodity stand for the expansive and intercultural regional and long-distance markets of coca chewing and other legitimate modes of consumption.[26] Contradictory as it may seem, the allure of indigenous rituals in urban and modern settings is in fact a de-exoticization of the indigenous, and the ritual consumption of coca in public becomes a symbolic assertion of the nation's dignity and sovereignty, crossing class and ethnic borders, and seducing the culturally weak, but politically dominant, mestizo-criollo minority.

Opposing these developments stands the war on drugs and the strategies of the U.S. embassy that pursue the liquidation of internal coca-leaf markets, the criminalization of all producers, the stigmatization of consumers, as well as a persistent political infiltration of the Bush administration into the internal structures of the Bolivian state. Behind this is the long-term complicity of the U.S. government with the corporate interests of transnational companies such as those in the pharmaceutical industry, those of the military-industrial complex, and the Coca-Cola Company; since 1961, the latter has been granted a world monopoly over the legal uses of coca leaves, as stated in article 27 of the *United Nations Single Convention on Narcotic Drugs*.

The new Bolivian government has up to now tried to cope with U.S. pressures in a contradictory way. The colonial inertia of the state apparatuses and procedures engenders ambiguous discourses and weakens state policies on the issue. In addition, the contradictory interests at play in the legal coca market supplied by the Yungas and in the recently legalized productive zone of the Chapare (where Evo Morales began his career as a cocalero leader) have resulted in a state of internal divisiveness among regional cocalero unions, along the lines of the arbitrary classification of coca productive zones ("traditional" vs. "surplus") introduced in 1988 by Law 1008, or the Regulation of Coca and Controlled Substances Law. Together, these factors show that launching a radically new coca policy is easier said than done.

New Urban Markets

Meanwhile, urban licit markets have continued to show a dynamic of their own. The lowland city of Santa Cruz is a case in point. In the city's central market one can see many stores managed by women *cocanis* (retail coca vendors) who supply a large clientele, ritual items, *chamairo* (a tropical plant used by lowland ethnic groups to flavor akhulliku), and other products.

Santa Cruz has the only modern factory that produces Chama Bico, a mixture of chamairo and bicarbonate of soda. Chama Bico is sold in large quantities in the local market, and according to the factory's owner, it is also exported to Argentina, Chile, and Brazil.

The Santa Cruz consumers of coca leaf belong to a wide range of social strata, from the highest entrepreneurial and agroindustrial elites to workers and indigenous migrants, including middle-class professionals, bus drivers, and all-night taxi drivers. On Avenida Japón there is a unique store called Cocanga that serves a select clientele of connoisseurs; it sells selected, packed, and cleaned coca leaf at 20 bolivianos (about $2.50) for a quarter pound, which in La Paz would sell for only 6 bolivianos (less than $1.00). In this store, in April 2004, I interviewed a young lawyer, a member of the judiciary, who told me he belonged to a group of coca-leaf chewers that got together every Friday to akhulliku, or "chew," and talk about the events of the week. While I was there, a young student bought a quarter pound. She told me that she used coca leaf to stay alert and work a double shift—studying and caring for her children—without getting tired. She also told me that chewing coca helped her keep her waistline with no apparent effort and that she has felt healthy and well nourished since she started to chew. In Santa Cruz coca leaf is not associated with indigenous users, but forms a part of a kind of regional gaucho style, given prestige and validated through its association with middle- and upper-class Argentine white people, frequent visitors to the city as tourists or entrepreneurs. In a region where the indigenous migrant population is routinely stigmatized and challenged on both the political and cultural fronts, coca does not factor as part of that stigma; instead, it has been appropriated for modern (one might say, postmodern), multifaceted, therapeutic, or recreational consumption.

But the world of the elites is not the only setting for the expansion of coca use in the regions of Santa Cruz and Beni. Among the sugarcane workers, chestnut growers, and logging-company workers, coca use is widely practiced, and many have adopted the coca-chewing habits of Amazonian indigenous groups, coca consumers from time immemorial. Such is the case of the users who flavor their coca wad with chamairo, a practice that has become common among urban and rural consumers of Santa Cruz. These expansive rural markets, associated with work and physical resistance, have their urban counterpart among the carriers, transport workers, taxi drivers, and self-employed artisans or merchants who use coca leaf to endure their long working days, though there are also young show-business and nightlife people who use the leaf for another kind of endurance. One might even posit that the growth of coca chewing in Santa Cruz is behind the surprising 33 percent of the vote that MAS got in that department in the December 2005 national elections.

In La Paz the promotion and legitimization of public consumption of coca leaf takes place during the annual Intercultural Fairs of Akhulliku, which began in El Alto in October 2004 and have continued in La Paz in October 2005 and October 2006.[27] During the ceremonies marking Evo Morales's taking of office, ceremonies that lasted from 18 to 23 January 2006, the sponsors of the Intercultural Fairs set up a Fair of Coca and Sovereignty in the colonial Plaza Alonso de Mendoza, showing the world the diverse legal uses of coca and the ritual and interpersonal meaning of the coca-chewing habit. In these marathon events there were exhibits of the best varieties of coca leaf selected from various regions of the country ("traditional" as well as "surplus"), a barter fair, and the sale of craft and industrial products made of coca leaf (including wines, soft drinks, breads, cookies, and flours). The fairs were sponsored by autonomous and independent organizations like the Workshop of Andean Oral History, the Coca Museum, the Institute of Sociological Research of UMSA, and the Committee for Coca and Drug Policies of the Chamber of Deputies, now led by cocalero representatives.

Dozens of leaders of the Peruvian coca-growers organizations came to La Paz from their regions, along with representatives from Colombian indigenous organizations of the Cauca. The de facto depenalization of akhulliku during those events, and its impact on the young population of La Paz and El Alto, as well as on visitors from various countries, was impressive. Among the most successful products were the breads, cakes, and cookies that used coca-leaf flour or syrup as a main ingredient. In the medicinal field there were also important initiatives, such as syrups and ointments and coca tonics. The Peruvian delegation brought samples of their energizing K-Drink, a successful product that had managed to attract an important foreign market in Asia, until the Peruvian government cancelled their export permit under the pressure of the International Narcotics Control Board (INCB) and the U.S. embassy, in application of the 1961 *United Nations Single Convention on Narcotic Drugs*. In January

2006 the Cauca indigenous enterprise Coca Nasa brought the famed Coca Sek, an energizing organic soft drink that is sold in southern Colombia as an alternative to Coca-Cola.

In these urban examples one can see a stratified market of modern consumers, who akhulliku the coca leaf for health, identity, or recreation, and who share, among themselves and with many other groups, qualities of a postmodern identity, which bears the mark of both globalization and its various styles, and the hegemonic indigeneity which characterizes the present-day Bolivian cultural scene. The existence of coca of diverse prices and qualities allows one a glimpse of a future consumer market that would supply ecologically certified coca to export markets such as today's northern Argentina; selected and ecological coca for urban consumers in general; top-grade coca for the wider popular market; and even second-grade coca for the rural poor.[28] The same could happen with the diverse "light" industrial products of coca: flours, soft drinks, energizing drinks, breads and pastries, pastas and other foods, and sweets and medicines made with coca flour or syrup, which are being developed for every pocket and stratum of the population.

Both the traditional and surplus producers of coca leaf thus face a demand for coca leaf that is not only growing but ever-more stratified and quality oriented, and that could grow even more if it had the proper international legislation and state and private support. This would amount to an alternative "war against drugs": one that would remove the surplus coca from the grip of the illegal economy by opening a high-value legal market of an expansive, quality-oriented world market. In the era of new-age medicines, energy supplements, and alternative body-and-mind health products, the export of high-value natural-coca-leaf products could be both a viable solution and a defense against illegal uses of the cheap raw material that have expanded out of control in many areas of South America. But this is only possible if the new government of Evo Morales succeeds in resisting U.S. pressures and resolutely poses to the United Nations the Bolivian demand for taking the coca plant out of List 1 of forbidden substances of the 1961 convention. This involves a shift in both foreign and domestic policies in order to seek international support for the Bolivian position and gradually dismantle the repressive policies and state-controlled agencies that are still devoted to the liquidation of the licit and healthy uses and markets for this indigenous commodity.

The Yungas at Stake: Drug Policies, Alliances, and Contradictions.

ADEPCOCA is one of the most successful enterprises of present-day Bolivia. It is a complex mixture of a union-type organization and a peasant
enterprise, and it is market oriented and capable of generating substantial
revenue. ADEPCOCA's general assembly gathers elected representatives from
every federation of the "traditional" or legal zone of coca and the "surplus" zone of Asunta, and has been granted a monopoly (by Law 1008,
Article 29) on the marketing of the legal coca crop from the Yungas, up to
a limit of 12,000 hectares.[29] Its officers are elected in *ampliados* (gather-
ings) *subcentrales and centrales*, which are intermediate-level local organizations of the cocalero families in the various cocalero provinces.

During the 2005 elections, all the cocalero regions of Cochabamba
and La Paz—both those of the legal or traditional zones and of the quasi-
illegal or surplus zones—voted massively for the MAS and Evo Morales.
Nevertheless, the potential hegemonic "indigeneity" in the new political
context, especially in cocalero regions that do not easily fit the stereotypical
traditional Indian identity of the indio permitido, faces difficult and unprecedented challenges.[30]

The official policies on coca and the war against drugs are now in the
hands of leaders of both the traditional and surplus zones of coca-leaf producers in the departments of Cochabamba and La Paz. Unfortunately, the
discussion is still narrowly related to a spatial redefinition of the extent to
which the surplus zones of the Yungas (particularly Asunta and Caranavi)
and the Chapare will be allowed to share the market for licit uses of coca
leaves with the traditional producers of the Sud Yungas, Nor Yungas, and
Inquisivi provinces of La Paz, and of Vandiola in Cochabamba (the only
legal producing areas recognized by Law 1008).

What remains to be seen is the stance that ADEPCOCA, the peasant organization and enterprise, will take with regard to the new policies on coca
that the government is trying to develop amid an aggressive press campaign
on coca's supposed lack of nutritional value and frequent public declarations made by U.S. embassy officials to discredit presidential intentions to
industrialize coca-leaf production and open new foreign markets (which
obviously imply a redefinition of the plant's international legal status).[31]
One of the main challenges for the new authorities is to conduct a study of
the legal demand for coca leaves based on a national survey of thousands

of households in order to determine how to "rationalize" the licit uses of coca leaves through the market. In addition, a national study on average productivity per hectare should be undertaken, with a sensitivity to the diverse regional variability in productivity, so as to associate the volume of dry coca leaves in the market with the number of hectares necessary for its cultivation. Provided the cocalero unions are able to surmount their internal divisions on this issue, these studies—which have the initial support of the European Union—could allow the Bolivian state to redefine the notions of "necessary" and "surplus" production zones and establish a sovereign policy of regulated markets for coca leaves. The challenge is therefore to successfully resist the U.S. embassy–imposed eradication program that has already caused some cocalero deaths in the Vandiola region of Cochabamba. These developments show how precarious the equilibrium is among the divergent interests in the legal coca market, and how limited governmental agency is on the coca issue.[32]

Nevertheless, the cautious policy of allowing a limited expansion of the legal coca crop and continuing manual eradication with the consensus of cocalero union leaders has kept the conflict with both the embassy and the cocalero grassroots under relative control. Up to now, there have been pacts between the state and the different actors in the coca-leaf market— the federations of producers, the legal retail distributors (*detallistas*), and the international cooperation funds and projects—so as to effect minimum changes and to slow down the continuity of the previous aggressive eradication policies. Moreover, the Estrategia de Lucha Contra el Narcotrafico y Revalorizacion de la Hoja de Coca (Strategy for the Struggle against Drug Traffic and Revaluation of the Coca Leaf), a radical departure from previous policies of aggressive eradication, was launched in December 2006.

A new marketing policy aimed at the expansion of the licit uses of coca has proven to be a more difficult task from a state-policy perspective. A formal prohibition of new commercialization licenses for retail vendors is still in force and has paradoxically resulted in a gray area of licit but illegal market expansion that addresses the increasing popularity and demand for coca in its natural state. High and rising prices for coca have nevertheless kept this market relatively immune to illegal trafficking. Suffice to say that the prices of coca in neighboring Peru are one-quarter and in Colombia one-sixth the prices in the legal markets of La Paz and Cochabamba. Industrial initiatives for any plant pursue the lowest possible prices for the raw materials, and the cocaine industry is no exception. This explains why the cocaine market is marginal in Bolivia, while it is booming in Colombia and Peru, where state policies follow more closely the U.S. strategy of repression and forced eradication.

But the limited entrepreneurial vision of ADEPCOCA, an enterprise that benefits from a virtual monopoly over the legal market and thus continues to endorse the traditional-surplus divide introduced by Law 1008, has kept the coca-growing enterprise in a limbo of indecisive policies, which only now are beginning to be challenged. On the other hand, a more thorough coca debate is taking place between the different actors of the legal coca markets and the state, as a result of which a new approach to the issue has been adopted by the government, as expressed in its Strategy for the Struggle against Drug Traffic and Revaluation of the Coca Leaf. As cocalero leaders of Chapare, Yungas, Caranavi, and other surplus zones become members of the legislative and executive powers and of the Constitutional Reform Assembly, they will need to create an integrated platform that articulates the interests of producers with those of licit consumers and industrializers and to arrive at some kind of consensus on issues such as regulation mechanisms, free-market expansion, rationalization of surplus production, and how to curb the influence of the illicit cocaine industry on the legal markets. Under the aegis of a modern, hegemonic indigeneity that is so well represented by this millennial Indian plant, the sovereign policies of the Bolivian state will soon have to move beyond a mere rejection of U.S. pressures for forced eradication toward an entirely new state policy that is capable of radically transforming the conditions and norms of the coca-leaf commodity chain.[33]

The Veiled Condition of Cocalero Identity

In discussing the dynamics of the legal markets and the contradictions of official Bolivian state policies under the aegis of a cocalero president, I have made little mention of the question of indigenous identity. This is due to the veiled condition of cocalero identity, which, despite the census figures, has translated historically into a growing invisibility. The years of the cocalero insurgency took place during the rise of neoliberalism, when the official policies of the indio permitido were at their peak, as expressed in the solitary figure of an indigenous vice president who was used as an ornamental figure that helped disguise the radically antipopular and anti-Indian policies of structural adjustment and the destruction of indigenous peasant economies. During the government of Sánchez de Lozada (1993–97), the Indian population was effectively reduced from a demographic majority to a residual minority through the manipulation of categories and the subjective impact of neoliberal hegemony, as expressed in the UNDP survey of 1996.

The Aymaras and Qhichwas of the highlands were no longer viewed as indigenous people in their own right, but only as poor peasants willing to accept the disciplines of modernization and subordinate integration in the world market. The cocaleros of the Yungas and the tropics of Cochabamba were viewed as even less indigenous than rural-urban migrants: many of them had become cocaleros after having been miners; they had union organizing experience; and, above all, nobody had to teach them how to deal with market forces—that is, they spoke a language that was in itself an intercultural translation of many languages. They were also acculturated Indians—an "acculturation from below," as Elizabeth Monasterios would call it—active agents of their own process of cultural and economic change who had been re-created as citizens by a migratory process that in some cases went back many generations.[34] Due to forced migratory experiences like the mining and manufacturing relocation of the 1980s, the cocaleros of the Chapare and some parts of the Yungas represent no ethnic identity with clear borders of self-identification or ethnic markers other than language. This is in sharp contrast with the hegemonic vision of the "tolerated Indian" spread by NGOs and by state development programs (including programs of alternative development) that have forced indigenous peoples of the lowlands to become just another part of nature, worthy of being preserved in a sort of timeless past for the delights of ecotourism. The indio permitido is a docile Indian when responding to the fetishistic strategy of the tourist's camera or the questions of the anthropologist or the biopiracy company that expropriates her/his exoticized image while stealing her/his knowledge of flora and medicinal plants. The indio permitido is an Indian satisfied with her/his minority status, domesticated and ready to play a role in the legitimization of multiculturalist policies endorsed by the neoliberal state. This neutralized and sanitized version of the indigenous excludes the Indian as a political and economic subject, denies the Indian the agency and right to become a successful entrepreneur, and does not recognize the Indian's capacity to face the challenges of regional and world markets of global commodities, not just those of the crafts, postcard, and tourist markets that are based in the reification of the Indian-as-Past.

In the context of this fetishistic and minority version of indigenous people, the Indian quality of the cocaleros of the Yungas is expressed not as discourse, but rather as practice. In a panel organized in 2003 to commemorate the twentieth anniversary of the Andean Oral History Workshop, Dionicio Núñez—the cocalero leader of COFECAY, elected to parliament in 2002—argued that the people of the Yungas were "Indians without ponchos or *chicotes* (whips)."[35] He argued that the cocalero ethnicity was revealed in the kinship and work relations that united people within communities and throughout a bigger external web in other communities and ecological regions.[36] At the same time, it was expressed in the exchange of work—mainly women's work—that wove together family networks and mobilized the workforce during the entire yearly cycle, which included at least three harvests of the leaves. To this one could add the multiple ways of conversion and interaction between reciprocity and market spheres, and the interactions of local, regional, and world circuits of exchange. On the other hand, cocalero systems of organization do not have—as in the highlands, for example—references to a long-term memory that can place claims on ethnic authorities with their traditional symbols like the poncho, the *ch'uspa*, or the whip. On the contrary, they have universally adopted Western costume, and they have transformed the coca-growers union into a kind of territorial microgovernment that rationally organizes daily life and the public representation of its members, including all the families of the surrounding communities. These organizations acquired a new dynamic with the Popular Participation Law of 1994 and have succeeded in gaining municipal power through the election of their own candidates. In this way, the cocalero grassroots organizations maintain territorial control over the entire region and organize the political power structure and the daily life of the region.

The power and organizational stability of cocalero unions and intermediate federations (centrales and subcentrales) has been recently eroded by the U.S. embassy's open intervention in the municipal politics in the region. The direct financial support of the embassy to communities in the northern and southern Yungas and its contribution to discouraging the mobilization of productive and commercial initiatives for promoting licit uses for the coca leaf are serious challenges facing Evo Morales's government.

The fact that the cocalero does not fit the stereotype of the indio permitido implicates that tradition as perverse and "orientalist," one that views things traditional as archaic icons—almost archeological pieces—that exist far from the market and its vices, imprisoned in the temple of nature (whether it's the jungle or some ethnic refuge in the Andean highlands) and subject to learned anthropological writing or tourist scrutiny and register.[37] The cocalero, on the contrary, is an acculturated Indian, skilled in the arts of buying and selling, and able to attain and negotiate power through political action, union organizing, and radical discourse. Nevertheless, political participation and mercantilism, both at the regional and national levels, have in no way erased the cocaleros' ethnic identities, as expressed in the use of Aymara and Qhichwa languages, kinship and communal networks, ritual life, and many other practices. The culture of coca is in itself an interesting example of coca's life history not only as an Indian sacred plant but also as one of the first regional Indian commodities since colonial times.[38] According to Alison Spedding, the coca field can be seen as a "total social fact" that has economic, social, spiritual, and political signification.[39] In the cocaleros' discourse there is frequent mention of coca's "sacred" and "millennial" dimensions, together with its importance for the peasant economy. Beyond the world of the producers, coca has also become a symbol of ethnic and national pride for the majority of the Bolivian population. Ritual uses of coca have also expanded and become connected with public and political life. In modern cities in Bolivia, Peru, and northern Argentina, rituals to the fertility goddess Pachamama and the mountain deities have become very popular as "invented traditions" in which coca leaf serves as a sort of connective tissue between the urban and the rural, indigenous and mestizo imagination, the political and the cultural.[40]

Within the CSUTCB, the cocaleros of the Yungas have also demanded "original community lands" and made territorial claims of their right to occupy and manage the Yungas space. Although these claims did not prosper in the previous legislative term, it is expected that the cocalero representatives in the new parliament—now a majority in the lower chamber—will take it up again and propose an integral treatment of the coca leaf as part of the indigenous rights of their cultivators and consumers. In such demands and in the territorial sweep of cocalero candidates in the 2005 elections, one can see that the coca issue involves ethnic as well as citizen identities, and the discourse on coca gets translated from cultural into political power.

Finally, the Yungas struggles since 1980 represent an articulation of class and ethnic identity, as well as a national anti-imperialist consciousness, all of which has attracted and articulated vast parts of the urban mestizo population and which constituted a powerful electoral alternative for the December 2005 elections. The cocalero capacity to bring together a broad front of dissent and civil disobedience in the face of the Bolivian state and its policies of repression and prohibition with regard to coca-leaf production and marketing leads one to conclude that ethnicity, or more precisely, indigeneity, is here the language in which counterhegemonic cultural and social power is expressed.[41] In practice, this translates into a slow and capillary invasion of huge regional and interregional markets for an indigenous commodity whose consumption articulates identity with recreational and instrumental behavior in a typically postmodern and multihued manner.

Disobedience to the empire thus has a national and even transnational connotation that is expressed in the massive adoption of coca leaf as a habitually consumed product and an expression of a cultural bond with indigenous roots. This characterizes the modern markets of cities and transborder spaces as sites of challenges to official policies sponsored under the aegis of the U.S. war on drugs. Dissent and alternative political options articulate identity and cultural demands with far-reaching political and economic issues that ultimately link coca producer and consumer interests with issues of national sovereignty and autonomy that have powerful political impact at the level of the Bolivian state.

The phenomenon of commercial expansion that articulates cocalero production with vast regional and interregional markets cannot be separated from the changes in the self-perception of the population as indigenous between the UNDP Survey of 1996 and the Bolivian National Census of 2001. That 62 percent of the Bolivian population, according to the latter census, self-identifies with one of the original peoples (Aymara, Qhichwa, Guarani, etc.) that inhabited Bolivian territory from time immemorial reveals the ideological impact of the indigenous social movements of 2000, of the cocalero struggle to protect and expand the legal market for coca leaves, and of efforts to develop coca's symbolic and economic potentials.

In the massive demonstrations and roadblocks of October 2003, expressions of this hegemonic indigenous identity proliferated in a multifaceted, postmodern way and were translated into the re-creation of a network of communal solidarities in which women, the rites, and akhulliku served as invisible, culturally distinct bonds of solidarity that opposed the homogenizing designs of the global market and its culturally Western model of individual citizenship. During those intense weeks, daily consumption of coca leaf doubtless expressed instrumental motives: in a context of food scarcity provoked by the roadblocks, akhulliku served to mitigate hunger and to enhance endurance for the marches, vigils, demonstrations, and hunger strikes. But there were also cultural motivations, a sense of belonging and ethnic bonding that was expressed in the use of coca as a symbol. Not only in the rituals that frequently accompanied the mobilizations, especially in rural areas, but also in the cocalero blockades, coca leaf came to be used as an emblem of a new sort of indigeneity, open to the recruitment of the acculturated, mestizo, and urban sectors of the population. The era of the hegemonic, mestizo, Spanish-speaking citizen who has erased all traces of her/his Indian past, and the era of the indio permitido, ornamental and instrumental to neoliberalism, seem to be coming to an end.[42]

But up to now—and until the Bolivian Constitution is rewritten in the Constitutional Assembly—the official discourse on ethnicity has translated into a formal recognition of the "multiethnic, multicultural" condition of Bolivian society. And it has also become a new type of "prose of counterinsurgency," in which the idea of "tradition" is used to neutralize the insurgent indigenous sectors and to convert the majority into docile minorities, subordinated to the patron-client web of the dominant parties.[43] This practice, which imprisons the ethnic condition in a kind of backyard of citizenship or a site of de-definition, construes the Indian as a subject lacking her/his own agency and political vision, fit only for hard manual work.[44] In this way, the profile of indigenous peoples remains subsumed, exiled from official discourse and recognized only in a formulaic way in the constitutional texts, devoid of any practical applicability. With Evo Morales's coming to power, this image is no longer totally true. Although there is still a monopoly of discursive power and of normative functions by mestizo elites coming from the Left, a monopoly that shadows the potential autonomy and agency of indigenous leaders and indigenous modes of thought, Morales serves as a sort of mirror that reflects the dignity of being Indian to millions of Bolivian workers, peasants, entrepreneurs, and intellectuals.

This alternative indigeneity exploded in the social mobilizations of 2000–2005 and was translated into identity practices that configured its demands and articulated its symbols and its political language to the point of overcoming stigma and winning a national election. In this dialectic, indigenous identity construction was transformed into a hegemonic cultural formula that sought to universalize its convocational appeal through the market, without losing its hereditary ownership of cultural artifacts like the coca leaf. Civil disobedience against the Bolivian state and against the policies of the empire thus became a commitment from below, for the nation and for its own modernity, anchored in long-term and long-distance markets and in ethnicity as a tacit consensus and cultural habitus with great capacity for political convocation and unification.[45] The challenge facing the Morales government lies in articulating the full potential of this new politics of identity, demanded by the actors of the coca-leaf market, into a national policy that is both sovereign and capable of gaining supporters in the world at large.

Notes

1. Mamani Ramírez, *El rugir de las multitudes*; Gómez, *El Alto de pie*.
2. Harris, Larson, and Tandeter, *La participación indígena en los mercados surandinos*.
3. See Muratorio, "Nación, identidad y etnicidad"; and Anderson, *Imagined Communities*.
4. República de Bolivia, Oficina Nacional de Inmigración, Estadística y Propaganda Geográfica, *Censo general de la población de la república según el empadronamiento de primero de Septiembre de 1900*, 41.
5. Grieshaber, "Fluctuaciones en la definición del indio."
6. República de Bolivia, Dirección Nacional de Estadística y Censos, *Censo demográfico de 1950*, 100–101.
7. Albó, Greaves, and Sandóval, *Chukiyagu*.
8. Rivera Cusicanqui, "*Oprimidos pero no vencidos.*"
9. Aymara-speakers and Qhichwa-speakers were by far the majority, but there were also significant numbers of speakers of Guaraní and dozens of other lowland indigenous languages, which were lumped together as "other." This census was later criticized for its "Andinocentrism" and blindness to lowland indigenous peoples.
10. República de Bolivia, Instituto Nacional de Estadística y Censos, *Censo nacional de población y vivienda* (1992).
11. The same illusion was embraced by the MNR leaders of the 1950s. Second-class citizenship for the Indians has been the dream of liberal elites in the country since the nineteenth century and the hidden agenda of many of the most progressive cultural reforms of the twentieth century.
12. Barth, *Ethnic Groups and Boundaries*.

13. Ibid.

14. Those years of triumphal neoliberal reforms were witness to an open erasure of the Andean Indians by international agencies and the World Bank, which assumed that the Aymaras and Qhichwas—precisely those who had been the most politically active since the 1970s—were no longer Indians and had become acculturated and integrated into the market. I have labeled this policy the *indio permitido*, or the tolerated ethnicity of the World Bank.

15. The idea of acculturation from above was suggested to me by Elizabeth Monasterios (personal communication) and is analogous to my concept of "forced citizenship" (Rivera Cusicanqui, "Mestizaje colonial andino").

16. Mamani Ramírez, *El rugir de las multitudes*.

17. United Nations Development Program, *Programas de empleo transitorio*.

18. I introduced this term at a public workshop at the University of Texas, Austin, on 25 April 2001. The workshop, conducted in Spanish and hosted by the Instituto Lozano Long de Estudios Latinoamericanos, was called "Descentralización del Estado y Derechos Culturales."

19. Due to limitations of space, I cannot deal here with the climactic moment of this process: the massive, countrywide mobilizations of rural and urban people against Sánchez de Lozada's second presidency in September–October 2003.

20. United Nations, *United Nations Convention against Illicit Traffic in Narcotic Drugs and Psychotropic Substances*, emphasis added.

21. United Nations, *United Nations Single Convention on Narcotic Drugs*, Article 49, paragraph 2(e).

22. Harris, Larson, and Tandeter, *La participación indígena en los mercados surandinos*.

23. Guha, "La prosa de contrainsurgencia."

24. See Appadurai, *The Social Life of Things*; and Chatterjee, *Our Modernity*.

25. See the essays compiled by William Carter in *Ensayos científicos sobre la coca*.

26. Due to coca's high content of vitamins, minerals, antioxidants, and medicinal alkaloids, there is presently a shift toward other forms of consumption of coca in urban settings, especially in Peru, Bolivia, and southern Colombia. Along with a longtime favorite, *mate de coca* (herbal tea), coca-leaf flour is being widely used in health-food stores, breads, cookies, noodles, and novo-Andean cuisine. Soft drinks, syrups, and cosmetic and hair-care products are also very popular.

27. See Campaña Coca y Soberanía, http://www.cocasoberania.org/.

28. See Rivera, *Las fronteras de la coca*.

29. República de Bolivia, Ley 1008, Ley de régimen de la coca y sustancias controladas, 1988.

30. Canessa, *Minas, maíz y muñecas*.

31. See *La Razón* (La Paz), 19 March 2006.

32. In September 2006 an incursion of the Bolivian army into the Vandiola region—

the only legal zone in the department of Cochabamba—caused two deaths and several injuries among cocalero peasants. The decision to repress was apparently taken outside the scope of the executive power, with the close supervision of the U.S. Drug Enforcement Agency. This episode reveals how internal conflicts among cocalero unions facilitate the U.S. embassy's strategy of imposing forced eradication on the Morales government. At the height of the "zero coca" policy of the 1990s, the Vandiola peasants remained aloof to the deaths of surplus-zone cocaleros in the Chapare, because their own rights as traditional coca cultivators were protected by Law 1008.

33. See Gootenberg, *Cocaine.*
34. See Elizabeth Monasterios's forthcoming work on the Andean avant-garde.
35. Núñez, "Originarios sin poncho ni chicote."
36. Spedding, "The Coca Field as a Total Social Fact."
37. See Said, *Orientalism.*
38. See Numhauser, *Mujeres indias y señores de la coca.*
39. Spedding, "The Coca Field as a Total Social Fact."
40. Hobsbawm and Ranger, *The Invention of Tradition*; Cáceres, La reinvención de la tradición en el Año Nuevo Aymara; Spedding, *Gracias a Dios y a los Achachilas.*
41. Canessa, *Minas, maíz y muñecas.*
42. Mamani Ramírez, *El rugir de las multitudes.*
43. Ibid.
44. Guerrero, "Una imagen ventrílocua"; Guerrero, "El proceso de identificación."
45. Bourdieu, *Le sens pratique.*

JEFFREY W. RUBIN

7   **HIGH STAKES IN BRAZIL**

Can Democracy Take on Empire?

In 2002 the trade unionist Luiz Inácio Lula da Silva
swept to victory in presidential elections in Brazil,
and since then he has surprised his own supporters
as well as international bankers by rigorously complying with the economic prescriptions of the International Monetary Fund (IMF). The result has been
a startling political story: a long-standing leader of
the leftist Workers Party (PT) has kept the Brazilian
economy stable, gained the support of domestic and
global financial leaders, and won re-election handily,
in 2006.[1] Equally startling was the corruption scandal
that erupted in May 2005, revealing that the PT, long
regarded as transparent and honest, made use of illegal
campaign funds in the 2002 elections and subsequently
paid opposition deputies to support its policies in Congress. Both sets of practices—economic orthodoxy and
political corruption—have been accompanied by the
marked absence of progressive socioeconomic reform
under the leftist Lula administration.

For advocates of neoliberalism, including former
President Fernando Henrique Cardoso and the centrist
and right-wing parties that supported him, Lula's adherence to mainstream economic doctrine and modest

social policy has been a triumph and relief. Many of those who voted for Lula, however, assumed that his orthodox economic stance was a first step, adopted to reassure financial markets and address inherited economic constraints. They expected Lula to move on to begin a new national project, prioritizing social inclusion and a more equal distribution of wealth by forging new bargains in such areas as land, labor, education, debt repayment, and trade.

Gessí Bonês, a women's movement activist in the southern state of Rio Grande do Sul, explained the leeway that supporters granted Lula during his first year in office by reflecting on the PT's experience in local government in her town of 7,000 people. "Before we entered government, we thought it was simple," Bonês told me. "You come into office, with that big budget, and you change everything. But now we see that things work differently. The budget isn't that big, and much of it is already allocated to basic salary expenses. And things change very slowly."[2]

As this slowness persisted through Lula's third and fourth years in office, however, with corruption scandals claiming center stage, it became clear that the president had eschewed reform and accepted the socioeconomic status quo. For those whose hopes for democracy are primarily long range, including many sympathetic commentators in the United States, Lula's presidency can nevertheless be deemed a success. In their view Lula has appropriately adjusted to the politics of the possible, focusing on economic stability and carrying out small reforms in social security, support for family farmers, and food for Brazil's poorest.[3] The popular Bolsa Família program, which offers small but crucial economic aid to poor families who keep their kids in school, reaches eleven million Brazilian families and has brought Lula considerable electoral support, as has a long-overdue 23 percent increase in the minimum wage. From a "realist" perspective, furthermore, the corruption scandals, while lamentable, fall within the norms of Brazilian politics and the exigencies of its weak party system.[4]

And Lula has played a key role in challenging the U.S. version of globalization on the international stage. From this perspective, the success of a leftist president in maintaining economic growth, gaining international stature, winning re-election, and handing over power to a successor in 2010 represents a significant democratic advance for Brazil. The corruption drama and widely publicized congressional investigations can even be seen as playing a complementary role in democratic consolidation. Riveted to their television sets during the summer of 2005 as politicians, bureau-crats, publicists, and their spouses moved from conspiracy to revelation, Brazilians gained a civics lesson in democratic norms and the rule of law.

But was it a civics lesson, or the fall of the dream and possibility of meaningful reform in one of the world's most unequal societies? For many PT supporters, the economic orthodoxy and political corruption of the Lula administration and the PT betray more than two decades of social-movement mobilization and leftist party building. World-renowned inno-vations such as participatory budgeting in Brazil's major cities and land occupations in the countryside were sidelined first by a commitment to debt repayment and a 4.25 percent budget surplus—higher even than the IMF required—and subsequently by ever-widening revelations of illegality, bribery, and influence-peddling at the heart of the PT. During his first term, Lula failed to implement any number of policies put forth in the *Concepts and Guidelines* adopted by the PT congress in December 2001, just before the initiation of the presidential campaign.[5] Most of these policies rep-resent long-term PT commitments to changing the economic model and lessening deprivation and inequality, and they include controlling interna-tional capital flows; carrying out a full-fledged land reform; renegotiating public debt to free resources for social-welfare programs, education, and infrastructure; and lowering interest rates to promote GDP growth. Fur-thermore, as fiscal orthodoxy continues apace, violence, unemployment, and drug trafficking are on the rise in Brazil's cities, while the rural divide between agribusiness and landless workers intensifies. In this context the notion that inclusion will occur gradually over decades through neoliberal growth and incremental social policy, presumably without upheaval or cataclysm, seems misguided and even delusional.

Amid the debate over Lula's economic policy, few acknowledge what is at stake in Brazil in the age of U.S. empire. As one of the best scenarios for democratically driven socioeconomic reform in the world today, Brazil since 2002 has put to the test the claims of those who champion democ-racy: that democracy can improve people's lives; that citizenship *within* political institutions fosters inclusion and well-being; and that nation-states can be significant forces for self-government and social justice in today's globalized world.

In Brazil reformist bargains within a market system could insure food, jobs, and education for ordinary people. And if innovation in Brazil—

including new economic relations with the United States and the IMF—were to lessen inequality, then promises made in the name of democracy and civil society would gain credence internationally. But if, as seems increasingly likely, the democracy flourishing in Brazil does not result in significant change in poverty and inclusion, then those who have worked credibly for reform through democratic politics may well return to the polarized positions of the past. Activists committed to change may fight for justice in the streets, instead of within political institutions, while Brazil's elites return to authoritarian visions of grandeur, defending themselves with political power and security forces.[6] In the broader Latin American context the failure of Brazil's democracy significantly to transform the lives of the poor may mean that, within democratic institutions, the populism of Hugo Chávez and the mass mobilizations of Bolivia and Ecuador surpass institutional activism as the most promising paths of resistance to empire.

Democracy, Inequality, and the Economy

Lula's government brought together many factors that made significant reform possible when he assumed office. The president led a political party with a long history of internal democracy, connection to social movements, and dedication to an alternative, egalitarian national project.[7] By 2002, the PT had demonstrated commitment to democratic rules and market principles, and it had governed with skill and innovation in Brazil's largest cities. The PT's originality, in innovations like participatory budgeting, lay in setting up processes of transparent deliberation and policymaking that avoided the constraints of conventional legislative politics.[8]

Lula's predecessor, Fernando Henrique Cardoso, had stabilized the economy—the world's eleventh largest—and brought balanced budgets to state-level government through federal legislation.[9] Although Cardoso gave a new degree of legitimacy and continuity to democratic institutions in Brazil, he did not grapple seriously with inequality. Lula won the 2002 elections with a large enough electoral mandate to address inequality directly, and he assumed office with great international prestige and charisma. At that moment, despite the fears and dismay of opponents of the PT, there was a palpable consensus, across the economic and political spectrum in Brazil, that it was essential to do something about misery, hunger, lack of education, and violence.[10]

The strongest factor behind the potential of the PT as a source of dissent and innovation was the social-movement activism that had flourished in Brazil since the late 1970s and had spurred the growth and developed the talent of the party. Brazil in 2002 represented a potential challenge to empire because its strong and pioneering social movements had crossed the divide between the streets and the institutions, making both into creative arenas for progressive politics.[11] Brazil under Lula put this institutional engagement on the part of social movements to the test. For those Brazilians who had worked hard for two decades to fight hunger, poverty, abysmal schools, violence, and joblessness in their communities, would citizenship *within the institutions* bring enduring reform?

Such citizenship might well have brought progressive reform had Lula used his early economic successes to press the United States and the IMF for better, more innovative rules regarding debt repayment and trade. Gains in these areas, resulting in funds for desperately needed investment in healthcare, education, and infrastructure, would have further encouraged activists and ordinary Brazilians to focus their political efforts on democratic institutions. And this in turn would have given Lula clout to publicly champion socioeconomic reform and press Congress to approve reformist initiatives. It would also have encouraged the PT to continue its successful two-pronged strategy for progressive change in Brazil: mobilizing within the institutions through conventional electoral and legislative processes; and mobilizing outside and around the institutions through such mechanisms as participatory budgeting, land occupations, socially responsible business associations, and the World Social Forum.

In contrast to this reformist scenario Lula's election did not prompt the PT at the national level to challenge the neoliberal status quo or to reimagine what national governments could do. Ironically, the success of its economic orthodoxy has enabled the Lula government better to weather revelations of widespread corruption. At the height of the corruption scandal in September 2005, Brazil became one of the only developing countries in the world to successfully sell bonds in its own currency on the international market, an achievement that demonstrated unprecedented confidence in the economy on the part of investors, who "appeared to largely shrug off the bribery scandal," according to the *Financial Times* of London.[12] This confidence reflected lower inflation rates, increases in exports, and a large trade surplus in 2005, as well as increases in anticipated growth for 2006. These economic indicators represent striking achievements and lent credence to the view, held consistently by Lula and his inner circle, that economic success should be the preeminent goal of national government, preceding other reformist efforts.

From the Streets to the Institutions

As a result of Brazil's democratic experimentation over the past two decades, the political activities of many ordinary Brazilians have moved from the streets to the institutions. In addition, the less overtly political aspects of people's cultural and community lives—their hopes, rumors, angers, faiths, and visions—entered institutionalized public spaces as well. It is precisely this broad presence of activist initiatives and cultures within formal political processes that made progressive reform possible during Lula's first term—especially in the context of Lula's "successful" management of the economy.

In Porto Alegre, a city of 1.3 million people in Brazil's south, the PT won municipal elections from 1988 to 2000 and instituted a successful experiment in urban government. Through participatory budgeting, ordinary people in the city's neighborhoods came together in a yearly cycle of meetings to decide how the city budget for municipal services would be spent.[13] Local residents, many of them with only grade-school educations, learned to argue, petition, make technical assessments, supervise project implementation, and vote. Dilecta Todoschini, a neighborhood activist and retired schoolteacher, compared the incremental approach of participatory budgeting to household improvements: "First, when you're living in one dark room, you hope for a window; and then you get the window and think about a floor, another room, indoor plumbing."[14] The highly structured deliberative process of participatory budgeting allowed moments for wide-ranging commentary and opinion as well. Even as the budgeting process provided a forum for developing skills of concise presentation and reasoned argument, it made space for emotion and storytelling, as people used the open-comment time at meetings to address what was most pressing or engaging in their lives.

Through such skills, gradualism, and open public discussion, Porto Alegre's shantytowns were transformed in fifteen years. Neighborhoods where sewage ran down hillsides or across muddy streets now enjoy basic infrastructural services and have begun to construct healthcare posts and daycare centers. When the residents of an illegal squatter settlement faced eviction, they learned skills of petitioning and argument in order to present their case.

Not everyone sees the benefit of such activity, of course. The CEO of a large Porto Alegre business told me over lunch in his executive dining room that participatory budgeting meetings were "just for people who have nothing to do."[15] The CEO's second in command, however, spoke very differently about the leftist government, with whose philosophy he disagreed: "These guys are far easier to work with than previous civilian and military politicians," he confided. "They're smart, they listen, and they take what I say seriously."[16] And later that day, when I visited one of the city's weekly neighborhood meetings in a distant slum, I saw women and men arriving after long workdays, with kids in tow, to discuss recent events and question (and challenge) representatives from city agencies. They did this week after week so that sometime in the future their children might receive subsidized bus fares or their streets gain potable water.

Another compelling example of grassroots innovation and institutionalization occurred in the rural towns of Rio Grande do Sul, the state of which Porto Alegre is the capital. In the late 1980s women from modest backgrounds withdrew from male-run organizations, such as the Movement of Landless Rural Workers, and formed the Rural Women Workers Movement (MMTR) in order to address women's economic and health issues, as well as gender relations within families.[17] Gessí Bonês, a leader of the movement, spent fifteen years supporting grassroots mobilizations and blocking highways to fight for social justice. From 2002 to 2005, in contrast, she ran the department of health in her small rural town while it was governed by a coalition that included the PT. Bonês's department monitored every at-risk child, set up a mobile dental clinic—constructed out of an old school bus—that provided free services to children in every rural neighborhood, and coordinated the street work of community health workers. In three years Bonês, who had only an eighth-grade education, assembled a team of eighty health-care workers, including doctors and nurses, who provided public services that were not available before the PT government took office locally.

Bonês says she has "dois coraçoes" (two hearts), one in the institutions and the other in the streets. When I visited in 2003, the summer after Lula took office, she suggested I come with her to meet with local bankers to request donations of pens and tablecloths—not money!—for the municipal health fair. The bankers learned about the realities of deprivation, which keeps the majority of local residents from making use of their banks, from the same woman who had blockaded their cars in years past.

Women in the rural women's movement can analyze pensions and budgets, plan takeovers of legislative offices, and critique the viability of genetically altered crops. In workshops in church basements, they discuss the nitty-gritty of how to change patriarchal gender relations in a place where many women still need their husbands' permission to leave the house. How does one steer a course between asking permission, on the one hand, and simply announcing one's departure, on the other? In role-playing workshops women find the words out of which discussion and negotiation are crafted in family relationships. Alongside these cultural changes, activists like Bonês run their towns, implementing new health and education policies and creating links between businesspeople and activists. They pay close attention to the things people want and need, and they respect the slowness of the democratic process while insisting that their participation in the institutions bear fruit.

Transformations of Life in the Favelas

If participatory budgeting is one urban story in Brazil, the favelas, or shantytowns, of Rio and São Paulo are another. The poverty of the favelas caught international attention in 1959, when Marcel Camus's *Black Orpheus* celebrated samba, black bodies, gossip, and the picturesque beauty of ramshackle hillsides overlooking one of the most beautiful bays in the world, with death lurking in the background. In *Child of the Dark*, the 1960 diary of a favela resident, Carolina Maria de Jesus wrote on her daughter's birthday, "I wanted to buy a pair of shoes for her, but the price of food keeps us from realizing our desires. . . . I found a pair of shoes in the garbage, washed them, and patched them for her to wear. I didn't have one cent to buy bread."[18]

Over the next forty years, millions of Brazilians migrated from the countryside to the city, commuting for hours to jobs as janitors, sweatshop workers, or domestic servants and struggling to keep their children in school. In the favelas mundane burdens and pleasures met extraordinary violence. In the 2003 film *City of God* brutal gangs traffic in drugs as ever-younger children become inured to shootings and death. The film's directors,

Fernando Meirelles and Katia Lund, reveal the dynamics of this spiraling violence in a documentary, *News from a Personal War,* in which Rio's then chief of police Helio Luz wonders how to keep two million people who earn less than $100 a month under control. He says bluntly, "I practice law enforcement to protect and serve the status quo." Captain Pimentel of Rio's Special Police Operations Battalion explains the excitement that surrounds this task: "I am in a war. The only difference is that I go home every day."

In an ironic twist the intensification of violence in the favelas has been accompanied by an influx of consumer goods. "Precarious shacks perched on unpaved streets with open sewage now boast refrigerators, TVs, and, in some cases, computers, as well as teenagers more educated than their parents. But education has not led to employment."[19] The Brazilian economy, even as it produces the world's largest soy crop and sells aircraft to the United States and Europe, provides few regular jobs for children of the favelas, encouraging many of them to take up drug trafficking and violence. As a result, people in the *não-asfalto,* the unpaved parts of the city, fear for their lives in the streets outside their houses. In April 2004, after shootouts between drug gangs shut down the roads that link Rio's beachfront neighborhoods, Governor Rosinha Matheus requested that federal troops occupy eight of the city's favelas, and President Lula authorized the deployment. In June 2005, in response to gun battles between drug-trafficking gangs and assaults on commuters, state legislators in Rio de Janeiro voted to build a six-and-a-half-foot high wall along some of the main highways in the city to block off the favelas that abut the roads.[20]

In the face of ongoing efforts further to divide the city, physically and metaphorically, young people in some of Rio's most violent and drug-ridden favelas have been learning to play drums in Afro-reggae bands and to perform in circus and theater troupes. They have done this as a result of the efforts of young black men and women who formed the Afro-Reggae Cultural Group in the wake of a 1993 police massacre in the favela of Vigario Geral.[21] The leaders of Afro-Reggae explicitly intend to lure children away from drug trafficking. One young woman told me how her family's dinner table was transformed when she and her brother joined the Afro-Reggae Health Troupe, a theater ensemble that staged plays about AIDS prevention; instead of watching telenovelas, her parents and siblings began to sing songs and tell stories, joke and discuss political issues. These very local changes in how people think and act are reinforced by Afro-Reggae's public activities, which include discussions about racism and police violence with government officials, as well as financial partnerships with city hall and prominent businesses to sponsor cultural activities in Rio's favelas.

Pressure from Below and Above

Lula's administration could get to the heart of exclusion and hunger in Brazil by addressing the contentious issue of land reform in the countryside, around which the Landless Rural Workers' Movement (MST) has mobilized with stunning success over two decades. In March of 2004, after quietly supporting Lula for more than a year and seeing little policy response, the MST resumed its illegal land occupations, seizing nearly 150 properties in twenty of Brazil's twenty-seven states. In May 2005, 13,000 landless workers marched to the nation's capital, Brasília, bringing the issue once again to the political forefront. The movement's goal is to pressure Lula to carry out a process of land reform that had been widely expected during Brazil's transition to democracy in the 1980s, but was blocked by rural landowners, who have disproportionate power in the federal legislature and employ private militias to intimidate opponents.[22]

Twenty years of MST organizing have produced solid support for land reform among Brazilians of all classes and regions. (A wildly popular nighttime soap opera, *The King of Cattle*, which portrayed landless squatters with sympathy and steamy romance, also contributed.) Many urban Brazilians see land reform as a way of keeping the rural poor in the countryside, rather than having them migrate to overcrowded urban slums. Still, land reform is expensive, because it involves buying idle land from its owners and subsidizing the early stages of settlement and production for new occupants. And some see land reform as threatening, because it makes societal claims on private property and supports alternatives to conventional agribusiness.

There is an opening for reform, albeit a fragile one, in the Brazilian countryside. The Lula government could shift the boundaries of the possible by addressing the issue of land reform regionally, rather than dealing with it as an all-or-nothing proposition. A creative policy, negotiated among competing groups, might focus redistributive efforts on Brazil's relatively unproductive northeast, where land redistribution and support for small-scale agriculture could make a real dent in poverty. In Brazil's powerhouse central regions, which produce the world's largest soy harvest on enormous tracts of land, Lula could ensure economic growth and foreign exchange by continuing his strong support of the agribusiness model. And in the south, where fertile land is more balanced between family farmers and big growers, Lula could also compromise, supporting MST and smallholder efforts at sustainable development, while leaving many big farms intact.[23] Carrying land reform to the international level, Lula might then press the IMF to allow payments for land buyouts to come out of the budget surplus or debt repayment. An imaginative policy of this sort, which cuts through old orthodoxies of left and right, risks pleasing no one. But in the hands of a skilled politician like Lula, it might point the way to a future of democratic compromise, where each contending group achieves some of its goals and the lives of the poorest are demonstrably improved.[24]

During the first two years of Lula's presidency, reform-minded Brazilians discussed a wide range of economic proposals that would maintain democratic and market principles but, like participatory budgeting and land reform, modify their rules and outcomes. For example, Lula has faced severe constraints on initiating social-welfare and economic-development programs—despite a healthy and growing economy—because the IMF has required a 3.75 percent budget surplus in order for Brazil to be deemed "credit-worthy. In response Brazilian officials have pressed the IMF to revise its accounting procedures, so as to distinguish between routine expenditures and productive investment in order to permit more of the latter.[25]

Jorge Gerdau, whose Gerdau SA ranks among the top ten steelmakers in the U.S. market, argues for controls on capital flows to limit the extent to which international investors can pull their money out of Brazil on a moment's notice. Gerdau, a fervent defender of free enterprise, explains that business planning cannot function when speculative investments enter and leave with lightning speed.[26] Leaders of the MST question the impact of agribusiness profits, pointing to tensions between generating needed foreign exchange and fostering a more equal society. Opening up these matters to discussion can yield solutions that avoid all-or-nothing logics, such as stimulating different forms of industry and agriculture in different regions to strike a balance among development goals.

Brazil's government debt, which skyrocketed under President Cardoso's 1995–2002 administrations, offers a striking example of the competing lenses through which current dilemmas can be viewed. Cardoso's efforts to clean up notoriously corrupt state-level finances led the national government to assume much of the states' unpayable debt. From one perspective, Cardoso presided over a very bad deal, assuming debt that the federal government can barely repay. From the perspective of strengthening democracy, however, Cardoso brought transparency and balanced budgets into the Brazilian mainstream in a way that avoided presidential decrees and authoritarianism, relying instead on negotiations among president, governors, and Congress.[27] It remains to be seen whether domestic elites and international power holders will allow any payoff for Brazil's democratic and fiscal triumphs—or even whether Lula will press for significant concessions.

In the 1980s Brazilian society campaigned against military dictatorship, and as a result the generals negotiated a transition to civilian rule. "Lula offers a tremendous opportunity," said then U.S. Ambassador to Brazil Donna Hrinak in 2004, "to show that a democratically elected government can implement a social agenda."[28] Hrinak herself spoke of the need for flexibility in U.S. policy, suggesting that Washington no longer felt tied to neoliberal economic orthodoxy and that the rules of the international economy could be modified. While Hrinak's words may have been disingenuous, a hard-hitting Lula bent on changing the economic rules of the game might have used such sentiments to promote reformist goals in public debate and private negotiations. Officials in the Brazilian foreign service spoke much as Hrinak did on economic matters, arguing that in exchange for greater access to their markets the United States should cut its domestic agricultural subsidies, which decrease the competitiveness of key Brazilian exports such as cotton and oranges.

Brazilian trade negotiators also wanted flexibility in industrial policy, so that if Brazilian auto or airplane exports were threatened in an economic downturn, the government could support these industries in targeted ways that might be deemed unfair under international trade guidelines. And Brazilians wanted the freedom to modify rules on trade-related intellectual-property rights, or TRIPS, in trade negotiations. (Already, by defying the patents on high-priced HIV drugs, Brazil's forward-looking Ministry of Health had established the most successful AIDS treatment and prevention program in the world.)[29] Despite such policy successes, Brazilian trade officials have spoken candidly about the constraints of U.S. domestic politics and their own very limited room for maneuver. To some PT observers,

Lula's trade representatives from the start ceded too much to the free-trade status quo. Beneath the recognition of "reality," however, was a challenge that echoed Hrinak's and Lula's own: this was as good as democratic legitimacy could be, and if negotiations failed to diminish poverty, claims for democracy would ring hollow throughout the Americas.

The Limits Posed by Empire

Innovation, however, is suspect where economic orthodoxy holds sway. So long as Lula honors this orthodoxy, he is widely praised among the world's financial powers. He has attended the International Economic Forum at Davos—the summit for economic leaders of the developed world—and was twice welcomed by President George W. Bush, at a time when few Latin American leaders gained Washington's attention. But in 2004, when Lula spoke of changing economic policy so as to promote redistribution of wealth, job creation, and social inclusion, Paulo Leme, director of emerging markets at Goldman Sachs, responded immediately that Lula's statement "weaken[ed] the government."[30] Paulo Vieira da Cunha, chief economist for Latin America for HSBC Securities, warned that "one of the questions behind the risk level of Brazil [was] political stability and the continuity of its economic policy."[31] HSBC was not worried about Brazil's macroeconomic stability in and of itself, Vieira da Cunha explained. Rather, "the threat is, as always, politics," where politics is understood as divergence from economic orthodoxy.[32]

The same economic orthodoxy that has pleased Brazilian bankers and international financial institutions initially dampened possibilities for growth.[33] Brazil's economic success has lain in paying its enormous foreign debt, balancing its budgets, and keeping inflation under control. The Lula administration achieves this by exceeding the 3.75 percent budget surplus required by the IMF and maintaining interest rates among the highest in the world. Together, these policies severely limit Lula's capacity to invest not only in such critical areas as education, healthcare, poverty alleviation, and land reform but in sorely needed economic infrastructure as well. They also make it difficult for Brazilian entrepreneurs to afford the credit necessary for investment and expansion. As a result, even domestic business groups that had valued the privatization and balanced budgets instituted by Lula's predecessor, Fernando Henrique Cardoso, argued that U.S.-promoted neoliberal policies hindered growth when carried to extremes. Together with many poor *and* middle-class supporters of the PT, these business-sector critics of neo-liberalism wanted Lula to defy international pressures and spend money to stimulate broad-based and sustainable growth. Instead, Lula did little to alter Brazil's development path, and he appears unlikely to do so during his second term.[34]

Domestic and international observers announced the demise of the progressive PT project—which was caught between the realisms of economic constraint and political-party interests—well before the onset of the 2005 corruption scandal. The *New York Times* made this official for U.S. readers in a magazine piece in June 2004. The *Times* praised Lula's intentions and underscored the need for change, but then, essentially, shrugged. Nothing much could be done, the article asserted, given the limits of what it called "democracy's great folk dance," a phrase echoed by the primitivist painting of Lula and the Brazilian countryside on the magazine's cover.[35] In a similar vein, many Brazilian leftists blamed the absence of progressive reform on the PT's decision to ally with centrist or right-wing parties in Congress in order to be able to pass legislation, or they located the demise of the PT project in Lula's own pre-election "Letter to the Brazilian People," in which he promised to honor international financial obligations if he were elected.[36]

Yet what was unprecedented about the first two years of the Lula presidency was that virtually all the key players were open to new thinking. While many U.S. leaders spoke for untrammeled free trade, voices within and outside the U.S. government favored modifying free-trade rules in light of Brazil's economic and political needs. Brazilian businessmen insisted that they were overtaxed, but they also understood that better schools were essential for sustained growth and believed that education was the responsibility of government. The PT emphasized its own short-term interests in the horse-trading fashion of democratic politicking, but sympathizers in the PT as well as in other parties wanted policy change, and many activists at the grassroots level began mobilizing in campaigns for agrarian reform, new economic approaches, and urban development. In this context, rather than seizing the reformist initiative, the Lula administration proceeded slowly, appearing to be mired in the status quo and exhibiting a surprising lack of new ideas.

Caution behooves any leftist party on a continent where popular mobilizations and calls for social justice in the 1960s and 1970s were met with

U.S.-supported military coups, torture, and killing. This history is always in the minds of today's Latin American leaders, many of whom survived the dictatorships. But the differences today are clear. Almost all current leftist players accept electoral rules and market principles, which was by no means the case in Latin America forty years ago, when communists and socialists sought equality and an end to capitalism through elections or armed revolution. Today much of the private sector in Latin America recognizes the insufficiency of neoliberal economic policy and the dire need for a well-educated workforce with a decent standard of living. And today there is no Cold War to obscure the difference between serious reform and communist takeover of the state.

Still, there are similarities. Like the Cold War, the war on terror encourages the equating of dissent with evil, and experimentation with instability. If Brazilian politics becomes more contentious, U.S. leaders may liken Brazil inappropriately to Venezuela, where populist President Hugo Chávez combines redistributive policies with antidemocratic sentiment and anti-Americanism.[37] Allegations about terrorist cells in the Iguassú Falls region of Brazil could be elevated to national-security threats, thus drawing Brazil into the emerging international-security framework. Private sectors have long been wary when ordinary people, especially poor people, enter the political scene in ways that challenge conventional norms. If popular protests—one of the few means available to press Lula toward reform—became bigger and more spirited, the Brazilian private sector might well scream instability, corruption, and terrorism as a means of forestalling change, and they would likely find a receptive audience in Washington.

Latin American efforts for socioeconomic change in the 1950s and 1960s used the languages of democracy and reform. Guatemala's democratically elected, leftist President Jacobo Arbenz sought land reform and labor rights, in the 1950s, through democratic institutions, as did Salvador Allende in Chile two decades later. Both efforts were met with U.S.-supported military coups and long periods of brutal government repression. Guerrilla movements arose in Central America only after state and paramilitary violence, justified in the name of anticommunism, became routine across the region. In 1968, in Mexico, students demonstrated for transparent government, autonomous universities, and an end to police violence (much as the Popular Assembly of Oaxacan Pueblos, or APPO, did in Oaxaca in 2006), and reformers in the countryside wanted

clean elections and honest development policies. It was only after government troops slaughtered hundreds of peaceful protesters in the Plaza of
Three Cultures at Tlatelolco that Mexican activists formed clandestine revolutionary networks and cities and countryside began to explode in radical
protest and guerrilla violence.

The period of democratic reformism in Latin America in the 1960s
has strangely returned, almost as if we—Latin Americans and the United
States alike—have been given a second chance, at the beginning of the
twenty-first century, to correct one of the enduring harms of the twentieth
century: the failure of economic development and democratic politics to
create decent lives for the global poor. The stakes this time are perhaps
even higher than they were before; in the post-9/11 world, it remains clear
that grinding poverty and cultural humiliation provide fertile ground for
violent extremism. In such an auspicious moment, what does it take to
bring moderation, openness, and imagination to the fore?

The Failure to Enact Meaningful Reform

Several factors appear to explain the failure of the Lula administration to
enact meaningful socioeconomic reform, from the constraints of the global
economy to the structure of Brazilian domestic politics. Economic pressures loom largest. The moment Brazil is deemed risky, its currency loses
value and foreign investment plummets. This occurred when Lula surged in
the polls before the 2002 elections; within three months, the Brazilian real
lost a third of its value against the dollar. Today, when New York bankers
respond to Lula's proposals with stern warnings, their words threaten real
economic havoc in Brazil. From this perspective, opposition on the part
of international financial institutions precludes innovative policymaking
in Brazil, even if innovations are economically sound, follow market principles, and promise political inclusion. Thus, redirecting debt repayment to
massive investment in education, so as to foster equality and strengthen the
capacities of Brazil's workers, would be deemed heretical by global financial powers, as would taxing speculative investment to fund land reform.

Domestic political factors severely limit reform as well. The electoral
system in Brazil is structured so as to favor weak parties and unaccount-
able representatives. Open-list proportional representation means that candidates gain office not because of the way they are ranked by their party,
which would favor party discipline and increase the likelihood of reform

coalitions, but by the number of votes they receive as individuals—which leads politicians to seek, above all else, access to government resources for their constituents. In addition, national party leaders have little control over candidate selection, politicians can change parties at will, and rural areas, where political clientelism and machine politics predominate, are over-represented in Congress.[38] In this context Lula has had to govern without a congressional majority, forcing him to make agreements with opposition parties that limit his ability to proceed with reform and probably legitimizing congressional payoffs in the eyes of some PT legislators.[39]

At the level of policy, Brazil's military and civilian elites over the past half-century have been more willing than their counterparts elsewhere to accept limited reforms in areas such as social security, healthcare, and cash transfers, but they have acted forcefully to prevent the deepening of those reforms in ways that might challenge elite privilege.[40] Leftist critics of the PT argue that the party had been on a path toward acceptance of the economic status quo for a decade and that it made fundamental compromises in order to win the 2002 elections.[41] Others add that those closest to Lula placed little value on participatory democracy and promoted centralized decision-making processes in the party and the administration alike.[42] PT leaders' acceptance of conventional strategies for gaining and holding national power, including distribution of large numbers of government jobs and management of pension funds, is invoked to explain their embrace not only of orthodox economics but of corrupt political practices as well. From this domestic perspective, institutional and party structures made successful reform unlikely.

These are compelling explanations. Yet Brazil right now exhibits a puzzling paradox. Lula's presidency represents the culmination of the greatest leftist success in challenging and transforming the status quo in Brazil since the late 1970s. Twenty years ago, many of the country's present achievements would have been unthinkable: Lula's assumption of office, the widespread legitimacy of the MST, participatory democracy in budgeting in scores of Brazilian cities, and Brazil's leading role in global trade negotiations. In the course of two decades of democracy and grassroots activism the Brazilian left and Brazilian civil society have transformed the realm of the possible in Brazilian politics. Why, then, when a leftist committed to social change assumes the presidency, does it suddenly appear self-evident that reform can go no further, that economic and institutional constraints are immutable? Such a position ignores the possibility of political challenge to structural constraints in the form of executive and party leadership at the national level and of mobilization at the grassroots.

Progressive reform in Brazil under Lula, though deeply constrained by domestic politics and the international economy, has faced a further and arguably more significant limit: lack of political vision and imagination. Few people or institutions in positions of power—including those who by interest or inclination might sympathize with claims for social justice or political inclusion—have been able to envision new relationships between economics and politics at the national level, new ideas about how economies might run, or alternative formulations of global rules, along with political strategies for achieving these. Similarly, it appears that PT leaders, despite the innovation they have initiated or observed at the level of social movements and municipal government, have little conception of what a *national government* might say or do to exercise power in new ways to further equality and inclusion.

A series of wide-ranging interviews with prominent PT activists and intellectuals carried out by the British journalist Hilary Wainwright in the summer of 2005 revealed again and again the absence of discussion of alternatives within the party and government.[43] Furthermore, when individual proposals concerning participatory democracy or land reform were brought to the attention of government leaders, the proposals were dismissed.[44] Without such discussion and imaginative policymaking, however, economic orthodoxy and political corruption appear inevitable and even legitimate. Wainwright's interviews illustrate the cultural component of hegemony, manifested in the perceived absence of "realistic" alternatives and reluctance to press for debate or policy change. Both within and outside the PT, support or tolerance for neoliberalism did not arise from imposition or map directly onto economic interest. Rather, a set of representations of the world and ideas about how it works influenced thinking about what is possible in economics and politics across the geographic and political spectrum. The Brazilian sociologist Francisco de Oliveira observed the colonizing capacity of the state, arguing that "rather than the seizure of the state apparatus by the party, what took place was the seizure of the party by the state."[45] In this view, the force of bureaucratic processes and worldview overran progressive commitments and imagination.

Democracy and markets alike are conceptualized in the narrowest terms to mean existing formal political procedures and economic rules of the game. For example, the IMF requires a 3.75 percent budget surplus not because that is what is required to pay the interest on Brazil's debt—indeed, it is insufficient—but because the IMF has decided that 3.75 percent denotes credit-worthiness. With another, equally market-based, perspective, the IMF might decide that a 2 percent budget surplus, along with investment in education, infrastructure, and land reform, was an even better indication of Brazil's credit-worthiness, because of the prospects for future economic growth and democratic inclusion such investment would generate. Thus there is nothing economically "necessary" about the enormous revenue withheld from productive investment in social welfare or infrastructure. But how many people know or can imagine that IMF guidelines, which make or break economies and political reforms with devastating force, are in part constructed and legitimated through belief and myth?

Social movements, NGOS, scholars, and local governments have long put forth new economic and political ideas, many of them publicized in arenas such as the World Social Forum. What is striking about many of these ideas is their practicality. Alternative forms of decision making, production, and distribution function in many places in Brazil and Latin America. To speak of multiple democracies and markets is not to invoke utopias, but rather working experiments. A cultural battle must be fought to make these experiments "real" and "natural," just as the transformed political landscape in Brazil is now taken for granted, and to extend experimentation, imaginatively, to the national level. In this battle cultural arguments, agents, and imaginaries play a central role. Just as the PT so effectively linked social movements to formal politics—bringing together the streets and the institutions—the PT and others need to connect this existing, practical world of out-of-the-box thinking to national and international politics.

The Corruption

Given the corruption scandals of 2004–2006, however, this is not likely to occur.[46] What is now the "myth" of PT honesty and transparency was widely accepted for twenty years, and virtually anyone who supported the PT or hoped it might carry out significant reform feels betrayed. In the course of the congressional investigations that have riveted Brazilians' attention Lula's chief of staff resigned, as did the head of the PT and the secretary of the treasury. Numerous legislators from parties in the PT coalition also resigned or were expelled. Lula has claimed throughout that he was unaware of the payment schemes, and so far there has been no evidence implicating him directly, but for many the idea of Lula's ignorance of these matters strains credulity.[47] Opponents of the PT who might have negotiated reformist bargains under pressure now see clear alternatives, in the form of a centrist and economically orthodox PT or the return of other centrist parties to power in future elections. And a great disenchantment with institutional politics can be felt across the country.

It is too early to characterize and explain the corruption in the PT if one doesn't fall back on either "all politics is corrupt" or "the inexorable weight of Latin American clientelism" as catchall explanations. There is little evidence about how widespread these practices have been or how they have evolved over time. Did forms of corruption involve primarily the São Paulo wing of the party, linked more to union bureaucracies than social movements, or were they prevalent throughout the party's internal groups and geographic diversity? Were kickbacks, illegal campaign financing, and congressional-vote buying the self-interested or perhaps strategic decisions of high-ranking national officials, separate from state and regional party officials and grassroots activists, or did they replicate practices common at the municipal and state level? To what extent were forms of payoff and patronage always a component of the PT's unprecedented ability to maintain numerous internal factions within one relatively democratic leftist party? And how have the balances among different kinds of internal political practices changed over time in the PT's twenty-five-year history?[48]

Most analysis of PT corruption focuses on its turn to the center some years before the 2002 presidential elections in a strategic move to win the presidency. This turn culminated in the recasting of Lula's image, alliance with a conservative party in the elections, the designation of a conservative businessman for the vice-presidential slot, and bargaining for congressional support for moderate social-security and tax reforms. Together, these are seen as evidence of a willingness to engage in any and all practices, from neoliberalism to corruption, for the sake of power. There is obvious slippage in this explanation, because it assumes that a political calculation to gain votes and win office by appealing to centrist voters, and then to govern pragmatically within perceived constraints, must correspond to the abandonment of ethical principles concerning electoral competition, business-government relations, and congressional politics. Such a conclusion is appealing to many in the PT who reject Lula's adherence to the neoliberal status quo; but even if true, in this case the explanation must be part of a more complex picture involving the historical mixtures of corruption, transparency, accountability, and political imagination within the PT.

What's at Stake?

Over the past twenty years, as participation in local movements and associations has grown and deepened worldwide, the concept of civil society has played a key role in theorizing about globalization and democracy.[49] Academics, policymakers, and politicians argue that a rich associational life in developing countries will provide the creative energy for free-market innovation and the civic skills essential for democratic government. Brazil puts this theorizing to the test. If a highly developed civil society like Brazil's cannot produce greater economic well-being through democracy, then there is no obvious underpinning for a better future along the lines envisioned in the West. Those who care passionately about hunger and poverty, violence and drug trafficking, and the juxtaposition of extreme wealth with extreme misery will look to other models.[50]

In nineteenth-century Latin America, as liberalism triumphed over conservative political philosophies, Indians, blacks, women, and workers were accorded few rights, and the minimal claims they could make depended on their conforming to subordinate social roles.[51] In the first half of the twentieth century subordinated people captured the spotlight through dramatic confrontations and reversals: when Mexican peasants fought for land and liberty in the century's first revolution; when Argentine workers marched from Buenos Aires's periphery to its exclusive center in support of Juan and Eva Perón; or when formerly disparaged Brazilian blacks took cultural center stage in samba and carnival.[52] From the 1930s to the 1960s, populist and revolutionary leaders recognized those formerly excluded groups—rhetorically and at times in practice—as deserving of well-being and inclusion. These groups did not, however, gain the rights of democratic citizenship.

In a curious reversal the transitions to democracy in Latin America in the 1980s offered precisely the democratic rights that had been lacking, but recognized no claims to economic well-being or inclusion. In this "second coming" of the people, democracy has taken shape in the framework of neoliberal globalization, which insists that sovereign citizens will sink or swim on the tides of free markets. Something has been lost along the way: the notion that all people have a legitimate claim to a materially decent life.

In this context, there has been a widespread failure to identify and articulate what is at stake in Brazil, to read from Brasilia both inward, to the favelas and the daily lives of tens of millions of desperately poor Brazilians, and outward, to the potential of democracy in the new age of empire and "war on terror." Pressing the boundaries of the possible today in Brazil requires transforming the unprecedented dialogues between people like Gessí Bonês and the bankers, favela activists and the police, MST settlements and local governments, and Porto Alegre squatters and the courts into meaningful national policy. So far, the alliances and the apparent governability established by Lula's administration to address the complexities of Brazilian society and its particular democratic politics have come at a high price: the loss of the excitement that social movements promote and a general disenchantment with politics. In contrast, the past successes of the PT in local governance and of the MST's land occupations, which stimulated broad networks of activism, derived from their ability to animate and enchant, even as they improved material conditions. Were Lula to reinvigorate policymaking with the spirit and participation of social movements, he might rescue the innovative and experimental aspects of Brazilian democracy, those most capable of bringing new cultural understandings and transforming the politics of the possible.

Notes

1. In the second round of voting Lula defeated the centrist candidate Geraldo Alckmin, 61 percent to 39 percent.
2. Gessí Bonês, personal interview, August 2003.
3. Hakim, "The Reluctant Partner"; Hunter and Power, "Lula's Brazil at Midterm."
4. For analysis of Brazil's party system, see Mainwaring, *Rethinking Party Systems in the Third Wave of Democratization.*
5. *Concepção e Diretrizes do Programa do Governo do PT para o Brasil.* This program was adopted at the PT National Party Congress, Olinda, Pernambuco, December 2001.
6. On the defenses of Brazilian elites—including the use of law, police, security forces, and violence to uphold elite privilege—see Caldeira, "Fortified Enclaves," 303–28; Caldeira and Holston, "Democracy and Violence in Brazil"; Payne, *Uncivil Movements.*

7. Keck, *The Workers Party and Democratization in Brazil*.

8. Avritzer, *Democracy and the Public Space in Latin America*, chap. 6.

9. Samuels, "Fiscal Straightjacket."

10. For beliefs about poverty and inequality among Brazilian elites, see Reis, "Perceptions of Poverty and Inequality among Brazilian Elites." For progressive business approaches to corporate responsibility in Brazil, see Instituto Ethos, http://www.ethos.org.br/. On private-sector beliefs about neoliberal reform, see Kingstone, *Crafting Coalitions for Reform*.

11. Dagnino, *Sociedade civil e espaços públicos no Brasil*.

12. Joanna Chung and Jonathan Wheatley, "Global Bond Is a Buoy for Brazil," *Financial Times* (London), 22 September 2005.

13. There is a rich literature on participatory budgeting in Porto Alegre and other Brazilian cities, including Santos, "Participatory Budgeting in Porto Alegre"; Abers, *Inventing Local Democracy*; Arvitzer and Navarro, *A inovação democrática no Brasil*; Baiocchi, *Militants and Citizens*.

14. Dilecta Todoschini, personal interview, May 2002.

15. Business executive, personal interview, March 2002.

16. Anonymous, personal interview, April 2002. In October 2004 the PT lost municipal elections in Porto Alegre after sixteen years in office. The winning center-right coalition has modified many aspects of the participatory-budgeting process and changed the names of many of its institutions and procedures.

17. Stephen, *Women and Social Movements in Latin America*: Part 3; van der Schaaf, *Jeito de Mulher Rural*.

18. de Jesus, *Child of the Dark*, 17.

19. Perlman, *Marginality from Myth to Reality*.

20. Governor Rosinha Matheus vetoed the plan, stating that it "would be a form of discrimination against good citizens who make up the vast majority of these communities" (Larry Rohter, "Brazil: Governor Vetoes Wall around Rio Slums," *New York Times*, 22 June 2005).

21. Gomes da Cunha, "Black Movements and the 'Politics of Identity'"; Yudice, *The Expediency of Culture*, chap. 4.

22. For an overview of the MST, see Fernandes, *MST*; Hammond, "Law and Disorder"; Navarro, "Mobilização sem emancipação"; Wright and Wolford, *To Inherit the Earth*; Wolford, "'Every Monkey Has Its Own Head.'"

23. Zander Navarro suggests looking at the issue of land reform regionally, though he believes that broad-based land reform no longer makes sense from an economic perspective ("O Brasil precisa da reforma agrária?").

24. In 2003 Plínio de Arruda Sampaio, a prominent land-reform expert and PT member, put together a land-reform proposal at the request of Lula's minister of agrarian reform, Miguel Rossetto. Sampaio produced a plan that he felt would "get enough people on the land to cause a rupture, not a total rupture,

but enough to start off a process" (Branford, "The Lula Government and Agrarian Reform," 57). Sampaio's plan would have settled a million families in three years and altered the Gini coefficient for land concentration by at least 10 percent. The plan, which Sampaio argued was both politically and economically feasible, was opposed by groups within the Ministry of Agrarian Reform and shelved by Rossetto, who told Sampaio that "we don't have the money" and that "we haven't the technical expertise" (ibid., 58).

25. In a three-year pilot program that began in 2005 the IMF agreed to permit $1 billion of the required 3.75 percent budget surplus to be spent for infrastructural investment. This amounts to a very small proportion—less than 4 percent—of the surplus. See Julie Ziegler, "Brazil Gets IMF Nod to Study Easing Budget Accounting Rules," *Bloomberg.com*, 25 April 2004, http://www .bloomberg.com/; Milani, "Brazil Cheers IMF Approval of Brazilian Pilot Plan."

26. Carta Capital, "O país é maior que sua elite."

27. For the details of Cardoso's efforts to insure balanced and transparent state budgets, see Samuels, "Fiscal Straightjacket." Jorge Domínguez underscored the democratic character of this process in his comments on Samuels's work in a presentation at the David Rockefeller Center for Latin American Studies at Harvard University, 22 October 2002.

28. Ambassador Donna Hrinak, personal interview, March 2004.

29. Tina Rosenberg, "Look at Brazil."

30. Cariello and Cardoso, "Para bancos, nota do PT desgasta governo."

31. Ibid.

32. Vieira da Cunha, "Brazil."

33. Brazil's 2.6 percent average rate of growth during Lula's first term, while steady, was only half that of the rest of Latin America.

34. In November 2005 the debate about economic policy flared publicly in sharp exchanges between Lula's then new chief of staff, Dilma Roussef, who favored change, and Finance Minister Antonio Palocci, whose orthodox policies had won widespread support from Brazilian elites and international financial institutions. After failing to win the 2006 elections in the first round, Lula began to speak once again about a more progressive economic policy. However, following his landslide second-round victory, when top officials like Rousseff and Minister of Institutional Relations Tarso Genro suggested, in Genro's words, that "the Palocci era has ended" (Santos, "Lula e a esquerda"), Lula quickly defended former minister Palocci, announced that central bank president Henrique Meirelles would continue in his post, and stated that there would be no shift away from orthodox economic policies of the past four years (Oliveira, "Lula in the Labyrinth," 7, 10).

35. Bearak, "Poor Man's Burden," 59.

36. Ricci, *Lulismo*; Hilary Wainwright, "Lula's Lament," *Red Pepper*, October 2005, http://www.redpepper.org.uk/.

37. For a more positive interpretation of Chávez's politics and its significance, see Ellner, "The Hugo Chávez Phenomenon," in this volume.

38. On the broad array of political characteristics that shape democratic institutions in Brazil and make reform coalitions difficult, see Lamounier and Meneguello, *Partidos políticos e consolidação democrática*; Mainwaring, *Rethinking Party Systems in the Third Wave of Democratization*; Power, *The Political Right in Postauthoritarian Brazil*; Ames, *The Deadlock of Democracy in Brazil*.

39. Fleischer, "The Politics of the Lula PT-led Coalition."

40. Hunter, "Democracy and Social Policy in Brazil."

41. Ricci, *Lulismo*.

42. Wainwright and Branford, *In the Eye of the Storm*, 35–36.

43. Ibid.

44. On Sampaio's experiences regarding agrarian reform, see Branford, "The Lula Government and Agrarian Reform," 56–58. On the experiences of Ubiritan dos Santos, one of the architects of participatory budgeting in Porto Alegre, Félix Sanchez, the coordinator of participatory-budgeting efforts in São Paulo, and Sergio Baierle, the head of the NGO Cidade in Porto Alegre, when they attempted to bring proposals regarding participatory budgeting to the attention of the Lula administration, see Wainright and Branford, *In the Eye of the Storm*, 7. For an account of the absence of participatory-budgeting processes at the national level by Olivio Dutra, who instituted the process in Porto Alegre as mayor and in Rio Grande do Sul as governor, see Wainwright and Branford, *In the Eye of the Storm*, 36. For the views of Roberto Gomes, a PT activist from the state of Ceara, see Wainwright and Branford, *In the Eye of the Storm*, 37.

45. Oliveira, "Lula in the Labyrinth," 17.

46. As of this writing (February 2007), it is clear that legislators in parties allied with the PT were paid $12,000 per month for their support in congress and that the highest PT officials in the government, including José Dirceu, Lula's chief of staff and a key organizer of his presidential campaign, were actively involved in or aware of these payments. It also appears that substantial illegal contributions to Lula's presidential campaign were made by individuals and businesses, some of them doing or hoping to do government work, and that these monies were illicitly deposited in offshore accounts. Finally, in September 2006, just before the presidential elections, PT operatives were discovered with close to $800,000 in cash, allegedly to buy dossiers they believed would discredit the presidential candidate Geraldo Alckmin and the gubernatorial (and former presidential) candidate José Serra.

47. Antonio Palocci, who maintains widespread private-sector support as Lula's orthodox finance minister, remained largely untouched by the scandal through the summer of 2005, but subsequently came under intense scrutiny and resigned.

48. Jonathan Fox emphasizes the importance of examining trajectories of voice and accountability over time to assess the degree of internal democracy in political parties and grassroots organizations. However, there has been very little research on the "anthropology of democracy" within the Workers Party, including the ways in which the party's internal practices have reflected the broader power relations of Brazilian society and how internal PT practices have varied at particular moments and over time (see Paley, "Toward an Anthropology of Democracy"). Two notable exceptions are Zander Navarro ("O 'Orçamento Participativo' de Porto Alegre") and Sergio Baierle ("The Porto Alegre Thermidor"), both of whom have argued that party patronage played a significant and negative role in participatory budgeting in Porto Alegre.

49. Cohen and Arato, *Civil Society and Political Theory*; Dagnino, *Sociedade civil e espaços públicos no Brasil*; Edwards, *Civil Society*.

50. In the absence of reform under Lula, for example, the anti-institutional stance of the MST will likely gain more adherents. Commenting on what he calls "institutional" and "parliamentary" forms of power, MST leader Gilmar Maruo explained, "I'm not saying that participation in elections is wrong. I'm not saying that we should ignore elections. But I think the question of building a popular power, *a duality of power in Brazil*, on the basis of organizational processes, such as popular councils, militant cells, is a very important part of a strategy for accumulating force" (Wainwright and Branford, *In the Eye of the Storm*, 36, emphasis added).

51. Grandin, *The Blood of Guatemala*; Hunefeldt, *Liberalism in the Bedroom*.

52. Womack, *Zapata and the Mexican Revolution*; James, *Resistance and Integration*; Vianna, *The Mystery of Samba*.

DANIEL A. CIEZA

8   **FROM MENEM TO KIRCHNER**

National Autonomy and Social Movements in Argentina

In 2001, in the midst of a serious economic, social, and political crisis, Argentina's provisional president, Adolfo Rodríguez Saa, announced one of the largest debt defaults in history. The default led international financial institutions (IFIs) to elevate Argentina to higher-than-ever levels of country risk, complicating the efforts of a series of Argentine governments to finance their way out of the deepening crisis.

Four years later, under the presidency of Néstor Kirchner, Argentina's fifth president in just over three years, the country maneuvered out of its default position in a manner that caused it to become a "bad example" for the IFIs, particularly the International Monetary Fund (IMF). In a short time, Argentina was able to improve its gross domestic product (GDP) and monetary reserves significantly while disregarding the criteria the IMF attempted to impose.

Just before the crisis hit, the Argentine economy had been widely praised by the IFIs as an exemplary model of the neoliberal structural adjustment advocated by the Washington Consensus. And beyond the technical economics, throughout the 1990s the government of Carlos Menem had made a show of its intimate relationship with the United States, which made the transformation of economic policy all the more dramatic. Between the presidencies of Menem and Kirchner, Argentina moved from closely aligning itself with the United States and enthusiastically obeying the IMF's instructions to searching for creative and autonomous alternatives within a new South American context.

This change in the political and economic scene has been driven by a nationalist sector of the Peronist movement and is supported by the social movements that emerged from the fragmented and dispersed forms of resistance to the neoliberal model. This political and economic transformation has been criticized by other political sectors, ranging from the Right, through the liberal Center, and including large parts of the traditional Left.[1]

This new course is not free of contradictions. While President Kirchner maintained a high level of unity and a positive image throughout his term in office, as reflected by the polls, the legislative elections of 2005, and by the election of his wife, Cristina Fernández de Kirchner, to succeed him in 2007, his popularity hasn't been translated into stable forms of political organization to accompany and strengthen the process. The limitations and ambiguities imposed by Peronism, the broad political grouping to which President Kirchner and most of the country's governors belong, have persisted.

A unique, progressive style of "Caesarism" has emerged, aligned with the new Latin American political movements, but with very peculiar characteristics.[2] In order to understand it, one must return to the structural changes of the 1990s and remember some aspects of Peronism, a difficult phenomenon to categorize in the academic world.

Structural Changes

Argentina began the 1990s with low levels of unemployment, relative social equality, and an average annual GDP growth rate of around 3 percent. It finished the decade as a society in crisis.[3] After a long period of historically low unemployment rates, Argentina entered a deep economic depression in 1998, reaching an open unemployment rate of 22 percent in 2001–2002, the highest in Latin America. The new joblessness was accompanied by strong social polarization and increases in all measures of inequality. All this began under the rule of Menem and remained the same or in some cases even worsened under the mandate of Fernando de la Rúa of the center-left coalition (called the Alliance) of the Radical Civic Union (UCR) and the Solidary Country Front (FREPASO). The changes occurred to a large degree because of the meticulous application of the neoliberal adjustment policies imposed by the IFIS.

The neoliberal policies applied in Argentina had already become familiar throughout the continent: an opening to private investment, the privatization of public-utility companies, economic deregulation, a decentralization of the state, and more "flexible" labor policies. This program was applied during Menem's two terms in office (1989–99), without compensations or palliative measures. Despite the fact that Menem promised a "productive revolution" during his 1989 campaign for the presidency—after "market forces" revolted against Raúl Alfonsín's UCR government—no such revolution took place. Menem's electoral discourse adopted the historical slogans of Peronism ("economic independence, political sovereignty, and social justice"), but the government went in exactly the opposite direction, as revealed by some of its most important measures.

The Convertibility Law and Economic Opening

The structural adjustments were preceded by a macroeconomic policy of "stabilization," anchored by the 1991 Convertibility Law that legally established parity between the Argentine peso and the U.S. dollar. This model, while eliminating the hyperinflation that characterized the last years of Alfonsín's government (1988–89) and the first stage of Menem's rule (1989–91), was lethal for the local economy because it made the dollar too cheap in relation to the peso. This situation, together with economic openings (lowered tariffs and elimination of controls), allowed for a devastating influx of foreign imports, which ruined small and medium-sized companies that could not compete, and destroyed the remains of the "national bourgeoisie."[4] A process of deindustrialization ensued, during which it became more feasible to import manufactured products from emerging Asian countries than to manufacture them locally.

The Privatization of Strategic Areas

Another neoliberal strategy was to privatize virtually all the public companies that had been nationalized during the classic Peronist period (1946–55). National companies in charge of mail, telephone, electricity, gas, water, oil, and aviation services were privatized, and the main beneficiaries were Spanish firms (Telefónica, Repsol, Iberia) and French firms (Telecom, Grupo Suez), with the participation of Chilean companies, especially in electric and gas services.

The privatization process was not transparent, but rather was rife with corruption. It was preceded by a strong publicity campaign that created consent among the majority of the population and was applied swiftly and deeply in the mid-1990s. Between 1993 and 1996, dozens of public companies were transferred to private hands.[5] The privatization of oil, electric energy, and gas created serious restrictions on the nation's autonomy.

Economic Deregulation

Another characteristic of the neoliberal period was the elimination or reduction of regulatory and control organizations that had been established after the dramatic crisis of 1930. The national grains and meats boards were suppressed, and the operative capacity of sanitary-control agencies was reduced, as was that of customs operations, despite an increase in imports.

Deregulation included the financial sector. International investors, especially speculative portfolio investors, found excellent opportunities for short-term businesses with high returns. The presence of speculative capital reinforced the creation of an investment "bubble." No controls or limits were placed on the Argentine business sector's capital flight or the multinationals' repatriation of profits.

State Decentralization

Following recommendations of the World Bank and the IMF, a variety of national governmental social functions were decentralized and delegated to the provinces. Education, health, and social assistance were decentralized. As a consequence, there was a reduction in social spending as well as a weakening of the national government and an increase in clientelism through local powers.

This disintegration of national public policies strengthened the power of local leaders (governors and mayors) and had medium-term consequences. Municipalities took on the responsibility for social programs, to the detriment of strategic planning, monitoring, and follow-up by centralized organizations.

"Flexible" Labor Policies and the Privatization of Social Security

Finally, a series of laws and decrees were passed that eliminated the supposed "rigidity" of labor legislation. The first step was the National Employment Law, which introduced "flexible contracts" for a determined period of time, some with reduced social-security benefits. The second step was the modification of work-related accident regulations, reducing costs for business owners. The third step was the modification of the traditional Work Contract Law, introducing a trial period of new, flexible contracts and differential regulations for small and medium-sized companies.

The provisional reform of the 1990s consisted of the introduction of a mixed, public-private retirement system. A reduction in employer contributions was established, as well as the transfer of large amounts of money to pension-fund managers, both for those who opted for this system and for those who did not make any decision. Pension funds were invested in financial markets and managed by private companies in the new capitalization system, which was particularly insecure. The transfer of moneys due to the privatization of the retirement system caused an approximately $2 billion annual loss of contributions to the national treasury, which had guaranteed the accounts. The public debt necessarily increased, in order to replace the loss of income.

Consequences of Neoliberal Policies and Adjustments

Despite the fact that inflation was controlled and significant growth took place between 1991 and 1994, the weakening of social protections combined with the international uncertainties provoked by the Mexican financial crisis and subsequent "tequila effect" caused Argentina to enter into a crisis that worsened and eventually, in 2001–2002, reached disastrous proportions.

The country suffered through the weakening of the national state, the bankruptcy of the productive apparatus, an agricultural crisis, the transfer of major parts of the economy into foreign hands, and the weakening of labor and social legislation. Furthermore, in addition to the somewhat positive consequence of a weakened military, the neoliberal restructuring led to the creation of a new political culture.

The Weakening of the State

In the 1990s the declining power of the public sector's regulatory and prosecutory functions created an "absent state." Corruption became more widespread; in particular, an illegal circuit sprang up around the massive number of imports ("parallel" customs, etc.). Public salaries and new appointments were frozen.

The decline in public health was notable; education became segmented due to the growth in private schools; and the fiscal role of the state in labor and health issues practically disappeared. With the national government's capacity for strategic governing diminished, feudalism made a comeback, characterized by the appearance of caudillo-type provincial governments and a justice system that depended on local political powers and violated basic freedoms.[6]

Deindustrialization and the Bankruptcy of the Productive Apparatus

In the 1990s the "productive poles" of the developmental stage and the old industrial belt practically disappeared. The automobile industry entered into crisis, affecting cities such as Cordoba and Rosario. Greater Buenos Aires's thriving working-class metropolis transformed, developing three concentric rings in which poverty increased as one moved away from the center. Old textile, metal, leather, and automobile industries closed shop and in many cases their properties were taken over by large foreign department stores with a high percentage of imported products.[7]

The industrial crisis was already under way, but in the 1990s the number of establishments, real salaries, and national manufacturing all declined. A speculative economy surfaced, encouraging the importation of products from emerging Asian countries, and small productive workshops were replaced by commercial businesses.

The Agricultural Crisis

Under the Convertibility Law of 1991, the Argentine agricultural sector was no longer profitable, due to the cheap dollar. The result was that producers—especially small producers—went into massive debt and land became concentrated in fewer hands. Cattle were progressively sold off, and a great deal of land was left idle. Little by little, the unused lands fell into the hands of foreign companies, who created very profitable planting "pools."[8]

One result was the development of applied biotechnology, which among other things allowed for the expansion of soy cultivation to regions that had previously not been viable for agricultural use. This generated controversy around the environmental problems of transgenic monoculture and the deforestation practiced in order to extend agricultural areas.[9]

The Transfer of the Economy into Foreign Hands

Over the course of the 1990s, wealth was progressively concentrated in the hands of large foreign companies. Not only did foreign capital control privatized public utilities, but large food companies were also sold to foreign firms. Long-standing Argentine national companies—such as Bagley and Terrabusi (producers of crackers and cookies), Quilmes (beer), several warehouses, and oil companies such as Perez Companc—were transferred to foreign control.

A similar process occurred in the financial sector, as Argentine banks disappeared through consolidations and buy-outs. In agriculture, too, transfers to foreign hands were also seen, with wealthy North Americans and Europeans purchasing thousands of hectares of land in Patagonia and in the Pampas, including border zones and freshwater reservoirs, such as the marshes of Ibera. In general, the "national bourgeoisie" disappeared, and the local business class was reduced to small urban businesspeople, agricultural producers, and social enterprises, especially cooperatives.

Rising Unemployment, Poverty, and Job Insecurity

In the 1990s social indicators became increasingly negative. Open unemployment rose from 5 percent at the beginning of the decade to 22 percent in 2002. More than 50 percent of the population lived under the poverty line during the major crisis of 2001, and jobs became increasingly unstable. This unprecedented decline was linked to the serious worldwide labor crisis. Without effective unemployment benefits, many families—including large parts of the middle class—slipped into poverty.

Social inequalities also increased. The wealthiest 10 percent of the population acquired more economic power than ever before, and the poorest 20 percent fell into extreme poverty. Argentina, a country with relative equality in terms of income distribution until the mid-1970s, had by the end of the 1990s become an example of extremely unequal income distribution.[10]

Weakening of the Unions

The high levels of unemployment and instability diminished the bargaining capacities of the country's labor unions. Affected by the replacement of national production by imports, long-powerful unions—especially the important Argentine metal, mechanics, and textile unions—suffered many setbacks. At the same time, the number of strikes and protests were greatly reduced. Instead of classic union protests, informally organized blockades of national roads through pickets, or *piquetes*, came to be the primary method of struggle.

Weakening of the Military

During the 1990s, Argentine military power weakened. Until the 1980s, an industrial-military complex functioned through the state-run Administration of Military Manufacturing, which at one point had more than twenty different types of companies. This complex was dismantled and privatized, the military budget was reduced, and the military leadership was de-politicized and effectively subordinated to civilian power.

This allowed for a successful consolidation of democracy. The substantial economic power of the armed-forces leadership, which had previously allowed it to operate as an ally of big business, had effectively disappeared.[11] However, the dismantling of the military companies affected certain aspects of national industry, especially the manufacturing of ships, the production of some medicines, weapons production, shipyards, and blast furnaces. In addition, the development of the nuclear industry was put on hold.

Rapprochement with Empire

Menemism was inseparable from U.S. foreign policy. The "intimate relationship" promoted by Chancellor Guido Di Tella and his advisor Carlos Escudé, a politician with a Harvard degree, included an automatic alignment with the United States in all international forums and frequent communication between President Menem and U.S. national and state authorities. At the request of the United States, Argentina sent ships to the Persian Gulf in 1990, withdrew from the Non-Aligned Movement, signed non–nuclear-proliferation treaties, and consistently voted against Cuba in international assemblies.[12]

In this context the president of the Buenos Aires provincial legislature received many U.S. members of Congress in his office. Hundreds of thousands of Argentine tourists traveled to various U.S. cities without needing to obtain a visa. Menem had a privileged relationship with George H. W. Bush, was the first Latin American president to receive Bill Clinton, and comfortably played the role of regional leader when dealing with U.S. diplomats.

Various social programs completed the new framework, some financed by the World Bank and the IMF. These were programs targeted to deal with "social contention" and extreme poverty, replacing the concept of social rights in classic Peronism with programs of assistance and temporary employment.[13] The mayors or municipal authorities were responsible for carrying out these social programs and thus acquired growing powers. Throughout all this, the Argentine peso's artificially sustained equivalence to the U.S. dollar created the illusion that Argentina was (or, at least, was becoming) a First World country.

The New Social Movements

In the mid-1990s new forms of protest emerged in remote parts of the country, led by laid-off workers from the recently privatized national oil and gas companies. The most common tactic used by these groups of unemployed workers was the blocking of national and provincial roads.

Since the late nineteenth century, the backbone of popular resistance to the dominant politics of Argentina had been the organized urban working class. After passing through a period of union anarchism and communism, Argentine workers mainly followed the Peronist movement and organized into large trade unions and confederations. The traditional methods of protest had been the general strike, the takeover of factories, and picketing in front of factories. The principal goals were better salaries and working conditions, though for more than twenty years, the call for the return of Juan Perón was linked to these struggles. A process of dissent from the bureaucratized union authorities emerged in the 1960s and 1970s, but was abruptly interrupted by the military coup of 1976, which cost the lives of thousands of union workers and delegates.

The structural reforms of neoliberal Argentina transformed the union structure and the organized working class. Most remarkable was the disappearance of the general strike under Menem. There had been an average of two general strikes per year throughout the twentieth century, and they had increased in number under the government of Alfonsín (the Peronist General Confederation of Labor called for thirteen general strikes during his rule). But with the neoliberal offensive, organized labor was weakened and new social actors emerged: the *piqueteros*, recently unemployed workers, and those who were systematically excluded from the productive sector as a result of deindustrialization. Women, many of whom had experience in the social organizations of the 1980s, predominated in piquetero groups.

Faced with the quiescence of union leaders and motivated by the pressures caused by unemployment, the piquetes—blockades of national roads as a form of pressure and protest—appeared in the mid-1990s. The first piquetes took place in remote areas of the country and were directly related to the layoffs caused by the privatization of Argentina's state oil company. Those layoffs had left hundreds of working families on the streets.

The piquetero movement presented both breaks and continuity with social-protest movements of the past; although it was a direct product of the country's new economic and social situation, many of its leaders had been involved in earlier movements. The movement now represents a wide range of political positions, a strong dependence on social-assistance programs, and a great mistrust of the political system, which paradoxically exercises political clientelism over participants through their dependence on a variety of social programs.

Faced with the bankruptcy of national companies and, in many cases, their abandonment by their owners, workers took control of many factories and maintained production. The recovery of bankrupt companies was thus led by the unions, by workers' delegate groups, and on occasion by municipal authorities. Toward the beginning of the 2000s, more than 300 cases of recovery were documented, but not all were able to continue.[14] Among the successful organizations were some graphic-arts workshops in Buenos Aires, a newspaper and a tractor factory in Cordoba, and warehouses in Mendoza.

The Alliance Experience

The triumph of the UCR-FREPASO Alliance, headed by Fernando de la Rúa and Carlos Álvarez, marked the end of Menem's rule and a heightening of the representative political system's crisis. During its first few months in office, because of its initial collection of progressive cabinet ministers, the alliance generated high expectations, but the experience of the alliance government was brief and tragic.

Despite its criticisms of Menem, the alliance did not abandon the Convertibility Law, and it remained obedient to the demands of the IMF. It was able to modify neither the economic nor the social aspects of the neoliberal model. The periodic missions of IMF representatives to monitor the refinancing of the foreign debt resulted in the imposition of laws strengthening the structures of labor flexibility and fiscal discipline. While the alliance was in power, social spending was reduced and the number of work-program beneficiaries was drastically diminished.

Danger signs appeared when the country defaulted on its national debt, but instead of trying out creative, energetic responses, the alliance government brought in Domingo Cavallo, another Harvard graduate and a former Menem minister, giving him extraordinary powers to implement orthodox measures. But the orthodox nature of transnational technocrats proved lethal.[15] The government's inability to confront the financial crisis, as well as a political confrontation with the Peronist Justicialist Party (PJ), precipitated a crisis.

Faced with capital flight and greater national risk, the Ministry of the Economy imposed bank-account restrictions in December 2001, including a banking *corralito* (freeze on assets) that impeded normal account withdrawals. These measures affected workers and employees who received their salaries through debit cards, but even more so the small and medium savers who had been depositing their layoff compensations in fixed-term dollar accounts.

The deepening crisis brought on the mobilization of the piqueteros. The main political slogan became *Que se vayan todos* (Get rid of them all). There were demonstrations not only against the legislators and the supreme-court justices who backed the banking corralito but also against the banks. The middle classes began to join the mobilizations.

The alliance government came to an end on the 19th and 20th of December 2001. On the first day, a mostly middle-class mobilization banging on their pots had a strong impact. On the second day, a march in Buenos Aires ended in a violent repression that left thirty-three people dead, and President de la Rúa decided to resign. He blamed his fall on the Buenos Aires "PJ apparatus."

On the resignation of de la Rúa, the PJ governor of San Luis, Adolfo Rodríguez Saa, was named provisional president. A week later, the government announced the debt default and committed itself to creating one million new jobs. Following an internal PJ struggle, Rodríguez Saa, in January 2002, was replaced by Senator Eduardo Duhalde, the former governor of the province of Buenos Aires. Duhalde led a transitional government that lasted a little more than a year.

The Duhalde government decided to abandon the Convertibility Law, thus devaluing the peso and converting bank deposits and debts into pesos. The cost of the dollar tripled from one to around three pesos.[16] This immediately improved growth possibilities for various sectors of the economy, especially manufacturing, agriculture, and construction. It also favored the tourist industry, as Argentina became a more economical option for international vacationers.

Kirchnerism: National Autonomy and Unexpected Development

The furor over the murder of two young piqueteros in June 2002 and the delayed economic recovery persuaded Duhalde to call for early presidential elections. As there were no other candidates with real possibilities within the PJ, Duhalde decided to back the governor of Santa Cruz, Néstor Kirchner, who was already campaigning. The other PJ candidates were former presidents Menem and Rodríguez Saa, both being allowed to proclaim their affiliation with the party in the first electoral round. In that first round, held in April, Menem took 24 percent of the vote, followed by Kirchner with 22 percent. When a number of independent polls showed that over 50 percent of all eligible voters "strongly disapproved" of Menem, the former president decided not to participate in the second electoral round. Kirchner thus began a four-year term of office on 25 May 2003.

Kirchner brought back the classic Peronist tradition of economic independence and applied an unorthodox development plan. The default declared by Rodríguez Saa and maintained by Duhalde allowed Kirchner to carry forward a growth model without having to follow the impositions and monitoring of the IMF.

During his four years in power, notable advances could be observed in economic growth, foreign-debt negotiation, and social control of privatized companies. This created a high level of public support for Kirchner, who, as he prepared to hand over the presidency to his wife, Cristina Fernández de Kirchner, elected in October 2007 to succeed him, continued to maintain almost a 60 percent approval rate among voters. In addition, according to all public-opinion polls, the population has continued to support President Kirchner's attitude of national independence.

Under Kirchner, Argentina's economic growth was unexpected, surpassing not only the predictions of international consulting firms but also those of the government itself. During Kirchner's first three years, Argentina's GDP grew at an annual rate of about 9 percent. Growth was particularly evident in industry, construction, tourism, and agricultural exports. Argentina accumulated large monetary reserves, and the fiscal surplus was more than sufficient to cover the government's commitments. Tax revenues also increased, and capital flight was contained. Some Argentine deposits in foreign banks returned to Argentina.

After successfully renegotiating the debt, the Argentine government blamed IMF officials for the failure of the model applied in Argentina in the 1990s and delayed the initiation of new negotiations. A group of politicians close to Kirchner evaluated the possibility of Argentina withdrawing from the IMF, while other groups proposed advance payments or medium-term agreements. In all of these scenarios, what Kirchner's government primarily sought to avoid was the permanent monitoring by IMF missions, which, it felt, affected national sovereignty.

The Argentine government also changed its relationship with the transnational companies that own the privatized utility companies. The government did not allow them to raise fees for water, electricity, or gas without making new investments. The Argentine mail service became public again, and a new energy company was created with the goal of slowly recovering the country's oil sovereignty. A small aviation company was also formed.

Néstor Kirchner's government had other successes as well. It was able to channel the acute social conflict that reached high levels in 2001–2002, and it has achieved international recognition for its human-rights initiatives. It also decriminalized social protests. While Menem's government had instructed federal prosecutors to apply the penal code to piquetero protesters, Kirchner's government instead attempted to create a dialogue with the piqueteros and to integrate part of the movement into the president's political project.

In order to channel the conflicts, Kirchner increased social spending and maintained the large employment program created by Duhalde. Even though the official program continued to subsidize the unemployed, it effectively reduced social protests. By mid-2005, piquetero mobilizations were limited to the Buenos Aires metropolitan area, and several groups had even decided to join the government. At the same time, the impact of popular assemblies and their slogan "Get rid of them all" was diluted when some traditional leftist groups tried to manipulate the assemblies and when the Kirchner phenomenon emerged, restructuring politics and creating new expectations among the middle class.

A New Type of Caesarism

With the consolidation of Kirchner's rule, Argentine politics underwent a complete turnaround. Domestically and internationally, Kirchner, who was active in combative Peronist movements of the 1970s, carried out a center-left program, which was supported by a group of Peronist leaders who had taken part in popular struggles as members of the "1970s generation." Kirchner also had the support of a part of the piquetero movement, as well as of FREPASO groups. He managed to gain this support without breaking agreements with local PJ leaders.

Internationally, he openly supported the left-of-center governments of Venezuela, Brazil, Uruguay, Chile, Bolivia, as well as the government of the Spanish leader José Luis Rodríguez Zapatero. In international forums he took an independent position on questions of U.S. power, as seen in his Organization of American States abstention on the issue of sanctions against Cuba. He was also publicly critical of the role of the IMF.

While it is very difficult to label the new movement, one could say that a Caesarist type of leadership—a leadership that places itself above the political parties and relates directly to the electorate—has emerged under the leadership of Néstor and Cristina Kirchner. At the peak of the crisis, Néstor Kirchner's strong personality melded with a power structure that allowed him to communicate directly with the people. Despite its negative implications, the Kirchners' leadership style clearly has progressive characteristics and has succeeded in establishing Argentine autonomy from the IMF, in promoting a national capitalism with social improvements, and in contributing to a South American bloc that can negotiate at the economic level with other nonhegemonic blocs, such as China and India. One is thus in the presence of a kind of "progressive Caesarism," of the type described three-quarters of a century ago by Antonio Gramsci in his *Notas sobre Maquiavelo, sobre la política y el Estado moderno.*

The midterm elections in October 2005, in which half the national deputies and a third of the federal senators were replaced, as were hundreds of legislative positions in the provinces, allowed for the first popular evaluation of the Néstor Kirchner administration's successes. The president's political program, represented in the Frente de la Victoria (Victory Front), garnered nearly 40 percent of the vote in the legislative elections of 2005—up from 22 percent in the first electoral round of 2003. The most significant triumph was the triumph of the future president, Cristina Fernández de Kirchner, in a senate race; she defeated the "invincible machinery" of Duhalde in the Province of Buenos Aires by 26 points.

In this context the relationship between Néstor Kirchner and the new social movements deserves special comment. One can say that a major division within the new social movements was created by the question of whether or not to identify with—and openly support—the first Kirchner government. (It is too early to tell how the presidency of Cristina Kirchner will get along with the movements.) Prestigious human-rights leaders such as Hebe de Bonafini of the Mothers of the Plaza de Mayo and Estela Carlotto from the Grandmothers of the Plaza de Mayo showed public support for Néstor Kirchner, as did many prominent piquetero leaders. Other social leaders linked with the traditional Left, however, harshly criticized his government and refused to support presidential proposals regarding IMF relations or debt negotiations.

Many Kirchner-supporting piqueteros joined the president's political alliance, Frente de la Victoria, and some successfully campaigned for office.[17] Indeed, by the end of his term of office, Kirchner had been able to incorporate several social-movement leaders into his government. By contrast, many anti-Kirchner piqueteros affiliated with leftist movements and parties that have little chance of coming to power.[18]

Conclusions

As always, the Argentine case is unorthodox. A recent essay by Adolfo Gilly discusses a rising radical populism in Latin America, which Gilly refers to as an "unidentified political subject"—a "political subject" that is very disturbing to the North American military.[19] At the same time, North American diplomacy oscillates as to how it defines Kirchner's rule and openly worries that it would consider Argentina's evolution toward Venezuelan *Chavismo* to be dangerous.

In a short time the Argentine government has gone from being the IMF's best student to being a relatively successful transgressor. Under Menem and de la Rúa, the IMF's and World Bank's directions were followed to the letter. Under Kirchner, Argentina is following its own path, with positive results so far. Beyond the positive macroeconomic numbers, Argentina has achieved a greater degree of independence from international economic organizations and a strong sense of national dignity.

These achievements attracted a number of Argentina's social leaders with anti-imperialist views to a position of support of—and, in some cases, incorporation into—Néstor Kirchner's government. Many of them saw this government as an instrument with which to achieve greater autonomy from the North American empire and to obtain historical demands that were suspended during the neoliberal period. This situation has created a conflict between the need to strengthen autonomous political organizations in order to deepen the long-term process and the government's desire to co-opt the social movements for immediate electoral purposes.

A stable, broad-based political organization to back the Kirchner project has not yet emerged.[20] Nor is there a well-defined opposition. The new political-institutional map shows a growing number of political groups allied with the successive Kirchner governments, mostly from the provinces, but the general environment is that of the "territorial" nature of politics and the strong political tensions within the PJ.

The social movements that support the Kirchners (human-rights and piquetero groups) are still very weak, and the various political sectors that back the government have not yet been able to consolidate their own political force. This explains, in part, why Néstor Kirchner renewed his electoral alliances with various PJ governors for the 2005 elections in order to defeat his opponents within the PJ, particularly the Buenos Aires political boss Eduardo Duhalde. By differentiating himself from the Buenos Aires caudillo, Kirchner has gained significant support from middle-class sectors.

A center-left political label, a certain dogmatic nationalism, a vertical methodology, an audacious pragmatism, and the search for support among the middle class appear to be some aspects of a very unorthodox program that is being carried out in Argentina. It is a type of "neopopulism" that has not yet been fully identified. It is a Caesarist phenomenon with many positive aspects, but it is difficult to understand and its future possibilities are complex. As Néstor Kirchner liked to repeat, "We are coming out of Hell." Just where the country is heading is not yet known, but the present is a lot better than the recent past.

Notes

1. For the traditional Left's attitude on new national-popular movements, see, for example, Laclau, *La razón populista*.
2. I have taken the concept of "progressive Caesarism" from Antonio Gramsci. See Gramsci, *Notas sobre Maquiavelo, sobre la política y el Estado moderno*.
3. In the mid-1960s the country's economic and social indicators were comparable to those of the less-developed Western European countries such as

Portugal, Greece, and Spain. By 2001–2002, however, a long period of decline was well under way, and Argentina fell far behind.

4. For a variety of interpretations of the decline of the national bourgeoisie, see *Realidad Económica* (Buenos Aires) 201 (2004), and especially Basualdo, "Burquesía nacional, capital extranjero y oligarquía pampeana"; and Schvarzer, "De nuevo sobre la burquesía nacional."

5. Rapoport, *Historia económica, política y social de la Argentina.*

6. Cieza, Crisis del mundo del trabajo y política de empleo.

7. Neffa, *Modos de regulación, regímemes de acumulación y crisis en la Argentina.*

8. Murmis, "El agro argentino."

9. Teubal, "Soja transgénica y crisis del modelo agro-alimentario argentino."

10. Rapoport, *Historia económica, política y social de la Argentina.*

11. Rouquié, *Argentina hoy.*

12. Rapoport, *Historia económica, política y social de la Argentina.*

13. Cieza, *Programas oficiales de empleo y capacitación en la Provincia de Buenos Aires.*

14. Sancha, "Recuperación de fuentes de trabajo."

15. Stiglitz, *El malestar en la globalización.*

16. Rodríguez Diez, *Devaluación y pesificación.*

17. The most visible case is that of Jorge Cevallos, director of emergencies in the Ministry of Social Development, but other cases of social militants with responsibilities in political and social areas of other organisms also exist.

18. These include Raúl Castel and Nina Peloso, leaders of the Independent Movement of Retired and Unemployed People, who ran for senator and deputy positions and won only 0.2 percent of the votes. The Trotskyist leaders Néstor Pitrola, of the Polo Obrero, and Gustavo Jiménez, of Teresa Vive, won 1.5 percent and 1.7 percent, respectively. The representative of the Popular Assemblies of the City of Buenos Aires, Margarita Meira, won 0.2 percent.

19. Gilly, "Populismo radical."

20. The Argentine government does not back centralized and organized political forces, such as the Partido de los Trabajadores (PT) in Brazil, the Bolivarian movement in Venezuela, the Socialist Party in Chile, or the Broad Front in Uruguay.

STEVE ELLNER

9 THE HUGO CHÁVEZ PHENOMENON

*Anti-imperialism from Above or Radical Democracy
from Below?*

The rapid unfolding in Venezuela of the three stages
of the Hugo Chávez presidency has generated con-
fusion regarding what, exactly, *Chavismo* stands for.
This difficulty is aggravated by the tendency among
both pro- and anti-Chávez observers to dwell on the
president's personality and discourse, rather than on
issues of substance such as the impact of concrete
policies on class and national interests.[1] An analysis
that distinguishes between the superficial and crucial aspects of Chavismo and evaluates its long-term
prospects is of particular importance because events
in Venezuela have implications that go far beyond its
borders. Indeed, the outcome of the Chávez experience
will undoubtedly influence the future of Latin America.
Chávez's prominent regional role is derived from his
widespread appeal to the general populace throughout
the continent, his diplomatic efforts to win over Latin
American governments to his bold initiatives, and the
emergence of an economic and political model that
neighboring nations may decide to imitate.

Furthermore, the Venezuelan case is crucial for understanding the current relations between nations of

the North and South and for assessing the feasibility of various forms of resistance by the latter in opposition to domination by the former. Throughout the Third World, these struggles have been propelled at two levels: from "above," by the state and political parties that seek to obtain and retain power; and from "below," by social movements and the unorganized sectors of the population. Confrontation from above centers on the assertion of sovereignty by Third World governments and consists of anti-imperialist policies and the strengthening of a bloc of Third World nations. It often leads to a "revolution of national liberation" in which a government bolstered by a well-institutionalized political party, a powerful labor movement, and sometimes a progressive national business sector plays a major role in the economy and clashes with foreign interests. Prior to the outset of globalization in the 1980s, nearly all those who supported far-reaching political change favored a statist strategy along these lines. Since then, however, globalization writers across the political spectrum have argued that a truly independent course of action on the part of Third World states is doomed to failure.

A second arena of resistance involves movements that are horizontally connected, internally democratic, and more loosely structured than political parties and the state. "Postmodern" writers who support the primacy of popular movements in effecting social change rule out government assertion of independence by force as unfeasible due to global constraints and the danger of international isolation. They also consider statist strategies to be hierarchical by nature and thus to possess only limited potential to effect meaningful and far-reaching change.[2] Advocates of the confrontation-from-below approach view relatively autonomous social movements and the large number of people whose daily lives clash with the logic of the established system—what one work calls the "multitude"—as more transformational than political parties, regardless of their ideological orientations.[3]

Important elements of both paradigms appear to apply to the Venezuelan case. Chávez has not only declared himself "anti-imperialist," but his defense of national sovereignty has in large part dictated his foreign policy. Thus, his government has taken important steps to diversify its economic ties and has consistently formulated independent positions on the world stage. Furthermore, Chávez's original political party, the Fifth Republic Movement (MVR), was designed to strengthen the government institutionally in the face of the acute conflict that inevitably erupts when anti-imperialist policies are deployed.

The bottom-up paradigm also applies to the *Chavista* phenomenon, not only because Chávez's discourse empowering the popular classes and lashing out at bureaucrats is compatible with this approach, but because the government's promotion of cooperatives and small-business ventures on a mass scale points in the direction of a decentralized economic model that counters the centralized structures of large companies. Furthermore, the emergence of a leftist labor confederation, the National Workers Union (UNT), whose leaders view themselves as constituting a vanguard of the Chavista movement, implies autonomy from the state and the party— another key feature of the bottom-up approach.

A final development favoring this strategy has been the widespread resentment among Chavistas, some of whom belong to social movements and organizations, toward the MVR and its allied parties in the ruling coalition. From the outset of his presidential campaign in 1997–98, Chávez employed an antiparty discourse (as did his major rival Henrique Salas Romer). Since then, the successes of the nonparty bloc of Chavistas have empowered its members. Thus, the Chavistas who were independent of political parties played a critical role and eclipsed the MVR when they took to the streets to demand Chávez's return to power at the time of the April 2002 coup. The nonparty Chavistas also formed independent structures that channeled the campaign in opposition to the president's removal in the recall election of August 2004.

Furthermore, in the eyes of some analysts a third pattern may be emerging. In the effort to strengthen the executive branch as the main guardian of national sovereignty (top-down strategy) and to promote participatory democracy (bottom-up strategy), political parties and intermediary social organizations may have been undermined, which could result in a caudillo-masses relationship between Chávez and the popular classes.

The following discussion is concerned with the international implications of the Chávez experience, particularly as it relates to North-South relations. In attempting to shed light on the influence that the Chavista government is likely to have on the rest of the continent, particularly with regard to certain policies and approaches that may be embraced by other governments, I set out to define the political and economic model that is emerging. My discussion of the salient features of Chavismo is also intended to ascertain which of the two change strategies—top-down or bottom-up—is most applicable to the Venezuelan case, and whether the two are complementary and reconcilable or contradictory and tension producing. In the first section

I overview the three stages of the Chávez presidency; in the ensuing discussion on the MVR, the Chavista social organizations, economic developments, and foreign policy, I seek to illuminate the significance of the Chávez phenomenon in the context of the two approaches to far-reaching change in Latin America.

The Three Stages of the Chávez Presidency

Chávez's 1998 presidential campaign emphasized political reforms over other issues, setting the tone for the first, moderate stage of his presidency in 1999 and 2000. His main electoral banner was the proposal of a constituent assembly, while more leftist socioeconomic demands, such as reformulating the terms of foreign-debt payment, were toned down. Venezuelan politics in 1999 centered on elections for the National Constituent Assembly, the drafting of a new constitution, and its approval in a national referendum held in December of that year. At this time, Chávez followed a moderate economic course, as demonstrated by his selection of the MVR congressman Alejandro Armas, who had ties with financial interests, to head a presidential subcommission on social security that would propose the privatization of the pension system.

From the outset, the Chavistas defended the concept of participatory democracy, which envisioned the direct involvement of the people in decision making, as an antidote to the excessive power of party elites. In proclaiming participatory democracy the 1999 Constitution spelled out the state's obligation to "facilitate" popular input in decision making (Article 62). It also cut off subsidies to political parties and obliged them to hold internal elections for choosing candidates and for filling leadership positions (Article 67). Participatory democracy was exemplified by the role played by social movements in presenting 624 proposals to the National Constituent Assembly, over half of which were incorporated into the new constitution.[4]

The most avid Chavista defenders of participatory democracy argued for replacing representative democracy and political parties with direct popular participation (what could be called "radical democracy").[5] This style of democracy, defended by the National Constituent Assembly's Citizen Participation Commission, was compatible with the movement-from-below approach put forward in theoretical writing. The attack by many Chávez supporters on the nation's political parties and the "political class" (meaning all politicians) lent itself to radical democracy, which favored placing parties on the sidelines of the political system.

In the course of the Chávez presidency, however, aspects of the radical version of participatory democracy, which best represents the bottom-up approach, have proven to be inoperative. The epitome of radical democracy was the holding of popular assemblies whose decisions were binding, as established in Article 70 of the 1999 Constitution. At the time, organizing "constituent assemblies" in the labor movement, the universities, and the oil industry became a Chavista rallying cry, but the idea failed to materialize. In early 2001, when worker councils chosen in rank-and-file assemblies attempted to run state-wide labor movements out of anti-Chávez union headquarters they had seized, they were criticized by the national Chavista leadership for excessive spontaneity and lack of discipline.[6]

An even more problematic application of the principle of radical democracy was articulated in Article 350 of the 1999 Constitution, which grants Venezuelans the right to "refrain from recognizing any regime, legislation or authority that goes against democratic values, principles and guarantees, or disrespects human rights."[7] When the opposition, beginning in 2002, questioned the legitimacy of the Chávez government, it invoked Article 350 to justify civil disobedience and its actions aimed at overthrowing the government.

The second stage of Chávez's presidency began in November 2001, when the government promulgated a package of forty-nine special laws designed to reverse the neoliberal trends of the 1990s. This legislation signaled a radicalization of the Chávez government and the initiation of its second, anti-neoliberal stage. The 2001 Hydrocarbons Law established majority government ownership of all mixed companies in charge of oil operations in order to reverse the neoliberal "oil opening" program of the preceding Caldera administration. Another law retained state control of social security, thus discarding the attempts to privatize the system undertaken by both the Caldera administration and the commission headed by Alejandro Armas. A third law, the Lands Law, was designed to break up and redistribute underutilized land.

In response, the business organization Federación de Cámaras y Asociaciones de Comercio y Producción de Venezuela (FEDECAMARAS) and the labor alliance Workers Confederation of Venezuela (CTV) called several civic strikes leading into the 11 April 2002 coup, which established a provisional government that lasted less than forty-eight hours. Later that year, the opposition again attempted to force Chávez out of power by staging a two-month general strike that greatly damaged the economy but proved to be a political fiasco.

The second stage, by going beyond the transformational discourse and structural political changes of the first stage, increased the importance of the Chavista project for Latin America. The passage of the forty-nine special laws in 2001 belied the argument that Chávez was a neoliberal disguised as a revolutionary.[8] His political survival punctured the Washington Consensus–promoted myth that in the age of globalization any deviation from the standard macroeconomic model was doomed to failure. Undoubtedly, Chávez's successes encouraged a shift in the political atmosphere of the continent, which contributed to the rise to power in Brazil, Argentina, Uruguay, Bolivia, Ecuador, and Nicaragua of leftists and center-leftists who at least initially stood for anti-neoliberalism and a degree of economic nationalism. The significance of this shift has been magnified by Washington's increasingly hostile stand toward Venezuela under the second Bush administration, including its support for the coup and general strike in 2002–2003.

The defeat of the general strike emboldened the Chávez government to go beyond mere rejection of ongoing neoliberal policies. A third stage set in, featuring innovative programs and the emergence of new structures that either defied or complemented the existing ones. Mission programs in the fields of health and education, for instance, functioned outside of the ministries. Likewise, a government chain of grocery stores called MERCAL competed with the private commercial sector.

At the outset of the third stage, Chávez declared his government "anti-imperialist," and by 2005, he was calling for the definition and construction of "socialism for the twenty-first century," at the same time that his government was reinterpreting the rights of private property. By late 2006, some Venezuelans in and out of the Chavista movement were criticizing the rudimentary structure of government and lack of mechanisms to ensure the successful implementation of programs and enforcement of policies. Nevertheless, the outline of a new social and economic model had just begun to emerge, and the process lacked definition and consolidation. Examining the role of the party, the state, and the Chavista bloc of independents is essential for understanding the new directions of the Chávez movement and presidency.

The MVR Party

Populist presidents such as Juan Domingo Perón, Lázaro Cárdenas, and Getúlio Vargas, who introduced anti-imperialist policies in the 1930s and 1940s, relied on political parties to bolster their position in the face of harsh opposition from national and international forces of reaction. Chávez also recognized the importance of developing a strong political party to counter the mobilization capacity of the opposition. In doing so, he differed from Peru's Alberto Fujimori (with whom he is sometimes compared), who spurned party organization and depended mostly on business and military allies.

The relative weakness of the MVR's institutionalization and ties with social movements largely confined the party to the electoral arena. Created in 1997 as a vehicle to promote Chávez's presidential candidacy, the MVR thus lacked ongoing links with civil society.[9] When Chávez gained power, his government attempted to institutionalize the party through various fronts such as the Constitutional Workers Front (FCT) and the Patriotic Circles, which were cells of about nine party members at the local level. However, Chavista labor leaders replaced the FCT with the Bolivarian Workers Force, which grouped workers both in and out of the party, while the Patriotic Circles were abandoned in favor of the Bolivarian Circles, which also had no special relationship with the MVR party. Chavista political leaders defended the decision to create broad fronts outside of the MVR on grounds that they guaranteed social-movement autonomy and deterred political-party control.

The MVR's experiences with internal elections to select party authorities and candidates, as mandated by Article 67 of the Constitution, have met mixed results. The most important election was carried out in April 2003 for the party's national executive committee, the Tactical National Command. On that occasion, the vast majority of the nearly 1,000 delegates to the party's national convention selected in internal elections belonged to the MVR's leftist current, headed by Congressman Willian Lara, even though the leftists accused the opposing current, headed by the retired officer Luis Alfonso Dávila, of having committed widespread electoral fraud. In spite of Lara's superiority in numbers of delegates, his effort to gain control of the MVR was thwarted when Chávez urged the convention to select the former officer Francisco Ameliach as the party's general director. Since then, however, Lara has overshadowed Ameliach in the MVR's national leadership.

The outcome of the 2003 convention highlighted two major impediments to the MVR's democratization. In the first place, Chávez has had the final word on all decisions, a prerogative that is accepted by everyone in the party. In the second place, Chávez has privileged military officers by naming them to important positions in accordance with his strategy of "civilian-military alliance." Both factors have interfered with party democracy as well as with the consolidation of internal currents that might have facilitated the MVR's much-needed ideological debate.

The Chavista movement's military current includes various governors and is headed by the former vice president and current governor of Miranda, Diosdado Cabello, who is allied with Ameliach. The MVR leftists who identify with Lara have insisted that with a few exceptions (such as the former president of the National Land Institute, Eiécer Otaiza), the Chavista military leaders have been resistant to further radicalization and have displayed but moderate enthusiasm for social programs. The special treatment accorded officers, however, obeys a political imperative: it bolsters the pro-Chávez current within the armed forces and in doing so preempts a possible opposition strategy of promoting disorder as a means to spur the military into staging another coup.

Lara and other MVR leaders have expressed support for the transformation of the party in order to establish links beyond the electoral arena.[10] These leaders have viewed Chávez's proposal to hold an ideological congress as the first step in the coalescence of pro-Chávez political organizations into a single party of the left which would be ideologically well defined, structurally viable, purged of corrupt leaders, and internally democratic.

Nevertheless, the leftists felt that for strategic reasons the party had to put off an all-out war on corruption. In addition, MVR leaders were reluctant to open the party up to ideological debate, fearing divisions that could prevent it from meeting the imminent challenges it faced. Their central argument as late as November 2007, as they prepared for the constitutional referendum in December, was the same that had prevailed throughout the party's history. Since its founding, the MVR has regularly faced emergency situations, due to the series of elections held in 1999 and 2000, followed by opposition-promoted insurgency. Chávez's announced goal of obtaining ten million votes in the December 2006 presidential elections, for which the congressional election of 2005 served as a springboard, once again shifted attention to the electoral arena. Pointing to these pressing challenges, MVR leaders have recommended postponement of party primaries, of exemplary measures against corruption, and of open ideological debate. However, following Chávez's resounding victories in the August 2004 recall election, the state and municipal elections three months later, and the 2006 presidential election (and before his narrow defeat in the 2007 constitutional referendum), the Chavistas found themselves in a comfortable position with an opposition that was highly discredited and demoralized, and thus the fixation on electoral battles seemed unfounded.

In spite of the MVR's failure to deal with the challenges of internal democracy, ideological clarity, and corruption, the party has been a major prop of the Chávez government. One of its most important achievements has been its success in maintaining majority control of the national congress, which has been essential for the survival of the Chávez government. Furthermore, even though many of Chávez's followers believe that the MVR has been discredited by the corruption and opportunism within its ranks, the party received the overwhelming majority of the Chavista vote in the August 2005 municipal elections. The Chavista leaders had structured their electoral tickets in order to allow the non-MVR organizations of the ruling coalition to test their backing by running their own slates, but none of them did well.

In spite of the decision to allow for multiple slates, Chávez and other leaders stressed the need to maintain unity and thus insisted that all MVR leaders support MVR slates. Following the municipal contests, a number of MVR leaders, including Gilmer Viloria, governor of the state of Trujillo and founding MVR member, were expelled from the party for supporting a separate ticket. In calling for unity Chávez stressed the importance of maintaining the MVR, even though he has occasionally expressed impatience and disappointment with the self-serving behavior and lack of discipline of many of its leaders. In contrast, he frequently praises the Communist Party for the discipline and unwavering commitment of its members.

The MVR's organizational weakness has opened space for actors who, as a whole, play a key role in the bottom-up approach, which privileges autonomous social movements and the direct participation of the rank and file of political and social organizations in decision making. Indeed, the MVR's avoidance of formal links with labor and social organizations was designed to respect their autonomy, in accordance with the bottom-up strategy. Nevertheless, contrary to this strategy, the Chavista social organizations have generally failed to achieve an autonomous status and furthermore have been short-lived.

Social Movements and Chavismo

The resentment commonly expressed by Chávez's followers toward the MVR, its allied parties, and Chavista politicians is unusual for a Latin American leftist movement in power. These rank-and-file Chavistas proudly affirm that they are independent of all political parties and claim they have no personal ambitions, unlike the Chavistas who participate in party politics. Many of the nonparty Chavistas belong to pro-Chávez social organizations, such as the Bolivarian Circles, which during the early years of Chávez's presidency held discussions on political issues such as the nation's new constitution.

The Bolivarian Circles and other organizations have been instrumental in rallying rank-and-file Chavistas to participate in mobilizations. Thus, for instance, through informal networks set in place by social organizations and enhanced by the use of cell phones, large numbers of slum dwellers converged on the presidential palace in Caracas and military bases throughout the country to demand Chávez's reinstatement in office at the time of the April 2002 coup. Significantly, the news that Chávez had not resigned but was being held captive, announced by the community radio station run by the Catholic organization Fe y Alegría, motivated residents of Caracas's low-income west side to join the protests. One leading member of a cultural organization, which in 2004 converted a police station in the west side's 23 de Enero district into a community radio station, recalled events of 13 April: "The members of our group were in close contact with one another and we marched together on Miraflores [the presidential palace]; but there was no central command that moved things that day."[11]

Chavista social organizations have been short-lived. The Bolivarian Circles, which were mostly community based, the Middle Class in Positive, which grouped professionals and others living in more affluent areas, and the Bolivarian Workers Force (FBT), which represented trade unionists, all faded out as their members switched over to other organizations and activities within the Chavista movement. In early 2004 some members of these organizations joined the Electoral Battle Units (UBES), which canvassed in neighborhoods in favor of the No Vote in the presidential recall election held in August of that year. UBE members were convinced that the structure created to lead the No Vote campaign, headed by nonparty Chavistas, would be subsequently retained and would serve to balance MVR input in the nomination of Chavista candidates in future elections. The UBES, however, also proved to be ephemeral.

The state's recruitment of Chavista-movement activists, and the opportunities it provided them, explains in large part the short duration of these organizations. The drain on social organizations has been exacerbated by the abundant oil-derived revenue at the state's disposal and the Chavista strategy of creating parallel structures in the fields of health, education, and food distribution. In some cases, various ministries and Chavista mayors and governors incorporated these activists into the public administration, granted them contracts, and provided them with start-up capital for cooperatives. Such relationships between activists and the state sometimes produced tensions within the social organizations. The militant, pro-Chavista Tupamaros movement, which originated in Caracas's west side in the 1990s, lost scores of members in 2004 when it decided to participate in electoral politics even as one of its leaders accepted a position in the Caracas police force. The dissidents accused the leadership of the Tupamaros of transforming the organization into a political party and thus of compromising its status as a movement.

The pro-Chavista labor movement has shown signs of achieving a degree of autonomy from the political parties and the state. In spite of conflicting internal currents, the Chavista labor confederation, the National Workers Union (UNT), has formulated proposals, demands, and slogans that were not officially shared by the MVR and its allied parties. The UNT, for instance, called for the implementation of an economic model based on production for internal consumption, reformulation of the foreign debt, and support for worker takeovers of companies that had closed down at a time when the government had not yet defined its position.[12] The self-perception of these trade unionists as representing a vanguard within Chavismo reinforced the notion of social-movement autonomy that is a keystone of the bottom-up approach.

The generally low level of social-movement autonomy under Chávez is not atypical for Latin America. The bottom-up approach favors maximizing social movement autonomy, which was virtually a banner in the 1980s, when writers influenced by the French sociologist Alain Touraine proclaimed "new social movements" to be the wave of the future. More recently, however, studies of leftist governments in Brazil at all levels, in Lima in the 1980s, and in other countries have documented the knotty problems and challenges that social movements face in defining their relationship with political parties and the state, even when those who are in power profess support for participatory democracy.

A study of the leftist-run government of Lima, for instance, points to how social movements that participated in municipal programs had to contend with reduction of funding from the central government, corruption charges exploited by the Shining Path guerrillas to discredit those movements, the dire poverty of their members, and political imperatives felt by the leftist parties, which limited autonomy.[13] In Venezuela, with the central government committed to popular input in decision making as spelled out in the 1999 Constitution, Chavista social movements were apparently at an advantage over their leftist counterparts elsewhere. Nevertheless, the failure of the MVR to reach out to social movements—itself an overreaction to party hegemonic practices of the past—deprived them of institutional links that would have facilitated their input into decision making.

Economic Transformation and Social Programs

During Chávez's first four years as president, the thinking behind the economic policy of his government was better defined on the basis of what it opposed than what it stood for. Indeed, Chávez's adversaries claimed that he was really a neoliberal, as demonstrated by his conservative fiscal policies.[14] Nevertheless, his reversal of the previous administrations' efforts to privatize the oil and aluminum industries and the social-security system, along with his refusal to accede to pressure from the opposition to reach an agreement with the IMF, established his credentials as an anti-neoliberal.[15] Similar to newly elected center-left presidents of the 1990s such as Rafael Caldera (Venezuela), Fernando de la Rúa (Argentina), and Ricardo Lagos (Chile), Chávez failed to define the specifics of his anti-neoliberalism, nor did he differentiate his policies from those of import-substitution–industrialization governments of the past.[16]

Following the defeat of the ten-week general strike in February 2003, pressure eased on Chávez, making possible the application of legislation and the implementation of social programs and practices that pointed in the direction of a new economic model. Many aspects of this new government orientation, such as the focus on the community and worker input in decision making, conform to the bottom-up paradigm. At the same time, however, the government's attempt to achieve self-sufficiency in food production for reasons of national security and its stiff requirements toward foreign capital accord with the anti-imperialist statist model.

The following government-sponsored activities, while drawing on practices of the past, suggest new goals and focuses.

The Mission Programs

The government has established special programs outside of the existing ministerial and legal structures, mainly in the fields of health and education at all levels. The programs employ innovative techniques such as using videocassettes and facilitators in place of classroom teachers, as well as granting stipends to those enrolled. In addition, twelve thousand Cuban doctors initiated the Barrio Adentro Mission, establishing residences in barrios throughout the country, with the hope—as yet unfulfilled—that they would gradually be replaced by young Venezuelan medical personnel. Due to the efforts of the Robinson Mission, the government was able to officially announce, in 2005, that all of the nation's 1.5 million illiterates had been taught basic reading and writing skills.

Worker Cooperatives

The Ministry of the Popular Economy (MINEP), Petróleos de Venezuela (PDVSA) and other state companies, various state banks, and some state and municipal governments have encouraged the creation of thousands of cooperatives by providing them with start-up capital and organizing training sessions. MINEP facilitators, who generally have a university or junior-college degree, are assigned two cooperatives each and are in charge of assisting them in dealing with problems that arise and of monitoring their activities. In May 2005, 300,000 unemployed workers graduated from the MINEP-sponsored Vuelvan Caras training program, and many of them subsequently formed cooperatives both in urban and rural areas that receive financial support from the ministry.

Co-Management *(Cogestión)*

Following the 2002–2003 general strike, Rafael Rosales and Nelson Nuñez, the presidents of two oil-worker federations, were selected to represent employees on the PDVSA board of directors. Although labor representation on state-company boards in Venezuela dates back to a 1966 decree, over the years the labor leadership affiliated with the old Democratic Action Party (AD) chose representatives who had no working or professional experience in the field, and thus their decision-making role was insignificant.[17] Since 2005, the Chavistas have made efforts to develop more authentic forms of co-management. In that year Chávez selected the veteran leftist Carlos Lanz to head the state aluminum company, Alcasa, with the express purpose of implementing co-management arrangements, which were then to be applied to other state companies in the industrial Guayana region. Lanz immediately announced that he would go beyond the token worker representation promoted by the European social-democratic movement and that Alcasa employees and community members would participate in drawing up the company budget for the year 2006. Unofficially, the government has tried to limit co-management to nonstrategic areas of the economy.

Worker Occupations and Government Expropriations

At the time of the 2002–2003 general strike, workers took over several large and medium-size companies, alleging that their owners had closed the firms without offering them legally required severance payments. At first the government deferred the matter to the courts, but in January 2005 President Chávez expropriated the paper company Venepal and then the valve company Constructora Nacional de Válvulas, and announced that he would do the same to all other private companies that had shut down. The UNT has played an active role in support of worker takeovers of other firms under similar circumstances. The confederation is also investigating scores of additional companies that meet the requirements for expropriation. The UNT insists that various enterprises, particularly hotels that faced bankruptcy and are temporarily being administered by the state financial agency, Fondo de Garantías de Depósito y de Protección Bancaria (FOGADE), be turned over to the workers, rather than to the former owners. In other cases, the government and employees have reached agreements with owners in which the state provides aid to facilitate recovery while management accepts co-management arrangements.

Land Distribution

In January 2005 Chávez announced the enforcement of the Constitution's Article 307 in opposition to the system of *latifundismo*, thus signaling the opening of a new front. At the same time, the governor of the State of Cojedes granted land titles to peasants who over a period of time had physically occupied an estate owned by a subsidiary of the large English company Vestey Group. In April a reform of the Lands Law authorized the National Land Institute (INTI) to proceed with land takeovers while cases are in the courts. As of late 2005, the government had begun to break up twenty-one large estates, turning some of the land over to cooperatives. The government reached an agreement on indemnification with a food-processing plant owned by Heinz in the State of Monagas, at the same time that it took over grain silos belonging to the powerful Polar Group in Barinas and allegedly inactive since 2002. The main government argument justifying these expropriations was Article 107 of the Lands Law, which defines latifundia as estates with less than 80 percent productivity. In addition, the INTI has contested the land claims of owners by presenting documents sometimes dating back to the nineteenth century and has also accused them of violating ecological legislation. This campaign is unique for Venezuela. The only other effective land reform in the nation's history was promulgated in 1960 and did not lead to the breakup of large estates.

Delegation of Authority to Community Organizations

On 4 February 2002 Chávez issued a decree which authorized urban land committees, constituted by inhabitants of individual slums, to undertake surveys, to distribute land deeds to longtime residents, and to develop public areas for recreational purposes. More recently, commissions of barrio dwellers—such as water commissions—have participated in the formulation and execution of public-works projects in their communities. And some twenty thousand neighborhood councils have been formed, each representing between two hundred and four hundred families, with authorization and eligibility for funding to develop local infrastructure.

Refusal to Appoint Business Representatives to Top Government Positions in Charge of the Formulation of Economic Policy

Since the outset of the modern democratic period in 1958, the positions of finance minister, development minister, planning minister, and Central Bank president were typically reserved for representatives of the business community. Since the early months of the Chávez presidency, the business sector has gone unrepresented in important government posts.

These and other programs and policies demonstrate the erroneousness of two critical assertions regarding the Chávez presidency. The first notion, formulated by labor and center-left members of the opposition during the government's early years, maintains that Chávez is a neoliberal disguised as an anti-neoliberal, but it has been belied by his refusal to move toward the privatization of crucial state-owned industries or the national system of social security, as well as by his refusal to reach an easy agreement with the IMF. The second thesis states that Chavismo is a throwback to the Latin American populist experience of the 1930s and 1940s. While there are important areas of similarity between the two, Chávez has established new goals and orientations that diverge from the policies and actions of the radical populism of those years.[18]

In the first place, Chávez's actions undermine the interests of the private sector to an extent unmatched by reformist and populist governments. Thus the Lands Law and the expropriation of closed-down companies reflect Chávez's rejection of private property as an absolute right devoid of social responsibilities. The government's commitment to the rights of private property under normal circumstances at the same time as it follows a policy of taking over uncultivated land and failing companies contrasts with socialist and radical experiences throughout history. Furthermore, the government's promotion of small-scale production is explicitly designed to challenge oligopoly control of the economy. The state-run food chain, Mercado de Alimentos (MERCAL), for instance, competes with privately owned supermarkets, as do state-financed cooperatives with regard to other larger companies. In another action taken against the private sector, the federal tax agency, Servicio Nacional Integrado de Administración Aduanera y Tributaria (SENIAT), implemented the plan "Evasion Zero, Contraband Zero," which doubled the revenue collected in 2004 over the previous year. In order to set an example, SENIAT has temporarily closed down and fined establishments of all sizes, including General Motors, McDonalds, and even the state-run PDVSA-Gas. These measures disprove the claim that in Latin America a viable income-tax system is unrealistic due to resistance from powerful economic groups.[19]

In the second place, Venezuelan politics has become a zero-sum game at the same time that Chávez's discourse reflects a clear class bias. For the first time in Venezuelan history, the head of state has declared that assisting the poor is more important for his government than is helping other sectors of the population. Expenditures in the areas of health and education as a percentage of the national budget have increased sharply, while income-tax collection has further contributed to the redistribution of wealth. Middle sectors in some cases have been adversely affected by this change in priorities. Thus, professional associations have expressed concern that the mission programs in the fields of health and education have lowered standards and are absorbing resources at the expense of established institutions. The social prioritization of Chavismo contrasts with radical populist movements in the 1930s and 1940s, which attempted to forge alliances linking the business sector with the workers, and whose leaders, unlike Chávez, shied away from references to class struggle in their discourse.

In the third place, government programs privilege lower-class communities in an attempt to incorporate them into the nation's life. Under the Barrio Adentro Mission, for instance, doctors are community-based and work with neighborhood organizations to promote preventive medicine. In the past, few doctors established their offices in slum areas. Furthermore, the educational missions promote student participation in community programs. The government also encourages the formation of cooperatives in communities where their members reside. Finally, the barrio-based commissions that distribute land deeds and develop programs for the supply of water bestow decision-making authority on the collectivity. The collective thrust of land distribution in slum areas contrasts with the practices of populist parties of the past, as well as with the prescriptions of neoliberal writers; populist elected officials granted land deeds in urban areas as part of a clientelistic transaction with electoral objectives, while some neoliberals supported programs of land ownership for the poor as a means to strengthen the system of private property.[20]

The success of Venezuela's emerging model, in which new structures (such as the missions) coexist with old ones, is contingent on continued high oil prices to finance parallel bureaucracies. In the long run, its viability also depends on the eradication of corrupt practices and the development of mechanisms to ensure the effective utilization of resources allocated to community programs and worker ventures. Indeed, the left wing of the Chavista movement views the struggle against corruption not only as a moral imperative but as a sine qua non for the nation's ongoing transformation. As long as the Venezuelan model depends on oil income, its applicability beyond its borders will be limited. Only by developing new institutions as a corrective to corruption and inefficiency can the nation's novel programs and policies develop into an alternative to neoliberalism for the rest of Latin America.

The narrow December 2007 defeat by popular referendum of a package of sixty-nine constitutional reforms proposed by Chávez and the National Assembly may provide some insight into the deepening of the social transformation of the third stage, as well as into some of its contradictions. The reforms were principally designed to promote direct participation by, and greater benefits to, non-privileged sectors of the population, as well as to strengthen state control of strategic industries. They included allocation of 5 percent of the national ordinary budget to the neighborhood councils; state promotion of national manufacturing and technology, particularly in the hydrocarbon sector; the provision that students and employees have the same weight as professors in the selection of university authorities; reduction of the work week to thirty-six hours; and creation of a "Social Stability Fund" financed by the state and workers in the informal economy to provide the latter with social security benefits. In the aftermath of the defeat, allies of the MVR, including the Venezuelan Communist Party and the Homeland for All Party, as well as many rank-and-file Chavistas, called for a critical debate over the reasons for the setback. Many stressed the need to deal with questions of corruption, internal democracy, and ideological clarification, which I have tried to present here as urgent tasks for the Chavista movement.

Conclusion

I have attempted to define the most significant aspects of the Chávez phenomenon and to explore their long-term implications for Venezuela and Latin America. Along these lines, I have examined government policies, strategies, and structural changes in order to discern the general outline of a new political and economic model. While some features of the new model, such as practices related to participatory democracy in its pure form ("radical democracy"), have proved to be unviable, a host of programs and policies are in an experimental stage.

The final outcome of the process, and the extent to which it proves to be viable, is of transcendent importance for the rest of Latin America and the Left worldwide. The Venezuelan government's anti-neoliberalism represents a point of reference throughout the hemisphere and in the process challenges the notion that in the age of globalization alternatives to the policies of the Washington Consensus are impossible.[21] Furthermore, the Venezuelan experiment speaks directly to the Left's attempt to devise a democratic, humanistic, anticapitalist model in the aftermath of the demise of the Soviet Union. The Venezuelan case serves as a corrective to abstract sterile debate on new models and ensures that the discussion be rooted in the search for feasible solutions based on concrete experiences. Indeed, Chávez himself often states that "trial and error" will lead the way to the new "socialist" model.

In many ways Chavismo resembles previous anti-imperialist governments in Latin America, such as those of Perón and Cárdenas, which nationalized foreign-owned industries and pursued independent foreign policies. The anti-imperialist approach was statist in that it favored government interventionism in the economy and assigned a major role to political parties. Chávez's determination from the outset of his political career to gain state power at the national level rather than target governorships or local governments (as the bottom-up approach supports), his command of power politics, and his government's assertion of national sovereignty reflect a statist orientation.[22] This preference is especially evident in Chávez's foreign policy, which attempts to promote a "multipolar world" as an antidote to U.S. imperialism. In keeping with his realpolitik approach, Chávez has cultivated friendly relations—at least for a time—with governments of diverse ideological orientations, including China, Jacques Chirac's France, and José Luis Rodríguez Zapatero's Spain. Internally, Chávez's defense of the MVR has also demonstrated his pragmatic and statist orientations. In spite of his attacks on bureaucracy and his appeal to the rank and file to vigorously assert itself, he defends unity from above and refuses to allow accusations of corruption and party opportunism to reach the extreme of undermining the MVR's electoral possibilities.[23]

Many of the novel features of the Chavista phenomenon—such as numerous credits granted to cooperatives, support for co-management, and the mission programs—contribute to the decision-making role and sense of empowerment of employees, agricultural laborers, and slum dwellers. In this respect, the programs are in accordance with the bottom-up approach. The distance between the rank and file of the Chavista movement and the governing party (particularly at the local and state level), as shown by the sharp criticisms leveled by the former against the latter, also lends itself to the bottom-up model and is without parallel in situations of radical transformation. In addition, the continuous reliance on mass mobilizations, which has been essential to Chávez's political survival, has few equivalents in Latin American history. Some of the Chavista actions contrast with the controlled mobilizations of radical populism and are particularly in keeping with the bottom-up model.[24] Thus, for instance, company takeovers at the time of the 2002–2003 general strike were the result of worker initiatives, and only with the expropriation of those firms two years later did the government define its position.

The thesis that Venezuelan politics since 1998 has been characterized by a caudillo-masses relationship between Chávez and his followers has to be evaluated in the context of the salient features of Chavismo. The characterization of Chávez as a caudillo recalls Gino Germani's writings half a century ago, which viewed the rank and file of populist movements as susceptible to demagogic manipulations.[25] Indeed, during the first years of the Chávez government, the Venezuelan media drew on negative stereotypes by depicting lower-class Chavistas as "hoards." Some writers point to the influence on Chávez of the Argentine theoretician Norberto Ceresole, who glorified the direct relationship between a nationalist military dictator and his followers in the absence of intermediary organizations.[26]

Nevertheless, these depictions do not take into account the highly critical attitude of the rank-and-file Chavistas toward their leadership and that many of them deny that their support is "unconditional."[27] To say that nothing stands between Chávez and the Chavista rank and file since all movement leaders are subservient to him is misleading because it passes over the critical role played by the middle-level leadership. Chavistas scrutinize the actions of these leaders, particularly mayors and governors, and have widely varying opinions of their performance. In one demonstration of independent thinking, Chavistas throughout 2006 were convinced that after the December presidential elections the movement would be relieved of pressure to maintain unity at all costs. As a consequence, they predicted a "revolution within the revolution" in which confrontations and mobilizations by Chavistas would be directed against corrupt and self-serving pro-Chávez leaders with the aim of purging them from the movement.

In addition, those Chavistas who represented a militaristic tendency within the Chavista movement were forced out during the early years. Ceresole himself was virtually declared persona non grata in 1999 as a result of his attacks against political parties in general, and he subsequently became a harsh critic of Chávez. Shortly thereafter, several of Chávez's former comrades-in-arms, voicing suspicions of politicians and hinting that military officers should lead the movement, left the ranks of Chavismo to join the opposition. One of the most influential of the disenchanted former Chavistas was Francisco Arias Cárdenas, Chávez's second-in-command in the 1992 coup.

The statist and bottom-up approaches are not in themselves contradictory, but they are sometimes fraught with tension. This relationship is particularly evident in the area of foreign policy. On the one hand, the Chávez government's diplomatic successes have been made possible by its tolerance toward, and friendly relations with, heads of state who adhere to widely diverse ideological positions. On the other hand, Chávez's fiery rhetoric in favor of revolutionary change and his glorification of Che Guevara and other revolutionaries have generated widespread active support among social-movement activists and the general population throughout Latin America, in accordance with the bottom-up strategy. Many of the social-movement activists from Brazil and Argentina who have attended government-sponsored festivals and forums in Venezuela (and who participated in the anti–Free Trade Area of the Americas rally in Mar del Plata, Argentina, where Chávez spoke at the time of the "Summit of the Americas" meeting in November 2005) are fervent opponents of Presidents Lula and Kirchner, respectively. A year after the Mar del Plata rally, tension between the two approaches again manifested itself, in the vote in the UN General Assembly on Venezuela's unsuccessful request for a nonpermanent seat on the Security Council. Chávez broadsided President George W. Bush and clashed with the presidents of Mexico and Peru, which invigorated radicals and unrepresented people throughout the hemisphere, but detracted from a diplomatic strategy designed to secure the necessary votes.

Similarly, Chávez's efforts to build a single governing party of the Left (statist approach) are at odds with his appeal to his followers to reject bureaucratic restraints and his call for a "revolution within the revolution" (bottom-up approach). Chávez's political survival has depended on his ability to retain the active support of the more militant members of his movement who are highly critical of all political parties, without undermining the MVR and its allies. Although achieving both objectives at times appears to be an awkward balancing act, the coexistence of the two approaches is what defines Chavismo and explains its political success.

On the socioeconomic front, the government implemented novel policies compatible with the bottom-up strategy, but also countered that approach with actions pointing in the opposite direction. Thus, at the same time that it promoted the mission programs and worker cooperatives, Chávez opened a dialogue with the business association FEDECAMARAS, and in October 2005 he proposed a "strategic alliance" with private economic groups. In the same month he raised the possibility of the nationalization of the foreign-owned steel company Siderúrgica del Orinoco (SIDOR). After nine years in power, Chavismo has employed a combination of the bottom-up and statist approaches on economic, political, and foreign-policy fronts, with no indication of a significant shift in favor of one of the two models in the short- or medium-term future.

Notes

1. The author is grateful to Fred Rosen for his critical comments on this chapter.
2. Laclau, "New Social Movements and the Plurality of the Social"; Hardt, "Porto Alegre," 114–15.
3. Evers, "Identity"; Hardt and Negri, *Multitude*.
4. Garcia-Guadilla, "Civil Society," 186–87.
5. This argument was most forcefully defended by the MVR's Haydee Machín, a member of the congressional Citizen Participation Committee.
6. Ellner, "Organized Labor and the Challenge of Chavismo," 171.
7. *Constitución de la República Bolivariana de Venezuela* (2001).
8. Parker, "Chávez and the Search for an Alternative to Neoliberalism," 64–66.
9. López Maya, "Hugo Chávez Frías," 80–84.
10. Lara, MVR, 14–15.
11. Antonio Alvarado, personal interview, Caracas, 6 October 2005.
12. Ellner, "Trade Union Autonomy and the Emergence of a New Labor Movement in Venezuela," 91–92.
13. The study's author, Gerd Schonwalder, credits the social movements for overseeing programs and, in the process, enhancing efficiency and accountability. He further argues that social movements have influenced leftist parties to abandon the vanguardism that previously characterized their behavior (Schonwalder, *Linking Civil Society and the State*, 187). Both Schonwalder and Hilary Wainwright (writing about social movements in Brazil) extol social movements while putting forward an implicit critique of the new-social-movement, anti-political-party paradigm. Wainwright argues that participatory democracy

must complement, not replace, representative democracy. She also points to the increasing number of political parties that recognize the importance of social movement independence (Wainwright, *Reclaim the State*, 186, 198).

14. Gómez Calcaño and Arenas, "Modernización autoritaria o actualización del populismo?" 122.
15. Wilpert, "Will Chávez's Project Survive?" 169.
16. Ellner, "Leftist Goals and Debate in Latin America," 15–19.
17. Ellner, *Organized Labor in Venezuela, 1958–1991*, 178.
18. Ellner, "The Radical Potential of Chavismo in Venezuela."
19. Castañeda, "Mexico," 32.
20. Parker, "Chávez and the Search for an Alternative to Neoliberalism," 68.
21. Ellner, *Neoliberalismo y antineoliberalismo en América Latina.*
22. Ellner, "Venezuela," 20–21.
23. In September 2005, for instance, Chávez defended the state TV channel's dismissal of a prominent news broadcaster, Walter Martínez, who had harshly attacked corruption and opportunism within the Chavista movement.
24. Collier and Collier, *Shaping the Political Arena*, 197.
25. Germani, *Authoritarianism, Fascism, and National Populism*, 153–208.
26. Steger, *The New Market Ideology*, 100–103.
27. Seawright and Hawkins, "Organizing Civil Society in Venezuela."

BIBLIOGRAPHY

Abel, Christopher, and Colin M. Lewis, eds. *Latin America, Economic Imperialisms and the State*. London: Athlone Press, 1985.

Abendroth, Hans Huber, et al. *La deuda externa de Bolivia: 125 años de renegociaciones y ¿cuántos más?* La Paz: CEDLA, 2001.

Abers, Rebecca. *Inventing Local Democracy: Grassroots Politics in Brazil*. Boulder, Colo.: Lynne Rienner, 2000.

Albó, Xavier, Thomas Greaves, and Godofredo Sandóval. *Chukiyagu: La cara Aymara de La Paz*. 4 vols. La Paz: CIPCA, 1981–87.

Alhadeff, Peter. "Dependency, Historiography, and Objections to the Roca Pact." In *Latin America, Economic Imperialisms and the State*, ed. Christopher Abel and Colin M. Lewis. London: Athlone Press, 1985.

Alvord, Clarence Walworth, et al., eds. *The Critical Period, 1763–1765*. British Series 1, Collections of the Illinois State Historical Library 10. Springfield: Illinois Historical Library, 1915.

Ames, Barry. *The Deadlock of Democracy in Brazil*. Ann Arbor: University of Michigan Press, 2002.

Anderson, Benedict. *Imagined Communities: Reflections on the Origin and Spread of Nationalism*. London: Verso, 1983.

Appadurai, Arjun. *The Social Life of Things: Commodities in Cultural Perspective*. Cambridge: Cambridge University Press, 1986.

Appleby, Joyce. *Inheriting the Revolution: The First Generation of Americans*. Cambridge, Mass.: Harvard University Press, 2000.

———. *Liberalism and Republicanism in the Historical Imagination*. Cambridge, Mass.: Harvard University Press, 1992.

Arriazu, Ricardo Héctor. *Lecciones de la crisis Argentina: Bases programáticas para un esquema de desarrollo sustentable*. Buenos Aires: Editorial El Ateneo, 2003.

Avritzer, Leonardo. *Democracy and the Public Space in Latin America*. Princeton: Princeton University Press, 2002.

Avritzer, Leonardo, and Zander Navarro. *A inovação democrática no Brasil*. São Paulo: Cortez Editora, 2002.

Baierle, Sergio. "The Porto Alegre Thermidor: Brazil's 'Participatory Budget' at the Crossroads." *Socialist Register* (2003).

Baiocchi, Gianpaolo. *Militants and Citizens: The Politics of Participatory Democracy in Porto Alegre*. Palo Alto, Calif.: Stanford University Press, 2005.

Barth, Frederik, ed. *Ethnic Groups and Boundaries: The Social Organization of Cultural Difference*. London: Allen and Unwin, 1969.

Bartra, Armando. "Rebellious Corn Fields." In *Mexico in Transition: Neoliberal Globalism, the State and Civil Society*, ed. Gerardo Otero. London: Zed Books, 2004.

Basualdo, Eduardo. "Burquesía nacional, capital extranjero y oligarquía pampeana." *Revista Económica* (Buenos Aires) 201 (2004).

Battistini, Osvaldo, ed. *La atmósfera incandescente*. Buenos Aires: Escuela de Economía y Sociedad, 2002.

Bearak, Barry. "Poor Man's Burden." *New York Times Magazine*, 27 June 2004.

Beccaria, Luis. *Empleo e integración social*. Buenos Aires: Fondo de Cultura Económica, 2001.

Belich, James. *Making Peoples: A History of the New Zealanders: From Polynesian Settlement to the End of the Nineteenth Century*. Aukland, Norway: Penguin, 1996.

Blasier, Cole. *The Hovering Giant: U.S. Responses to Revolutionary Change in Latin America, 1910–1985*. Pittsburgh: University of Pittsburgh Press, 1985.

Bonelli, Marcelo. *Un país en deuda: La Argentina y su imposible relación con el FMI*. Buenos Aires: Planeta, 2004.

Borón, Atilio. "Poder, contrapoder y antipoder: Notas sobre un extravío teórico-político en el pensamiento crítico contemporaneo." *Revista Chiapas* 15 (2003).

Bourdieu, Pierre. *Le sens pratique*. Paris: Minuit, 1980.

Branford, Sue. "The Lula Government and Agrarian Reform." In *In the Eye of the Storm: Left-wing Activists Discuss the Political Crisis in Brazil*, ed. Hilary Wainwright and Sue Branford. London: Trans National Institute, 2006.

Brogan, Denis W. *America in the Modern World*. Westport, Conn.: Greenwood Press, 1960.

Bronstein, Sergio. *Reforma laboral en América Latina: Evolución y tendencias recientes*. San José, Costa Rica: International Labor Organization, 1996.

Brown, Christopher Leslie. *Moral Capital: The Foundations of British Abolitionism*. Chapel Hill: University of North Carolina Press, 2006.

Bruno, Eugenio Andrea. *El default y la restructuración de la deuda*. Buenos Aires: Nueva Mayoría, 2004.

Burguete, Araceli. "Chiapas: Nuevos municipios para espantar municipios autónomos." In *El Estado y los Indígenas en tiempos del PAN: Neoindigenismo, legalidad e identidad*, ed. Rosalva Aída Hernández, Sarela Paz, and María Teresa Sierra. Mexico City: Centro de Investigaciones y Estudios Superiores en Antropología Social, 2004.

Burns, E. Bradford. *The Unwritten Alliance: Rio-Branco and Brazilian-American Relations*. New York: Columbia University Press, 1966.

Cáceres, Sandra. La reinvención de la tradición en el Año Nuevo Aymara. Unpublished undergraduate thesis, Universidad Mayor de San Andrés (UMSA), La Paz, 2003.

Caldeira, T. P. R. "Fortified Enclaves: The New Urban Segregation." *Public Culture* 8 (1996).

Caldeira, T. P. R., and James Holston. "Democracy and Violence in Brazil." *Comparative Studies in Society and History* 41.4 (1999).

Calvert, P. A. R. *The Mexican Revolution, 1910–14: The Diplomacy of Anglo-American Conflict*. Cambridge: Cambridge University Press, 1968.

Candia, Jose Miguel. "América Latina: Modernización capitalista y reforma neoliberal." In *La encrucijada del desempleo ante el tercer milenio*, ed. Daniel Cieza. La Plata, Argentina: H.C.D. (City Council), 2000.

Canessa, Andrew. *Minas, maíz y muñecas: Identidades e indigeneidades en Larecaja*. La Paz: Mamahuaco, 2006.

Canny, Nicolas. "England's New World and the Old, 1480s–1630s." In *The Origins of Empire: British Overseas Enterprise to the Close of the Seventeenth Century: Oxford History of the British Empire*, ed. Nicholas Canny. Oxford: Oxford University Press, 1998.

———, ed. *The Origins of Empire: British Overseas Enterprise to the Close of the Seventeenth Century: Oxford History of the British Empire*. Oxford: Oxford University Press, 1998.

Cariello, Rafael, and C. Cardoso. "Para bancos, nota do PT desgasta governo." *Folha de São Paulo*, 3 November 2004.

Carothers, Thomas. *In the Name of Democracy: U.S. Policy toward Latin America in the Reagan Years*. Berkeley: University of California Press, 1991.

Carrera, Íñigo, and Celia Cotarelo, "La protesta en Argentina Jan-April, 2001." *Observatorio Social de América Latina (OSAL)* (Buenos Aires) 4 (June 2001).

Carta Capital. "O país é maior que sua elite." *Carta Capital*, 24 December 2003.

Carter, William. *Ensayos científicos sobre la coca*. La Paz: Juventud, 1996.

Castañeda, Jorge. "Mexico: Permuting Power." *New Left Review* 7 (2001).

Castel, Robert. *La metamorfosis de la cuestión social: Una crónica del salariado*. Buenos Aires: Piados, 1997.

———. *Las trampas de la exclusión*. Buenos Aires: Editorial Topía, 2001.

Castle, Kathryn. *Britannia's Children: Reading Colonialism through Children's Books and Magazines*. Manchester, U.K.: Manchester University Press, 1996.

Cayton, Andrew R. L. "Noble Actors upon 'the Theatre of Honour': Power and Civility in the Treaty of Greenville." In *Contact Points: American Frontiers from the Mohawk Valley to the Mississippi, 1750–1830*, ed. Andrew R. L. Cayton and Fredrika Teute. Chapel Hill: University of North Carolina Press, 1998.

Cayton, Andrew R. L., and Fredrika Teute, eds. *Contact Points: American Frontiers from the Mohawk Valley to the Mississippi, 1750–1830*. Chapel Hill: University of North Carolina Press, 1998.

Centro de Estudios Legales y Sociales. *El Estado frente a la protesta social, 1996–2002*. Buenos Aires: SIGLO XXI, 2003.

———. *Plan jefes y jefas: Derecho social o beneficio sin derechos?* Buenos Aires: Centro de Estudios Legales y Sociales, 2003.

Chang, Ha-Joon. *Kicking Away the Ladder*. London: Anthem Press, 2002.

Chatterjee, Partha. *Our Modernity*. Manila: SEPHIS-SEASREP, 1996.

Cieza, Daniel. Crisis del mundo del trabajo y política de empleo. Ph.D. diss., Universidad Nacional de La Plata, 2005.

———. *De la cultura del trabajo al malestar del desempleo: Desarrollo económico y conflicto laboral en la Argentina*. La Plata, Argentina: H.C.D. (City Council), 2000.

———. *Programas oficiales de empleo y capacitación en la Provincia de Buenos Aires*. La Plata, Argentina: H.C.D. (City Council), 1998.

Clark, Bruce. *Native Liberty, Crown Sovereignty: The Existing Aboriginal Right of Self-Government in Canada*. Montreal: McGill-Queens University Press, 1990.

Cline, William. *International Debt Reexamined*. Washington: Institute for International Economics, 1995.

Cohen, Jean, and Andrew Arato. *Civil Society and Political Theory*. Cambridge, Mass.: MIT Press, 1994.

Colley, Linda. *Britons: Forging the Nation, 1707–1837*. London: Yale University Press, 1993.

Collier, George, with Elizabeth Quaratiello. *Basta! Land and the Zapatista Rebellion in Chiapas*. Oakland: Food First Books, 1999.

Collier, Ruth Berins, and David Collier. *Shaping the Political Arena*. Princeton, N.J.: Princeton University Press, 1991.

Connell-Smith, Gordon. *United States and Latin America*. London: Heinemann, 1974.

Constitución de la República Bolivariana de Venezuela. Caracas: Talleres Gráficos de la Asamblea Nacional, 2001 [1999].

Coupland, Reginald. *The Empire in These Days: An Interpretation*. London: Macmillan, 1935.

Dagnino, Evelina, ed. *Sociedade civil e espaços públicos no Brasil*. São Paulo: Paz e Terra, 2002.

Davis, David Brion. *Inhuman Bondage: The Rise and Fall of Slavery in the New World*. New York: Oxford University Press, 2006.

———. "The Problem of Doing History by Ahistorical Abstraction." In *The Antislavery Debate: Capitalism and Abolitionism as a Problem in Historical Interpretation*, ed. Thomas Bender. Berkeley: University of California Press, 1992.

———. *The Problem of Slavery in the Age of Revolution, 1770–1823*. Ithaca, N.Y.: Cornell University Press, 1975.

———. *Revolutions: Reflections on American Equality and Foreign Liberations*. Cambridge, Mass.: Harvard University Press, 1990.

de Jesus, Carolina Maria. *Child of the Dark: The Diary of Carolina Maria de Jesus*. New York: Dutton, 1962.

Deloria, Vine, and Ray De Mallie, eds. *Documents of American Indian Diplomacy*. 2 vols. Norman: University of Oklahoma Press, 1999.

Deloria, Vine, and Clifford Lytle. *The Past and Future of American Indian Sovereignty*. New York: Pantheon, 1984.

Derrida, Jacques. *Politics of Friendship*. London: Verso, 1994.

———. "Remarks on Deconstruction and Pragmatism." In *Deconstruction and Pragmatism*, ed. Chantal Mouffe. London: Routledge, 1996.

Dickason, Olive P. "Concepts of Sovereignty at the Time of First Contacts." In *The Law of Nations and the New World*, ed. L. C. Green and Olive P. Dickason. Edmonton: University of Alberta Press, 1989.

Domínguez, Jorge. *Cuba: Order and Revolution*. Cambridge, Mass.: Harvard University Press, 1978.

———. "U.S.-Cuban Relations: From the Cold War to the Colder War." *Interamerican Studies and World Affairs* 39.3 (1997).

Dowd, Gregory Evans. *A Spirited Resistance: The North American Indian Struggle for Unity, 1745–1815*. Baltimore: Johns Hopkins University Press, 1992.

Drake, Paul. *The Money Doctor in the Andes: The Kemmerer Missions, 1923–33*. Durham, N.C.: Duke University Press, 1989.

Drescher, Seymour. *Econocide: British Slavery in the Era of Abolition*. Pittsburgh: University of Pittsburgh Press, 1977.

———. *The Mighty Experiment: Free Labour versus Slavery in British Emancipation*. New York: Oxford University Press, 2002.

Dresser, Madge. "Squares of Distinction, Webs of Interest: Slavery, Gentility and Urban Development in Bristol." *Slavery and Abolition* 21 (2000).

Dye, Alan. *Cuban Sugar in the Age of Mass Consumption*. Palo Alto, Calif.: Stanford University Press, 1998.

Eakin, Hallie, and Kirsten Appendini. "Subsistence Maize Production and Maize Liberalization in Mexico." *Newsletter of the International Human Dimensions of Global Environmental Change* 1 (2005).

Edwards, Michael. *Civil Society*. Cambridge: Polity, 2004.

Egle, William, and John Blair Linn, eds. *Pennsylvania Archives, Series 2*. 19 vols. Harrisburg, Penn.: Lane S. Hart, 1874–1893.

Eichengreen, Barry. *Globalizing Capital: A History of the International Monetary System*. Princeton: Princeton University Press, 1996.

Eichengreen, Barry, and Albert Fishlow. "Contending with Capital Flows: What Is Different about the 1990s?" In *Capital Flows and Financial Crises*, ed. Miles Kahler. Ithaca, N.Y.: Cornell University Press, 1998.

Elespe, Douglas R., et al. *Default y reestructuración de la deuda externa*. Special ed. Buenos Aires: La Ley, 2003.

Ellis, Joseph J. *Founding Fathers: The Revolutionary Generation*. New York: Knopf, 2000.

Ellner, Steve. "Leftist Goals and Debate in Latin America." *Science and Society* 68.1 (2004).

———. *Neoliberalismo y antineoliberalismo en América Latina: El debate sobre estrategias*. Caracas: Editorial Tropykos, 2006.

———. "Organized Labor and the Challenge of Chavismo." In *Venezuelan Politics in the Chávez Era: Class, Polarization and Conflict*, ed. Steve Ellner and Daniel Hellinger. Boulder, Colo.: Lynne Rienner, 2003.

———. *Organized Labor in Venezuela, 1958–1991: Behavior and Concerns in a Democratic Setting*. Wilmington, Delaware: Scholarly Resources, 1993.

———. "The Radical Potential of Chavismo in Venezuela: The First Year and a Half in Power." *Latin American Perspectives* 28.5 (2001).

———. "Trade Union Autonomy and the Emergence of a New Labor Movement in Venezuela." In *Venezuela: Hugo Chávez and the Decline of an "Exceptional" Democracy*, ed. Steve Ellner and Miguel Tinker Salas. Lanham, Md.: Rowman and Littlefield, 2007.

———. "Venezuela: Defying Globalization's Logic." NACLA *Report on the Americas* 39.2 (2005).

Evers, Tilman. "Identity: The Hidden Side of New Social Movements in Latin America." In *New Social Movements and the State in Latin America*, ed. David Slater. Amsterdam: CEDLA, 1985.

Feijoó, María del Carmen. *Nuevo país, nueva pobreza*. Buenos Aires: Fondo de Cultura Económica, 2001.

Ferguson, Niall. *Colossus*. New York: Penguin, 2004.

———. *Empire*. London: Basic Books, 2002.

Fernandes, Bernardo Mançano. MST: *Formação e territorialização*. São Paulo: Editora Hucitec, 1996.

Fernández Sotelo, Antonio Diego. "El último rescate." Unpublished master's thesis, Department of Information Science and Technique, Universidad Iberomericana (Mexico City), 1994.

Ferrante, Juan. "Reflexiones en torno al trabajo y la política: Los cambios en la conformación del trabajador colectivo." In *El trabajo y la política en la Argentina del fin de siglo*, ed. Claudio Lozano. Buenos Aires: EUDEBA-CTA-UBA, 1999.

Fieldhouse, D. K. *The Theory of Capitalist Imperialism*. London: Longman, Green, 1967.

Fladeland, Betty. *Men and Brothers: Anglo-American Antislavery Cooperation*. Urbana: University of Illinois Press, 1972.

Fleischer, David. "The Politics of the Lula PT-led Coalition." Paper presented at the Conference of the Latin American Studies Association, Las Vegas, October 2004.

Fleras, Augie, and Jean Leonard Elliot. *The Nations Within: Aboriginal-State Relations in Canada, the United States, and New Zealand*. Toronto: Oxford University Press, 1992.

Galazo, Norberto. *De la Banca Baring al FMI: Historia de la deuda externa Argentina*. Buenos Aires: Editorial Colihue, 2003.

Gallagher, John, and Ronald Robinson. "The Imperialism of Free Trade." *Economic History Review* 6.1 (1953).

Garcia-Guadilla, María Pilar. "Civil Society: Institutionalization, Fragmentation, Autonomy." In *Venezuelan Politics in the Chávez Era: Class, Polarization and Conflict*, ed. Steve Ellner and Daniel Hellinger. Boulder, Colo.: Lynne Rienner, 2003.

Garrone, Valeria, and Laura Rocha, *Néstor Kirchner: Un muchacho peronista y la oportunidad del poder*. Buenos Aires: Planeta, 2003.

Gellman, Irwin F. *Good Neighbor Diplomacy: United States Policies in Latin America, 1933–1945*. Baltimore: Johns Hopkins University Press, 1979.

Germani, Gino. *Authoritarianism, Fascism, and National Populism*. New Brunswick, N.J.: Transaction Books, 1978.

Gilly, Adolfo. "Entre Babel y la ciudad futura." *Cuadernos del Sur* (Mexico City) 20 (1995).

———. "Populismo radical: Un sujeto político no identificado." *Le Monde Diplomatique de Buenos Aires* (June 2004).

Gleach, Fredric W. *Powhatan's World and Colonial Virginia: A Conflict of Cultures*. Lincoln: University of Nebraska Press, 1997.

Gleijeses, Piero. *Shattered Hope: The Guatemalan Revolution and the United States*. Princeton: Princeton University Press, 1991.

Godio, Julio. *Sociología del trabajo y política*. Buenos Aires: ATUEL, 2001.

Godio, Julio, et al. *La incertidumbre del trabajo*. Buenos Aires: Editorial Corregidor, 1998.

Goldberg, Carole E. "Review Essay: A Law of their Own." *Law and Social Inquiry* 25 (2000).

Gomes da Cunha, O. M. "Black Movements and the 'Politics of Identity.'" In *Cultures: Revisioning Latin American Social Movements*, ed. Sonia Álvarez, Evelina Dagnino, and Arturo Escobar. Boulder, Colo.: Westview, 1998.

Gómez, Luis. *El Alto de pie: Una insurrección Aymara en Bolivia*. La Paz: Comuna e Indymedia, 2003.

Gómez Calcaño, Luis, and Nelly Arenas. "Modernización autoritaria o actualización del populismo? La transición política en Venezuela." *Cuestiones Políticas* (Maracaibo) 26 (2001).

Gootenberg, Paul. *Cocaine: Global Histories.* London: Routledge, 1999.

Gorz, André. *Estrategia obrera y neocapitalismo.* Mexico City: ERA, 1969.

———. *Miserias del presente: Riquezas de lo posible.* Buenos Aires: Paidos, 1998.

Gramsci, Antonio. *Notas sobre Maquiavelo, sobre la política y el Estado moderno.* Buenos Aires: Nueva Visión, 1984.

Grandin, Greg. *The Blood of Guatemala.* Durham, N.C.: Duke University Press, 2000.

———. *Empire's Workshop: Latin America, the United States and the Rise of the New Imperialism.* New York: Henry Holt, 2006.

Grassi, Estela, et al. *Políticas sociales, crisis y ajuste estructural.* Buenos Aires: Editorial Espacio, 1994.

Green, L. C. "Claims to Territory in Colonial America." In *The Law of Nations and the New World,* ed. L. C. Green and Olive P. Dickason. Edmonton: University of Alberta Press, 1989.

Green, L. C., and Olive P. Dickason, eds. *The Law of Nations and the New World.* Edmonton: University of Alberta Press, 1989.

Greenberg, Kenneth R., ed. *Nat Turner: A Slave Rebellion in History and Memory.* New York: Oxford University Press, 2003.

Grieshaber, Ervin. "Fluctuaciones en la definición del indio: Comparación de los censos de 1900 y 1950." *Historia Boliviana* (La Paz) 2 (1986).

Grotius, Hugo. "The Law of War and Peace." In *The Classics of International Law,* trans. Francis W. Kelsey, ed. James Brown Scott et al. Vol. 3. Oxford: Clarendon Press, 1925.

Guerrero, Andrés. "El proceso de identificación: Sentido común ciudadano ventriloquía y transescritura." In *Etnicidades,* ed. Andrés Guerrero. Quito: FLACSO, 2000.

———. "Una imagen ventrílocua: El discurso sobre la desgraciada raza indígena en el Ecuador." In *Imágenes e imagineros: Representaciones de los Indígenas Ecuatorianos,* vols. 19–20, ed. Blanca Muratorio. Quito: FLACSO, 1994.

Guha, Ranajit. "La prosa de contrainsurgencia." In *Debates postcoloniales: Una introducción a los estudios de la subalternidad,* ed. Silvia Rivera and Rossana Barragán. La Paz : Historias / SEPHIS / Aruwiyiri, 1997.

Gurría, José Angel. *La política de la deuda externa.* Mexico City: Fondo de Cultura Económica, 1993.

Gwynne, Robert N., and Cristóbal Kay, "Latin America Transformed: Globalization and Neoliberalism." In *Latin America Transformed: Globalization and Modernity,* ed. Robert N. Gwynne and Cristóbal Kay. London: Arnold, 2004.

Hakim, Peter. "The Reluctant Partner." *Foreign Affairs* 84.1 (2004).

Hamilton, Milton Wheaton, et al., eds. *The Papers of Sir William Johnson.* 13 vols. Albany: State University of New York Press, 1921–1962.

Hammond, John L. "Law and Disorder: The Brazilian Landless Farmworkers' Movement." *Bulletin of Latin American Research* 18.4 (1999).

Hardt, Michael. "Porto Alegre: Today's Bandung." *New Left Review* 14 (2002).

Hardt, Michael, and Antonio Negri. *Empire.* New York: Penguin, 2000.

———. *Multitude: War and Democracy in the Age of Empire.* New York: Penguin, 2004.

Haring, Sidney L. *Crow Dog's Case: American Indian Sovereignty, Tribal Law, and United States Law in the Nineteenth Century.* New York: Cambridge University Press, 1994.

Harris, Olivia, Brooke Larson, and Enrique Tandeter. *La participación indígena en los mercados surandinos: Estrategias y reproducción social.* Vols. 16 and 20. La Paz: CERES, 1987.

Harvey, David. *A Brief History of Neoliberalism.* London: Oxford University Press, 2005.

Harvey, Neil. *The Chiapas Rebellion: The Struggle for Land and Democracy.* Durham, N.C.: Duke University Press, 1998.

Haya de la Torre, Agustín. "El modelo neoliberal autoritario en el Perú: Sus efectos sociales." In *La encrucijada del desempleo en el tercer milenio,* ed. Daniel Cieza. La Plata, Argentina: H.C.D. (City Council), 1999.

Healy, David. *Drive to Hegemony: The United States in the Caribbean, 1898–1917.* Madison: University of Wisconsin Press, 1988.

Henry, Alexander. *Travels and Adventures of Alexander Henry.* Ann Arbor, Mich.: University Microfilms, 1966.

Hershberg, Eric, and Fred Rosen. "Turning the Tide?" In *Latin America after Neoliberalism: Turning the Tide in the Twenty-first Century?* ed. Eric Hershberg and Fred Rosen. New York: New Press, 2006.

Hexter, J. H. "The Historical Method of Christopher Hill." In *On Historians,* by J. H. Hexter. Cambridge, Mass.: Harvard University Press, 1979.

———. *On Historians.* Cambridge, Mass.: Harvard University Press, 1979.

Higgins, Nicholas. "Mexico's Stalled Peace Process: Prospects and Challenges." *International Affairs* 77.4 (2001).

Hinderaker, Eric. "The 'Four Indian Kings' and the Imaginative Construction of the First British Empire." *William and Mary Quarterly,* Third Series 53 (1996).

Hobsbawm, Eric, and Terence Ranger. *The Invention of Tradition.* Cambridge: Cambridge University Press, 1983.

Holloway, John. "Dignity's Revolt." In *Zapatista! Reinventing Revolution in Mexico,* ed. John Holloway and Eloina Pelaez. London: Pluto Press, 1998.

Holm, Tom. *Strong Hearts, Wounded Souls: Native American Veterans of the Vietnam War.* Austin: University of Texas Press, 1996.

Hopkins, A. G. "Informal Empire in Argentina: An Alternative View." *Latin American Studies* 26.2 (1994).

Horsman, Reginald. "American Indian Policy in the Old Northwest, 1783–1812." *William and Mary Quarterly*, Third Series 18 (1961).

Huggins, Martha K. *Political Policing: The United States and Latin America*. Durham, N.C.: Duke University Press, 1998.

Humphreys, R. A. *Latin America and the Second World War*. 2 vols. London: Athlone Press, 1981–82.

———. "Lord Shelburne and the Proclamation of 1763." *English Historical Review* 49 (1934).

Hunefeldt, Christine. *Liberalism in the Bedroom: Quarreling Spouses in Nineteenth Century Lima*. University Park: Pennsylvania State University Press, 2000.

Hunter, Wendy. "Democracy and Social Policy in Brazil: Advancing Basic Needs, Preserving Privileged Interests." Paper presented at the "Democracy and Human Development: A Global Inquiry" conference, Boston University, fall 2004.

Hunter, Wendy, and Timothy J. Power. "Lula's Brazil at Midterm." *Democracy* 16.3 (2005).

Ibañez Aguirre, José Antonio. *México: Ciclos de deuda y crisis del sector externo*. Mexico City: Plaza y Valdes, 1997.

Ignatieff, Michael. *Empire Lite: Nation Building in Bosnia, Kosovo, Afghanistan*. New York: Vintage, 2003.

Immerman, Richard. *The CIA in Guatemala*. Austin: University of Texas Press, 1988.

Ingram, Edward. *The Beginning of the Great Game in Asia, 1828–1834*. Oxford: Oxford University Press, 1979.

Instituto de Estudios Económicos y Fiscales. "Empleo, desempleo y programas oficiales: La experiencia reciente." *Informe iefe* (La Plata) 80 (1998).

International Monetary Fund. *International Capital Markets*. Washington: International Monetary Fund, 1995.

James, Daniel. *Resistance and Integration: Peronism and the Argentine Working Class, 1946–1976*. Cambridge: Cambridge University Press, 1988.

Jennings, Francis. "The Imperial Revolution: The American as a Tripartite Struggle for Sovereignty." In *The American Indian and the American Revolution: Occasional Papers, the Newberry Library Center for the History of the American Indian*, ed. Francis Jennings. Chicago: Newberry Library, 1983.

Jennings, Francis, et al. *The History and Culture of Iroquois Diplomacy*. Syracuse, N.Y.: Syracuse University Press, 1985.

Johnson, Chalmers. *Blowback: The Costs and Consequences of American Empire*. New York: Holt, 2000.

Jones, Dorothy. *License for Empire: Colonialism by Treaty in Early America*. Chicago: University of Chicago Press, 1982.

Juliá, Carlos, et al. *La memoria de la deuda*. Buenos Aires: Editorial Biblios, 2002.

Kagan, Robert. "Benevolent Empire." *Foreign Policy* 111 (1998).

Kawashima, Yasu (Yasuhide). "Jurisdiction of the Colonial Courts over the Indians in Massachusetts, 1689–1763." *New England Quarterly* 42 (1969).

Keck, Margaret. *The Workers Party and Democratization in Brazil*. New Haven, Conn.: Yale University Press, 1992.

Kennedy, Paul. *The Rise and Fall of the Great Powers*. New York: Vintage Books, 1987.

Kent, Donald H., ed. *Pennsylvania and Delaware Treaties, 1629–1737*. Vol. 1 of *Early American Indian Documents: Treaties and Laws, 1607–1789*, gen. ed. Alden T. Vaughan. Washington: University Publications of America, 1979.

Keohane, Robert O. *After Hegemony: Cooperation and Discord in the World Political Economy*. Princeton: Princeton Classic Editions, 1984.

Kielstra, Paul Michael. *The Politics of Slave Trade Suppression in Britain and France, 1814–48: Diplomacy, Morality and Economics*. London: Macmillan, 2000.

Kingstone, Peter R. *Crafting Coalitions for Reform: Business Preferences, Political Institutions, and Neoliberal Reform in Brazil*. University Park: Pennsylvania State University Press, 1999.

Kirkpatrick, Jeane J. "Dictators and Double Standards." *Commentary* 68 (1979).

Klein, Herbert. *The Atlantic Slave Trade*. Cambridge: Cambridge University Press, 1999.

Kliksberg, Bernardo. "Desocupación y exclusión en América Latina." *Encrucijadas* (Buenos Aires) 2 (2000).

Knight, Alan. *The Mexican Revolution*. 2 vols. Cambridge: Cambridge University Press, 1986.

———. *U.S.-Mexican Relations, 1910–40: An Interpretation*. San Diego: Center for U.S.-Mexican Studies, 1987.

Kolchin, Peter. *American Slavery*. London: Penguin, 1995.

Krugman, Paul. "Dutch Tulips and Emerging Markets." *Foreign Affairs* 74.6 (1995).

Kuczynski, Pedro-Pablo, and John Williamson, eds. *After the Washington Consensus: Restarting Growth and Reform in Latin America*. Washington: Institute for International Economics, 2003.

Kupperman, Karen Ordahl. *Indians and English: Facing Off in Early America*. Ithaca, N.Y.: Cornell University Press, 2000.

Laclau, Ernesto. "Can Immanence Explain Social Struggles?" In *Empire's New Clothes: Reading Hardt and Negri*, ed. Paul Passavant and Jodi Dean. London: Routledge, 2003.

———. "New Social Movements and the Plurality of the Social." In *New Social Movements and the State in Latin America*, ed. David Slater. Amsterdam: CEDLA, 1985.

———. *La razón populista*. Buenos Aires: Fondo de Cultura Económica, 2005.

Lafeber, Walter. *The Panama Canal: The Crisis in Historical Perspective*. Oxford: Oxford University Press, 1979.

Lal, Deepak. *In Praise of Empires*. New York: Palgrave Macmillan, 2004.

Lamounier, Bolívar, and Rachel Meneguello. *Partidos políticos e consolidação democrática*. São Paulo: Brasiliense, 1986.

Lara, Willian. MVR: *De aparato electoral a partido político orgánico*. Caracas: Self-published, 2005.

Laurell, Asa Cristina, and Luisa Mussot. "El empleo y los nuevos modelos de Relaciones laborales y del seguro social." In *La encrucijada del desempleo en el tercer milenio*, ed. Daniel Cieza. La Plata, Argentina: H.C.D. (City Council), 1999.

Lehman, Kenneth D. *Bolivia and the United States: A Limited Partnership*. Athens: University of Georgia Press, 1999.

Leogrande, William M. *Our Own Backyard: The United States in Central America, 1977–1992*. Chapel Hill: University of North Carolina Press, 1998.

Leopold, Richard W. *Elihu Root and the Conservative Tradition*. Boston: Little, Brown, 1954.

Lepore, Jill. *The Name of War: King Philip's War and the Origins of American Identity*. New York: Knopf, 1998.

Levin, N. Gordon. *Woodrow Wilson and World Politics*. Oxford: Oxford University Press, 1968.

Levine, Barry B., ed. *El desafío neoliberal*. Bogotá: Grupo Editorial Norma, 1992.

Leyva, Xochitl, and Gabriel Ascencio. *Lacandonia al filo del agua*. Mexico City: Fondo de Cultura Económica, 1996.

Lieuwen, Edwin. *U.S. Policy in Latin America: A Short History*. New York: Frederick A. Praeger, 1965.

Linebaugh, Peter. "The Secret History of the Magna Carta." *Boston Review* 28.3 (2003).

Lipson, Charles. "International Debt and National Security: Britain and America." In *The International Debt Crisis in Historical Perspective*, ed. Barry Eichengreen and Peter Lindert. Cambridge, Mass.: MIT Press, 1991.

Lobato, Mirta, and Juan Suriano. *La protesta social en la Argentina*. Buenos Aires: Fondo de Cultura Económica, 2003.

López Echagüe, Hernán. *El otro: Una biografía política de Eduardo Duhalde*. Buenos Aires: Planeta, 1996.

López Maya, Margarita. "Hugo Chávez Frías: His Movement and His Presidency." In *Venezuelan Politics in the Chávez Era: Class, Polarization and Conflict*, ed. Steve Ellner and Daniel Hellinger. Boulder, Colo.: Lynne Rienner, 2003.

Louis, William Roger, ed. *Imperialism: The Gallagher and Robinson Controversy*. New York: New Viewpoints, 1976.

Lozada, Salvador María. *La deuda externa y el desguace del Estado nacional*. Cuyo, Argentina: Ediciones Jurídicas, 2002.

Lundestad, Geir. "Empire by Invitation? The United States and Western Europe, 1945–52." *Peace Research* 23 (1986).

Lynn, Martin. "British Policy, Trade and Informal Empire in the Mid-Nineteenth Century." In *The Oxford History of the British Empire: The Nineteenth Century*, ed. Andrew Porter. Oxford: Oxford University Press, 1999.

MacDonald, C. A. "The Politics of Intervention: The United States and Argentina, 1941–46." *Latin American Studies* 12.2 (1980).

Mainwaring, Scott P. *Rethinking Party Systems in the Third Wave of Democratization: The Case of Brazil.* Palo Alto, Calif.: Stanford University Press, 1999.

Mamani Ramírez, Pablo. *El rugir de las multitudes: La fuerza de los levantamientos indígenas en Bolivia-Qullasuyu.* La Paz: Aruwiyiri, 2004.

Marichal, Carlos. *A Century of Debt Crises in Latin America.* Princeton: Princeton University Press, 1989.

———. "La devaluación y la nueva crisis de la deuda externa mexicana: Reflexiones y recomendaciones." *Este País* (Mexico) 51 (1995).

Marshal, Adriana. "Para que sirve la reforma laboral? Si se propuso crear mas empleo fracasó." *Encrucijadas* 2 (2000).

Martínez, Daniel, and Víctor Tokman. "Efectos de las reformas laborales: Entre el empleo y la desprotección." In *Flexibilización en el margen: La reforma del contrato de trabajo*, Organización Internacional de Trabajo. Buenos Aires: Organización Internacional de Trabajo, 1999.

May, Ernest R. *Imperial Democracy: The Emergence of America as a Great Power.* New York: Harcourt, Brace, and World, 1961.

Mayer, Henry. *All on Fire: William Lloyd Garrison and the Abolition of Slavery.* New York: St. Martin's Press, 1998.

McHugh, P. G. "Constitutional Questions and Maori Claims." In *Waitangi: Maori and Pakeha Perspectives of the Treaty of Waitangi*, ed. I. H. Kawharu. Auckland, New Zealand: Oxford University Press, 1989.

Merrell, James H. "Declarations of Independence: Indian-White Relations in the New Nation." In *The American Revolution: Its Character and Limits*, ed. Jack Greene. New York: New York University Press, 1988.

Midgley, Clare. "Slave Sugar Boycotts, Female Activism and the Domestic Base of British Antislavery Culture." *Slavery and Abolition* 17 (1996).

Milani, Aloísio. "Brazil Cheers IMF Approval of Brazilian Pilot Plan." *Brazzil*, 23 February 2005.

Monasterios, Elizabeth. "The Andean Avant-garde: A Latin American Decolonizing Debate." In *Companion to Post-colonial Studies*, ed. Elizabeth Monasterios. Nuremberg: Nuremberg University Press, forthcoming.

Monza, Alfredo. "Evolución reciente y perspectivas del mercado de trabajo en Argentina." *Aportes* 5 (1996).

Moore, Charles, ed. "Gladwin Manuscripts." *Historical Collections of the Michigan Pioneer and Historical Society* 27 (1897).

Moore, Robin J. "Imperial India, 1858–1914." In *The Oxford History of the British Empire: The Nineteenth Century*, ed. Andrew Porter. Oxford: Oxford University Press, 1999.

Morgan, Edmund S. *Inventing the People: The Rise of Popular Sovereignty in England and America*. New York: Norton, 1989.

Morgan, Kenneth. *Slavery, Atlantic Trade and the British Economy, 1660–1800*. Cambridge: Cambridge University Press, 2000.

Muñoz Ramírez, Gloria. "Los Caracoles: Reconstruyendo la nación." *Rebeldía* (Mexico City) 23 (2004).

Muratorio, Blanca. "Nación, identidad y etnicidad: Imágenes de los indios ecuatorianos y sus imagineros a fines del siglo 19." In *Imágenes e imagineros: Representaciones de los Indígenas Ecuatorianos*, vols. 19–20, ed. Blanca Muratorio. Quito, Ecuador: FLACSO, 1994.

Murillo, Victoria. "La adaptación del sindicalismo argentino a las reformas de mercado en la primera presidencia de Menem." *Desarrollo Económico-Revista de Ciencias Sociales* 37.147 (1997).

Murmis, Miguel. "El agro argentino: Algunos problemas para su análisis." In *Las agriculturas del MERCOSUR*, ed. Norma Giarraca. Buenos Aires: La Colmena, 1998.

Mussa, Michael. *La Argentina y el FMI: Del triunfo a la tragedia*. Buenos Aires: Planeta, 2002.

NACLA (North American Congress on Latin America). *New Chile*. New York: NACLA, 1973.

Navarro, Zander. "O Brasil precisa da reforma agrária?" Paper presented at the 10th Seminario Nacional de Direito Agrario conference, São Paulo, December 2002.

———. "Mobilização sem emancipação: As Lutas Sociais dos Sem-Terra no Brasil." In *Produzir para viver: Os caminhos da produção não capitalista*, ed. Boaventura de Sousa Santos. Rio de Janeiro: Civilização Brasileira, 2002.

———. "O 'Orçamento Participativo' de Porto Alegre (1989–2002): Um conciso comentário crítico." In *A inovação democrática no Brasil*, by Leonardo Avritzer and Zander Navarro. São Paulo: Cortez Editora, 2002.

Neffa, Julio César. *Actividad, empleo y desempleo*, Buenos Aires: Association of Work and Society, 2000.

———. *Modos de regulación, regímemes de acumulación y crisis en la Argentina*. Buenos Aires: Eudeba, 1998.

Neffa, Julio César, et al. *Exclusión en el mercado de trabajo: El caso de Argentina*. Santiago de Chile: Ford Foundation, 1999.

Nichols, Roger L. *Indians in the United States and Canada: A Comparative History*. Lincoln: University of Nebraska Press, 1998.

Numhauser, Paulina. *Mujeres indias y señores de la coca: Potosí y Cuzco en el siglo 16*. Madrid: Cátedra, 2005.

Núñez, Dionisio. "Originarios sin poncho ni chicote: Los cocaleros de los Yungas." Panel presentation at the Veinte Años del Taller de Historia Oral Andina conference, Tambo Kirkinchu, La Paz, 16–18 November 2003.

Nye, Joseph S. *Bound to Lead: The Changing Nature of American Power*. New York: Basic Books, 1990.

O'Brien, Jean M. *Dispossession by Degrees: Indian Land and Identity in Natick, Massachusetts, 1650–1790*. New York: Cambridge University Press, 1997.

O'Brien, Patrick, and Armand Clesse, eds. *Two Hegemonies*. Burlington, U.K.: Ashgate, 2002.

O'Callaghan, Edmund B., and B. Fernow, eds. *Documents Relative to the Colonial History of the State of New York*. 15 vols. Albany: Weed, Parsons, 1853–1887.

Oldfield, J. R. *"Chords of Freedom": Commemoration, Ritual and British Transatlantic Slavery*. Manchester, U.K.: Manchester University Press, 2007.

———. *Popular Politics and British Anti-slavery: The Mobilization of Public Opinion against the Slave Trade, 1787–1807*. Manchester, U.K.: Manchester University Press, 1995.

Olesen, Thomas. *International Zapatismo: The Construction of Solidarity in the Age of Globalization*. London: Zed Books, 2005.

Oliveira, Francisco de. "Lula in the Labyrinth." *New Left Review* 42 (2006).

O'Mellin, Liam Séamus. "The Imperial Origins of Federal Indian Law: The Ideology of Colonization in Britain, Ireland, and America." *Arizona State Law Journal* 31 (1999).

Organización Internacional de Trabajo. *El sistema argentino de relaciones laborales*. Madrid: MTSS, 1995.

O'Shaughnessy, Andrew Jackson. *An Empire Divided: The American Revolution and the British Caribbean*. Philadelphia: University of Pennsylvania Press, 2000.

Owen, Roger, and Bob Sutcliffe, eds. *Studies in the Theory of Imperialism*. London: Longman, 1972.

Pagden, Anthony. *Lords of All the World: Ideologies of Empire in Spain, Britain and France, c. 1500-c.1800*. New Haven, Conn.: Yale University Press, 1995.

Paley, Julia. "Toward an Anthropology of Democracy." *Annual Review of Anthropology* 31 (2002).

Parker, Dick. "Chávez and the Search for an Alternative to Neoliberalism." In *Venezuela: Hugo Chávez and the Decline of an "Exceptional" Democracy*, ed. Steve Ellner and Miguel Tinker Salas. Lanham, Md.: Rowman and Littlefield, 2007.

Pastor, Robert A. "The Carter Administration and Latin America: A Test of Principle." In *United States Policy in Latin America: A Quarter Century of Crisis and Challenge, 1961–1986*, ed. John D. Martz. Lincoln: University of Nebraska Press, 1988.

Pauly, Louis W. *Who Elected the Bankers? Surveillance and Control in the World Economy*. Ithaca, N.Y.: Cornell University Press, 1997.

Payer, Cheryl. *The Debt Trap: The IMF and the Third World*. Rev. ed. New York: Monthly Review Press, 1975.

Payne, Leigh A. *Uncivil Movements: The Armed Right Wing and Democracy in Latin America*. Baltimore: Johns Hopkins University Press, 2000.

Peckham, Howard. *Journals of Robert Rogers*. New York: Corinth Books, 1961 [1765].

Pennsylvania Gazette, 1728–1800. CD-ROM. 4 disks. Accessible Archives, 1990.

Pérez, Louis A., Jr. *Cuba under the Platt Amendment, 1902–34*. Pittsburgh: University of Pittsburgh Press, 1986.

Perlman, Janice E. "Marginality from Myth to Reality: The Favelas of Rio de Janeiro, 1969–2003." Paper presented at the "Brazil in Bold: Dialogues across Disciplines" conference, University of Massachusetts, Amherst, 13 February 2004.

Piven, Frances Fox, and Richard Cloward. *Poor People's Movements: Why They Succeed, How They Fail*. New York: Vintage, 1978.

Platt, D. C. M. *Finance, Trade and Politics in British Foreign Policy, 1815–1914*. Oxford: Oxford University Press, 1968.

———. "The Imperialism of Free Trade, Some Reservations." *Economic History Review* 21.2 (1968).

Porter, Andrew, ed. *The Oxford History of the British Empire: The Nineteenth Century*. Oxford: Oxford University Press, 1999.

Power, Timothy J. *The Political Right in Postauthoritarian Brazil: Elites, Institutions, and Democratization*. University Park: Pennsylvania State University Press, 2000.

Prucha, Francis Paul, S.J. *The Great Father: The United States Government and the American Indians*. 2 vols. Lincoln: University of Nebraska Press, 1984.

Pulsipher, Jenny Hale. " 'Subjects . . . unto the Same King': New England Indians and the Use of Royal Political Power." *Massachusetts Historical Review* 5 (2003).

Quirk, Robert E. *An Affair of Honor*. New York: Norton, 1967.

Rabe, Stephen C. *Eisenhower and Latin America*. Chapel Hill: University of North Carolina Press, 1988.

Rakove, Jack N. *Original Meanings: Politics and Ideas in the Making of the Constitution*. New York: Knopf, 1996.

Rapoport, Mario. *Historia económica, política y social de la Argentina*. Buenos Aires: Editorial Macchi, 2003.

Recalde, Hector. *Política laboral 1989–1995*. Buenos Aires: Paidos, 1995.

Reis, Elisa P. "Perceptions of Poverty and Inequality among Brazilian Elites." In *Elite Perceptions of Poverty and Inequality*, ed. Elisa P. Reis and Mick Moore. London: Zed Books, 2005.

Repetto, Fabián. "Notas para un análisis de las políticas sociales: Una propuesta desde el institucionalismo." *Perfiles Latinoamericanos* (FLACSO) 12 (1998).

República de Bolivia, Dirección Nacional de Estadística y Censos. *Censo demográfico de 1950.* La Paz: Dirección Nacional de Estadística y Censos, 1955.

————. *Censo nacional de población y vivienda.* La Paz: Instituto Nacional de Estadística y Censos, 1976.

————. *Censo nacional de población y vivienda.* La Paz: Instituto Nacional de Estadística y Censos, 1992.

————. *Censo nacional de población y vivienda.* La Paz: Instituto Nacional de Estadística y Censos, 2001.

República de Bolivia, Oficina Nacional de Inmigración, Estadística y Propaganda Geográfica. *Censo general de la población de la república según el empadronamiento de primero de Septiembre de 1900.* 2 vols. La Paz: Oficina Nacional de Inmigración, Estadística y Propaganda Geográfica, 1901–1904.

Ricci, Rudá. "Lulismo: Três discursos e um estilo: Movimentos sociais e governo Lula." *Revista Espaço Acadêmico* 45 (February 2005).

Richardson, David. "The British Empire and the Atlantic Slave Trade, 1660–1807." In *The Eighteenth Century,* ed. P. J. Marshall. Vol. 2 of *The Oxford History of the British Empire.* Oxford: Oxford University Press, 1998.

Rifkin, Jeremy. *El fin del trabajo.* Buenos Aires: Paidos, 2001.

Rivera Cusicanqui, Silvia. *Las fronteras de la coca: Epistemologías coloniales y circuitos alternativos de la hoja de coca: El caso de la frontera Boliviano-Argentina.* La Paz: IDIS / Aruwiyiri, 2003.

————. "Mestizaje colonial andino: Una hipótesis de trabajo." In *Violencias encubiertas en Bolivia,* ed. Xavier Albó and Raúl Barrios. La Paz: CIPCA / Aruwiyiri, 1993.

————. *"Oprimidos pero no vencidos": Luchas del campesinado Aymara y Qhichwa, 1900–1980.* La Paz: HISBOL-CSUTCB, 1984.

Robinson, Ronald. "Non-European Foundations of European Imperialism: Sketch for a Theory of Collaboration." In *Studies in the Theory of Imperialism,* ed. Roger Owen and Bob Sutcliffe. London: Longman, 1972.

Robinson, Ronald, and John Gallagher, with Alice Denny. *Africa and the Victorians: The Official Mind of Imperialism.* London: Macmillan, 1961.

Robinson, W. Stitt, "The Legal Status of the Indian in Colonial Virginia." *Virginia Magazine of History and Biography* (1953).

————, ed. *Virginia Treaties, 1607–1722.* Vol. 4 of *Early American Indian Documents, Treaties and Laws, 1607–1789,* gen. ed. Alden T. Vaughan. Frederick, Md.: University Press of America, 1983.

Rodríguez Diez, Alejandro. *Devaluación y pesificación.* Buenos Aires: Bifronte Editorial, 2003.

Rodríguez Lascano, Sergio. "¿Slogan Moral? Otra forma de hacer la política." *Rebeldía* (Mexico City) 23 (2004).

Roorda, Eric Paul. *The Dictator Next Door: The Good Neighbor Policy and the Trujillo Regime in the Dominican Republic, 1930–45.* Durham, N.C.: Duke University Press, 1998.

Rosen, Fred. "From Mexico to New York, Labor Joins the Struggle." NACLA Report on the Americas 38.6 (2005).

Rosenberg, Emily S. *Financial Missionaries to the World: The Politics and Culture of Dollar Diplomacy, 1900–30.* Cambridge, Mass.: Harvard University Press, 1999.

Rosenberg, Tina. "Look at Brazil." *New York Times Magazine,* 28 January 2001.

Rouquié, Alain. *Argentina hoy.* Buenos Aires: SIGLO XXI, 1982.

———. *The Military and the State in Latin America.* Berkeley: University of California Press, 1987.

Rubertone, Patricia E. *Grave Undertakings: An Archaeology of Roger Williams and the Narragansett Indians.* Washington: Smithsonian, 2001.

Rus, Jan, Rosalva Aída Hernández Castillo, and Shannan L. Mattiace, eds. *Mayan Lives, Mayan Utopias: The indigenous peoples of Chiapas and the Zapatista Rebellion.* Lanham, Md.: Rowman and Littlefield, 2003.

Said, Edward W. *Orientalism.* New York: Pantheon, 1978.

Samuels, David J. "Fiscal Straightjacket: The Politics of Macroeconomic Reform in Brazil, 1995–2002." *Latin American Studies* 35.3 (2003).

Sanabria, Harry, ed. *Coca, Cocaine and the Bolivian Reality.* New York: State University of New York Press, 1997.

Sancha, José. "Recuperación de fuentes de trabajo." *Realidad Económica* (Buenos Aires) 183 (2001).

Sánchez Aguilar, E. The International Activities of U.S. Commercial Banks: A Case Study: Mexico. Ph.D. diss., Harvard University, 1973.

Santos, Boaventura de Sousa. "Lula e a esquerda." *Folha de São Paulo,* 22 November 2006.

———. "Participatory Budgeting in Porto Alegre: Toward a Redistributive Democracy." *Politics and Society* 26.4 (1998).

Savelle, Max. *The Origins of American Diplomacy: The International History of Angloamerica, 1492–1763.* New York: Macmillan, 1967.

Schlemenson, Aldo. "Hombres no trabajando." *Encrucijadas* (Buenos Aires) (2000).

Schonwalder, Gerd. *Linking Civil Society and the State: Urban Popular Movements, the Left, and Local Government in Peru, 1980–1992.* University Park: Pennsylvania State University, 2002.

Schoultz, Lars. *Beneath the United States: A History of U.S. Policy toward Latin America.* Cambridge, Mass.: Harvard University Press, 1998.

———. "Latin America and the United States." In *Latin America after Neoliberalism: Turning the Tide in the Twenty-first Century?* ed. Eric Hershberg and Fred Rosen. New York: New Press, 2006.

Schvarzer, Jorge. "De nuevo sobre la burguesía nacional." *Revista Realidad Económica* (Buenos Aires) 201 (2004).

Scribano, Adrián, and Federico Schuster. "Protesta social en la Argentina de 2001: Entre la normalidad y la ruptura." *Observatorio Social de América Latina (OSAL)* (Buenos Aires) 5 (2001).

Seawright, Jason, and Kirk Hawkins. "Organizing Civil Society in Venezuela: A Study of the *Círculos Bolivarianos.*" Paper presented at the Twenty-Fifth Congress of the Latin American Studies Association, Las Vegas, Nevada, October 2004.

Secretaría de Hacienda, Mexico. *Deuda externa pública mexicana.* Mexico City: Fondo de Cultura Económica, 1988.

Seoane, José, and Emilio Taddei. "Protesta social, ajuste y democracia: La encrucijada latinoamericana." *Observatorio Social de América Latina (OSAL)* (Buenos Aires) 4 (2001).

Shannon, Timothy. *Indians and Colonists at the Crossroads of Empire: The Albany Congress of 1754.* Ithaca, N.Y.: Cornell University Press, 2000.

Shoemaker, Michael, ed. "Bouquet Papers." *Collections of the Michigan Pioneer and Historical Society* 19 (1892).

Smith, Gaddis. *Last Years of the Monroe Doctrine, 1945–1993.* New York: Hill and Wang, 1994.

Smith, Tony. *America's Mission.* Princeton: Princeton University Press, 1994.

———. *The Pattern of Imperialism: The United States, Great Britain and the Late-industrializing World since 1815.* Cambridge: Cambridge University Press, 1981.

Snapp, J. Russell. *John Stuart and the Struggle for Empire on the Southern Colonial Frontier.* Baton Rouge: Louisiana State University Press, 1996.

Sosin, Jack. *Whitehall and the Wilderness: The Middle West in British Colonial Policy, 1760–1775.* Lincoln: University of Nebraska Press, 1961.

Spedding, Alison. "The Coca Field as a Total Social Fact." In *Coca, Cocaine and the Bolivian Reality*, ed. Barbara Leons and Harry Sanabria. New York: State University of New York Press, 1997.

———, ed. *Gracias a Dios y a los achachilas: Ensayos de sociología de la religión en los Andes.* La Paz: Plural / ISEAT, 2004.

Stallings, Barbara. *Banker to the Third World: U.S. Portfolio Investment in Latin America, 1900–1986.* Berkeley: University of California Press, 1987.

Starr, Rebecca. *A School for Politics: Commercial Lobbying and Political Culture in Early South Carolina.* Baltimore: Johns Hopkins University Press, 1999.

Steger, Manfred B. *The New Market Ideology: Globalism.* Lanham, Md.: Rowman and Littlefield, 2002.

Stephen, Lynn. *Women and Social Movements in Latin America: Power from Below.* Austin: University of Texas Press, 1997.

Stevens, Sylvester K., et al., eds. *The Papers of Henry Bouquet.* 19 vols. Harrisburg: Pennsylvania Historical and Museum Commission, 1951–1994.

Stevens, Sylvester K., and Donald H. Kent, eds. *The Papers of Col. Henry Bouquet.* 19 vols. Harrisburg: Pennsylvania Historical and Museum Commission, 1940–1943.

Stiglitz, Joseph. *El malestar en la globalización.* Madrid: Taurus, 2002.

Stoll, David. *Is Latin America Turning Protestant?* Berkeley: University of California Press, 1990.

Suarez Godóy, Enrique. *San Luis, una política social diferente*. Buenos Aires: Government of San Luis, 2004.

Svampa, Maristella, et al. *Entre la ruta y el barrio*. Buenos Aires: Editorial Biblos, 2003.

Swanberg, W. A. *Citizen Hearst*. New York: Scribner, 1961.

Temperley, Howard. "British and American Abolitionists Compared." In *The Antislavery Vanguard: New Essays on the Abolitionists*, ed. Martin B. Duberman. Princeton: Princeton University Press, 1965.

———. *British Anti-slavery, 1833–1870*. London: Longman, 1972.

Teubal, Miguel. "Soja transgénica y crisis del modelo agro-alimentario argentino." *Realidad Económica* (Buenos Aires) 196 (2003).

Thomas, Hugh. *The Slave Trade: The History of the Atlantic Slave Trade, 1440–1870*. New York: Simon and Schuster, 1997.

Thompson, Andrew. "Informal Empire? An Exploration in the History of Anglo-Argentine Relations, 1810–1914." *Latin American Studies* 24.2 (1992).

Topik, Steven C. *Trade and Gunboats: The United States and Brazil in the Age of Empire*. Palo Alto, Calif.: Stanford University Press, 1996.

Torres Molina, Ramón, *Absolutismo presidencial: Decretos de necesidad y urgencia*. Buenos Aires: EDIAR, 2001.

Toussaint, Eric. *Deuda externa en el Tercer Mundo: Las finanzas contra los pueblos*. Caracas: Nueva Sociedad, 1998.

Toynbee, Paget, ed. *The Letters of Horace Walpole, Fourth Earl of Orford*. Oxford: Clarendon Press, 1904.

Ugarteche, Oscar. *Adios estado, bievenido mercado*. Lima: Fundación Friedrich Ebert, 2004.

———. *El falso dilema: América Latina en la economía global*. Lima: Fundación Friedrich Ebert, 1996.

United Nations. *United Nations Convention against Illicit Traffic in Narcotic Drugs and Psychotropic Substances*. New York: United Nations, 1988.

———. *United Nations Single Convention on Narcotic Drugs*. New York: United Nations, 1961.

United Nations Development Program. *Programas de empleo transitorio: La experiencia de Barrios Bonaerenses. Aspectos conceptuales, metodológicos y operatives*. La Plata, Argentina: United Nations Development Program, 1999.

U.S. Department of State. *Foreign Relations of the United States, 1964–1968*. Vol. 31, *South and Central America: Mexico*. Washington: U.S. State Department, 2004.

Van Cott, Donna Lee. "Explaining Ethnic Autonomy Regimes in Latin America." *Studies in Comparative International Development* 35.4 (2001).

van der Schaaf, Alie. *Jeito de mulher rural: A busca de direitos sociais e da igualdade de gênero no Rio Grande do Sul*. Passo Fundo, Brazil: Editora Universidade de Passo Fundo, 2001.

Vega Ruiz, María Luz. *La reforma laboral en América Latina*. Buenos Aires: Organización Internacional de Trabajo, 2001.

Vianna, Hermano. *The Mystery of Samba: Popular Music and National Identity in Brazil*. Chapel Hill: University of North Carolina Press, 1999.

Vicario, Tiziana. "Argentina y el FMI: Una visión integrada de los factores internos y externos de la crisis." *Revista Ciclos en la Historia, la Economía y la Sociedad* (Buenos Aires) 14.27 (2004).

Vieira da Cunha, P. "Brazil: The Threat Is, As Always, Politics." *Latin America Economics Insight* (2004).

Vilas, Carlos. *La democratización fundamental*. Mexico City: CONACULTA, 1995.

Vitoria, Francisco de. *Political Writings*. Ed. Anthony Pagden and Jeremy Lawrence. New York: Cambridge University Press, 1991.

Wainer, Valeria, and Juan Montes Cató. "Flexibilización de la jornada de trabajo en el marco de la desregulación del mercado laboral." *Magazine Epoca* 2.2 (2000).

Wainwright, Hilary. *Reclaim the State: Experiments in Popular Democracy*. London: Verso, 2003.

Wainwright, Hilary, and Sue Branford, eds. *In the Eye of the Storm: Left-wing Activists Discuss the Political Crisis in Brazil*. London: Trans National Institute, 2006.

Wallerstein, Immanuel. *The Modern World-System*. New York: Academic Press, 1974.

Waltz, Kenneth N. *Foreign Policy and Domestic Politics*. London: Little, Brown, 1968.

Walvin, James. *Black Ivory: A History of British Slavery*. London: HarperCollins, 1992.

———. *Making the Black Atlantic: Britain and the African Diaspora*. London: Cassell, 2000.

Ward, J. R. "The British West Indies in the Age of Revolution, 1748–1815." In *The Eighteenth Century*, ed. P. J. Marshall. Vol. 2 of *The Oxford History of the British Empire*. Oxford: Oxford University Press, 1998.

White, Richard. *The Middle Ground: Indians, Empires and Republics in the Great Lakes Region, 1650–1815*. New York: Cambridge University Press, 1991.

Wilkins, David. *American Indian Sovereignty and the Supreme Court: The Masking of Justice*. Austin: University of Texas Press, 1997.

Wilkinson, Charles F. *American Indians, Time, and the Law: Native Societies in a Modern Constitutional Democracy*. New Haven, Conn.: Yale University Press, 1987.

———. *Blood Struggle: The Rise of Modern Indian Nations*. New York: Norton, 2005.

Williams, Eric. *Capitalism and Slavery*. Chapel Hill: University of North Carolina Press, 1944.

Williams, Robert. *The American Indian in Western Legal Thought: The Discourses of Conquest.* New York: Oxford University Press, 1990.

Williamson, John, ed. *Latin American Adjustment.* Washington: Institute for International Economics, 1990.

Wilpert, Gregory. "Will Chávez's Project Survive?" In *Coup against Chávez in Venezuela: The Best International Reports of What Really Happened in April 2002,* ed. Gregory Wilpert. Caracas: Fundación Venezolana para la Justicia Global, 2003.

Wolford, Wendy. " 'Every Monkey Has Its Own Head': Rural Sugarcane Workers and the Politics of Becoming a Peasant in Northeastern Brazil." Paper presented at Colloquium in Agrarian Studies, Yale University, New Haven, Connecticut, 21 January 2005.

Womack, John. *Rebellion in Chiapas: An Historical Reader.* New York: New Press, 1999.

———. *Zapata and the Mexican Revolution.* New York: Random House, 1968.

Wood, Bryce. *The Dismantling of the Good Neighbor Policy.* Austin: University of Texas Press, 1985.

———. *The Making of the Good Neighbor Policy.* New York: Columbia University Press, 1961.

Wood, Gordon. *The Radicalism of the American Revolution: How a Revolution Transformed a Monarchical Society into a Democratic One Unlike Any that Had Ever Existed.* New York: Knopf, 1992.

World Bank. *World Debt Tables, 1992–1993.* Vol. 2, *Country Tables.* Washington: World Bank, 1993.

Wright, Angus Lindsay, and Wendy Wolford. *To Inherit the Earth: The Landless Movement and the Struggle for a New Brazil.* Oakland, Calif.: Food First, 2003.

Yúdice, George. *The Expediency of Culture: Uses of Culture in the Global Era.* Durham, N.C.: Duke University Press, 2004.

Zibechi, Raúl. "The New Popular Movements." NACLA *Report on the Americas* 38.5 (2005).

CONTRIBUTORS

DANIEL A. CIEZA is a professor of legal sociology at the National University of La Plata and an associate professor of Argentine socioeconomic structure in the labor-relations department of the University of Buenos Aires. He is the national coordinator of the Argentine Network of Human Rights Observers, which reports to the Human Rights Secretariat of the Argentine government.

GREGORY EVANS DOWD is the director of Native American Studies and a professor of history and American culture at the University of Michigan, Ann Arbor. He is the author of *A Spirited Resistance: The North American Indian Struggle for Unity, 1745–1815* (1992) and *War under Heaven: Pontiac, the Indian Nations and the British Empire* (2002).

STEVE ELLNER has published extensively on Venezuelan politics and history. Since 1994, he has taught graduate courses at the School of Law and Political Science at the Central University of Venezuela. He is the author of *Organized Labor in Venezuela, 1958–1991: Behavior and Concerns in a Democratic Setting* (1993). One of his most frequently cited publications is "Venezuelan Revisionist Political History, 1908–1958: New Motives and Criteria for Analyzing the Past," *Latin American Research Review* (1995).

NEIL HARVEY is an associate professor of government at New Mexico State University. He is the author of *The Chiapas Rebellion: The Struggle for Land and Democracy* (Duke University Press, 1998) and is a frequent contributor to the editorial page of the Mexican daily *La Jornada*.

ALAN KNIGHT is a professor of Latin American history at St. Anthony's College, Oxford University. He is the author of *The Mexican Revolution* (2 vols., 1986); *U.S.-Mexican Relations, 1910–1940: An Interpretation* (1987); and *Mexico: From the Beginning to the Conquest* and *Mexico: The Colonial Era*, the first two volumes of a three-volume general history of Mexico (2002).

CARLOS MARICHAL is a professor of history at El Colegio de Mexico and is the president of the Mexican Association of Economic History. He is the author of *A Century of Debt Crises in Latin America: From Independence to the Great Depression, 1820–1930* (1989) and *The Bankruptcy of the Viceroyalty, 1780–1810: New Spain and the Finances of the Spanish Empire* (1999).

JOHN RICHARD OLDFIELD is a senior lecturer in modern history at the University of Southampton. He has published numerous articles on slavery and abolition in the Atlantic world. He is the author of *Mobilization of Public Opinion against the Slave Trade, 1787–1807* (1995) and the editor of *The Abolitionist Struggle: Opponents of the Slave Trade* (2003).

SILVIA RIVERA CUSICANQUI is professor emeritus at the University Mayor de San Andrés, La Paz, and is a founding member of the Andean Oral History Workshop. She is a leading expert on the coca leaf, with long experience in the Yungas region of Bolivia. She is the author of *Oprimidos pero no vencidos* (Oppressed but not conquered) (2003) and *Las fronteras de la coca* (The frontiers of coca) (2003).

FRED ROSEN is an independent journalist and political economist based in New York and Mexico City. He is a senior analyst at the North American Congress on Latin America (NACLA) and a contributing editor to the *NACLA Report on the Americas*. He coedited, with Eric Hershberg, *Latin America after Neoliberalism: Turning the Tide in the Twenty-first Century?* (2006).

JEFFREY W. RUBIN is an associate professor of history at Boston University and a research associate at the university's Institute on Culture, Religion and World Affairs. He is the author of *Decentering the Regime: Ethnicity, Radicalism, and Democracy in Juchitán, Mexico* (Duke University Press, 1997), which the New England Council of Latin American Studies awarded the Best Book Prize for 1997.

INDEX

Abolition Act of 1807, 83

Abolition movement: Abolition Act of 1807 and, 83; American groups and, 81; American Revolution's influence on, 79–80; American revolutionary slaveholders and, 82, 85; Anti-Slavery Society and, 83–86; British imperial crisis and, 79–80, 84–85; culture of, 86–87; economic self-interest of, 78, 84–85; emancipation and, 84–86; empire "without slaves" and, 87; European opposition to, 83, 86; Foreign Slave Bill and, 83; free labor ideology and, 84–86; "imagined community" of reformers and, 81–82; indentured labor and, 86; moral elements of, 78–79; public opinion mobilization for, 80–81; SEAST and, 81; slave registration and, 83–84; slave revolts and, 84–85; transnational networks and, 81. *See also* Atlantic slave trade

ADEPCOCA, 145, 151–53

African Institution, 83

Afro-Reggae Cultural Group, 170–71

akhulliku, 144–45, 147–50, 158

Alfonsin, Raúl, 190, 196

Alliance for Progress, 29, 41

Amherst, Jeffery, 55, 62

Anti-neoliberal policies. *See* Neoliberal policies: resistance to

Anti-slavery. *See* Abolition movement

Anti-Slavery Society (Society for the Mitigation and Gradual Abolition of Slavery Throughout the British Dominions), 83–84, 86. *See also* Abolition movement

APPO, 134–35, 176

Argentina: "Caesarist" leadership in, 200–202; growth under Kirchner, 199–200; new social movements in, 196–97, 202 (*see also Piquetero* movement); postwar external debt paid, 97; UCR-FREPASO alliance and, 197–99. *See also* Kirchner, Néstor; Menem, Carlos

—financial crisis, 2001–2002: government declares sovereign default, 108–10, 188, 192, 197–99; IMF halts lending, 107–8; recovery from, 199–200

Cold War, 4, 31, 34; functions of imperialism and, 39–41; U.S. interventionism and, 42–44
Colosio, Luis Donaldo, 104
Comisión Federal de Electricidad (CFE), 100–101
Commission for Peace and Reconciliation in Chiapas (COCOPA), 122–23; PRD failure to defend, 128–30
Committee for the Abolition of Third World Debt (CADTM), 100, 110
Communism, containment by United States of, 35–36
Confederation of Bolivian Rural Workers (CSUTCB), 142, 156
Convertability Law, 190, 193, 198
Corn, cultural and ecological significance of, 124–25
Council of Federations of Peasant Coca Growers of the Yungas (COFECAY), 146, 155
Countryside Can Endure No More (El Campo No Aguanta Más), 125
Coupland, Reginald, 87
Crown subjects. See Indians
CSUTCB, 142, 156
Cuba, 26, 31–33, 37–40. See also Imperialism: U.S.
Cuban missile crisis, 28
Cuban Revolution, 31, 34–36. See also Imperialism: U.S.
Cuillerier, Alexis, 63–64

Debt crisis. See Foreign debt
Debt negotiations. See Foreign debt
Debt politics, 93
De la Rúa, Fernando, 107–8, 189, 197–98, 216
Delegado Cero (Delegate Zero). See Marcos, Subcomandante
Democratic model. See Brazil

Democratic National Convention (CND), 134
Democratic reform in Latin America, violent responses to, 176–77
Departmental Association of Coca Growers (ADEPCOCA), 145, 151–53
Dissent: from above, 12, 14, 18, 121–22, 206; from below, 12–14, 17 (see also Cocaleros, "Other Campaign"; Piquetero movement; Zapatista movement); against empire, 84 (see also Slave revolts); within empire, 84, 120, 131 (see also Abolition movement; Zapatista movement)
Dissent, containment of: by elites, 33–36; by interventions, 30–31, 32–24, 37–39; by noncoercive means, 35–36
Dissent against neoliberalism, 118. See also Chavez, Hugo; Chavista movement; Zapatista movement
Dollar as international currency reserve, 95
Dominion, Indian. See Sovereignty
Duck test, 34
Duhalde, Eduardo, 108, 198–99, 200–203

Economic globalization, resistance to, 118–19, 126–27, 129. See also Neoliberal policies: resistance to
Eice, John, 61–62
Elites, "collaborating," 25, 33–34
Emancipation movement. See Abolition movement
Empire: "American," 1; "disobedience" to, 157–59; dissent in, 34–36; European, in North America, 57–58; "false," 54–55, 67–68; foreign threats to, 36–40; "formal" vs. "informal," 24–27, 30–32, 35;

103–4; GATT and, 104; NAFTA and, 104; repayment to creditors and, 106; similarities to 1980s, 106; *tesebonos* and, 105

—financial crisis in postwar period, 97

Migrant workers, 16–17

Military coups, U.S.-supported, 176

Minavavana, 55–56, 58, 68. *See also* Indians

Ministry of the Popular Economy (MINEP), 217

MNR, 139

MMTR, 168

Monroe Doctrine, 37–38

Morales, Evo, 12, 14, 137, 143, 146–47, 149–51, 155, 158–59. *See also* Coca leaf; *Cocaleros*, Indigenous peoples: in Bolivia

MST, 168–71

MVR, 206, 211–14

Multilateral development banks, establishment of, 95

Multitude, concept of, 120, 131, 133. *See also* Zapatista movement

NAFTA, 37, 43, 104, 118, 122, 125

National Action Party (PAN), 123–24

National Democratic Convention (CND), 134

National Employment Law, 191

National Institute of Statistics (INE), 140

Nationalist Revolutionary Movement (MNR), 139

National Workers Union (UNT), 207, 215, 218. See also *Chavista* movement

Nation building, 27

Native Americans. *See* Indians

Negri, Antonio, 7–8. *See also* Empire

Neoliberal policies, 9–11, 103; in Argentina, 9, 189–92; as impediment to growth, 174–75; indigenous peoples and, 140, 153–54. *See also* Empire

—resistance to: in Argentina, 209–10; in Bolivia, 141–43; in rural Mexico, 118–19, 124–27, 129; in Venezuela, 121–22, 125, 209–10, 216–22. *See also* Chávez, Hugo; *Chavista* movement; Zapatista movement

"Network movements," 131–33

New York Manumission Society, 81

Núñez, Dionicio, 155

"Other Campaign," 15, 118, 131–34; no media attention to, 132. *See also* Marcos, Subcomandante; Zapatista movement

PAN, 123–24

Panama Canal, 32, 27, 39

Participatory budgeting, 167–69

Participatory democracy, 208–10

Party of the Democratic Revolution (PRD), 117; loss of Zapatista support and, 129–32

PDVSA, 217–18

Pemberton, James, 81

PEMEX, 100, 106

Penn, William 57

Pennsylvania Abolition Society (PAS), 81

Perón, Juan, 97, 182, 196, 211, 223

Peronism, 190, 195–96, 199, 201

Peronist Justicialist Party (PJ), 198–99

Petrodollars, Latin American loan boom and, 98–101

Petróleos de Venezuela (PDVSA), 217–18

Petróleos Mexicanos (PEMEX), 100, 106

Pickering, Timothy, 68

Pinochet, Augusto (general), 100

Fred Rosen is a senior analyst at the North American Congress on Latin America and a contributing editor to the NACLA *Report on the Americas*.

Library of Congress Cataloging-in-Publication Data
Empire and dissent : the United States and Latin America / edited by Fred Rosen.
p. cm. — (American encounters/global interactions)
Includes bibliographical references and index.
ISBN 978-0-8223-4255-7 (cloth : alk. paper)
ISBN 978-0-8223-4278-6 (pbk. : alk. paper)
1. Latin America—Relations—United States.
2. United States—Relations—Latin America.
3. Imperialism—History. I. Rosen, Fred
F1418.E48 2008
303.48'28073—dc22   2008013872